Rethinking School Reform

VIEWS FROM THE CLASSROOM

Edited by Linda Christensen and Stan Karp

Rethinking School Reform: Views From The Classroom
Edited by Linda Christensen and Stan Karp

Rethinking Schools, Ltd. is a nonprofit educational publisher of books, booklets, and a quarterly journal on school reform, with a focus on issues of equity and social justice. To request additional copies of this book or a catalog of other publications, or to subscribe to the Rethinking Schools journal, contact:

Rethinking Schools
1001 East Keefe Avenue
Milwaukee, Wisconsin 53212 USA
800-669-4192
www.rethinkingschools.org

Special thanks to the Joyce Foundation for its generous support of this project.

Cover and book design by Mary Jane Karp.
Cover photos by Jean-Claude Lejeune.

Project Editor: Leon Lynn
Editorial Assistance: Stacie Williams
Proofreader: Joanna Dupuis

ISBN 0-942961-29-3

Contents

Preface

School reform: two of the most overused words in educational discourse today. Ever since the 1983 publication of *A Nation at Risk* — a report characterized by alarmist predictions of a "rising tide of mediocrity" in our nation's schools — all manner of recommendations on how to rescue public education have been made and tried: more testing for students and for teachers, stricter gatekeeping for prospective teachers, longer school days, more phonics, less attention to multiculturalism, a more rigorous curriculum, more courses in science and math, *ad infinitum.*

Nearly everyone, in fact, has been heard from except those closest to the issues being discussed: teachers, families, and students themselves. Their voices, although clamoring to be heard, have been largely silenced in school reform conversations.

On the other hand, the voices of powerful individuals and organizations representing the interests of administrators, policymakers, politicians, and academics have been loud and clear. It is not surprising, then, that while words such as standards and standardized tests, rubrics, best practices, vouchers, "choice," and others have made their way into everyday life, words such as social justice, equity, and equality have been conspicuously missing from most discussions of school reform.

Rethinking School Reform: Views from the Classroom provides welcome relief from the conventional wisdom that technical responses will somehow solve the problems of inequality in our nation's schools. Understanding that the problems faced by our public schools are not technical glitches but instead ethical problems, the authors in this book — most of whom are themselves classroom teachers — bring into focus the work and ideas of those who most care about, and work toward, social justice in education. The book actually moves beyond its title somewhat, because not only do we get views from the classroom, we also hear about implications for the district, state, and national levels. We hear from teachers and their students, from parents and concerned community members, about what it will take to truly reform our public schools. Addressing school reform in this way provides a bold agenda for change, an agenda that heretofore has not been brought into the wider conversation on reform.

Editors Linda Christensen and Stan Karp and the other authors of this book take on sacrosanct policies and practices such as rigid ability tracking and standardized testing, while also addressing issues as diverse as Ebonics and bilingual education, hero-worship in the curriculum and slaveholding presidents, racism and queer-friendly schools, Helen Keller and Christopher Columbus. They look with a thoughtful eye and a critical lens at such issues as privatization and vouchers, busing and language diversity, and through it all they speak with a clear voice about what too many educators, in their rush to implement reform at any cost, seem to have forgotten: that public schools are meant to serve children and the public good, not testing companies or textbook publishers, not politicians or administrators. Yet, in this age of "school reform," our public schools have become havens of testing and standardization, losing their joy and hope. Schools have strayed far from their task. Christensen, Karp, and the others bring us back to where they belong.

This is an inspiring and important book. Rather than simply pointing out the problems with school reform as currently defined — something they do with great insight — the authors of this book concentrate on what those who support real reform can actually *do*. They provide abundant ideas to help teachers rethink their classroom practices, from using action research to "talking back" to the text. They describe skillful ways to take advantage of "teachable moments." They write about powerful classroom experiences that challenge racism and other biases in the classroom and the community. They provide numerous resources that all teachers and others can use to change schools and classrooms.

But they also make it clear that school reform does not end at the door to the classroom, or even the door to the school. It must also be districtwide and statewide, and it must reach into the streets, as well as into the halls of Congress. In a word, as this book makes abundantly clear, effective, nurturing, and loving schools will result only when teachers and others work together to make change.

This is also a hopeful book. In its pages, you will find that those of us who work for equitable and joyful schools are not alone. We are joined by many others: teachers, administrators, parents and families, community members, and others who want to make the world of public schools better for all children. Increasingly, radical right-wing ideologues have hijacked the discourse of progressives, using terms such as "all children can learn" or "no child left behind." Rather than stand by while these terms are used to fashion a mean-spirited reform that does little to fulfill our nation's stated ideals of equality and fair play, the authors in this book urge us to take back both the discourse and our responsibilities to change the nature of the conversation. It is time to break out of the reactionary mold of school reform and take courageous action on behalf of all our children. *Rethinking School Reform* can start us on the journey.

— *Sonia Nieto*

Introduction

The journal *Rethinking Schools* was started by Milwaukee-area classroom teachers in the mid-1980s. It appeared soon after a commission appointed by then-President Ronald Reagan sparked a new national debate on education with a report entitled "A Nation at Risk."

That report opened two decades of high-profile school reform efforts that continue today. Throughout the period, corporate and elite political interests have dominated the debate. Governors have held numerous education summits, corporate leaders have organized countless roundtables and conferences, and the media have echoed a relentless critique of public schools and the people who work in them.

Rethinking Schools was originally formed so that Milwaukee teachers, parents, and students might have a voice in the debates that promised to reshape their daily lives. The journal soon grew beyond Milwaukee concerns, and over the past 17 years has established itself as a leading grassroots voice for teachers on educational issues of national concern. At a time when school reform is too often something done to teachers, rather than a productive response to their needs and daily experience, *Rethinking Schools* reaffirms that the "view from the classroom" is a key missing link in the process of reform.

In *Rethinking School Reform*, we have collected some of the journal's best writing. Taken together, these articles present a vision of schooling and reform quite different from the one emanating from official sources.

The organization of the book reflects our priorities as teachers and as education activists. It begins where too many school reform efforts never go: inside our classrooms.

We start in Part 1, "Critical Teaching," with a look at this "indispensable and much-neglected missing piece in the puzzle of school improvement." In defining what we consider good instructional practices, we present the kinds of curriculum choices and classroom values that we think schools in a democratic society should promote. Taken together these choices outline "a common social and pedagogical vision that...strives toward what we call a social justice classroom." We argue further that "unless our schools and classrooms are animated by broad visions of equity, democracy, and social justice, they will never be able to realize the widely proclaimed goal of raising educational achievement for all children." Other articles in this section offer specific examples of what such teaching looks like in social studies and language arts classes. Critical classroom practice is our point of departure because we believe it is the central element against which all reform efforts should be judged.

One major obstacle to sustaining democratic classrooms and schools is the accumulated baggage of history. When we go to school in the morning we bring with us our families, our cultures, our racial heritages, our class and gender experiences. Like the society they serve, schools have always struggled with these differences, sometimes pretending they don't exist, at other times imagining we can "celebrate diversity" without examining why some differences translate into access to privilege and power, while others become a source of oppression and injustice.

In *Rethinking School Reform*, we maintain that the difficult and complicated issues of race, class, gender, and sexual orientation must be confronted head-on. They permeate every aspect of our educational experience, and public schools — which are perhaps the last place where an increasingly diverse and divided population still meets to a common purpose — cannot avoid them. There are no easy answers to addressing these challenges, in school or out, but Part 2, "Taking Bias Seriously," offers some examples of how these issues present themselves to teachers and students, and how we might respond in constructive and courageous ways.

While classrooms are at the center of our efforts to rethink school reform, they are not the only battleground. Part 3, "Education Policy and Politics," looks at how school issues have become hotly contested at the national, state, and district levels. Battles over vouchers, desegregation, privatization, and federal education policy reflect crucial political choices that will have a lasting impact not only on schools, but on public life as a whole, and on whether the United States will realize the promise of a pluralistic, multicultural democracy in the 21st century or abandon it. We need to understand how decisions made in legislatures and courtrooms impact our classrooms and our schools, and how we, in turn, might impact those decisions.

Within schools, the clearest reflection of this larger struggle between multicultural, democratic values and privatized, corporate interests is the struggle over standards and testing. Today standardized curricula imposed through ever more suffocating layers of standardized testing constitute the primary agenda of anti-democratic schooling. Like all effective political strategies, this agenda speaks to real concerns held by large numbers of people, including concerns over low student achievement, the lack of institutional accountability, and the seemingly intractable school failure in low-income communities. These very real problems provide a platform for school reformers of all shapes and sizes to posture as champions of the underserved and underprivileged.

But most of the official remedies being offered would perpetuate and legitimize an inequitable status quo, while squeezing the life out of alternative reform efforts that hold much more promise of real progress. In Part 4, "Standards and Testing," we examine how the issues of academic achievement and assessment can promote or prevent the kind of schooling our children need. We consider the difference between "standards" and "standardization," and look at ways that equitable assessment practices can support schools in their efforts to serve all students well, instead of sorting and labeling them into new categories of failure.

Finally in Part 5, "Roads to Reform," we consider the challenges and possibilities involved in trying to promote positive change. Addressing such key elements as school funding, staff development, untracking, curriculum reform, and the role of teachers unions, we present a vision of reform that might start to measure up to the tasks at hand. These articles suggest how a social justice perspective can inform the many different components that are needed for successful school change.

Throughout *Rethinking School Reform*, we keep coming back to the view from the classroom. It is a common thread. What kinds of policies, resources, people, and purpose do we need in our nation's classrooms so that they might become not only places of individual academic achievement, but also "laboratories for a more just society"?

Teachers do not have all the answers to the issues raised by school reform, and the view from the classroom is not always the clearest. But classrooms are where the core business of schooling takes place, and it's where the measure of all reform proposals must ultimately be taken. If a given initiative supports more effective critical teaching and creates more equitable and democratic classrooms, it is worth pursuing. If it retards or restricts such efforts, then it's part of the problem. In the final analysis, that is the test that every school reform needs to pass.

— *The Editors*

PART I

Critical
Teaching

Rethinking Our Classrooms: Teaching for Equity and Justice

The Editors of Rethinking Schools

In rethinking our classrooms we begin from the premise that schools and classrooms should be laboratories for a more just society than the one we now live in. After more than a decade of high-profile national debate on school reform, we think this proposition is more central than ever to the success, perhaps even the survival, of public education.

Schools have crucial obligations not only to individual students and families, but to our society as a whole. Their success or failure is tied not just to personal well-being, but to the prospects of creating a multiracial democracy capable of addressing the serious social and ecological problems that cloud our future. We live in a world plagued by economic inequality, endemic violence, and racial injustice. A me-first, dollar-driven culture undermines democratic values, and seems to invent daily new forms of alienation and self-destruction. Over the long term, the production and consumption patterns of industrially overdeveloped and underplanned economies like ours threaten global ecological disaster.

Given such unpleasant but inescapable realities, education reform must be driven by a far broader vision than it has been in recent years. What happens every day in our classrooms both shapes and is shaped by the larger social currents that define who we are as a society and where we are headed. Accordingly, to be truly successful, school reform must be guided by democratic social goals and values that provide a deeper context for more traditional academic objectives.

Unfortunately, too many schools foster narrowly self-centered notions of success and "making it." Too many, especially in poor areas, provide a dismal experience based on tests, tracking, and a sanitized curriculum that lacks the credibility or sense of purpose needed to engage students or to connect with their communities. Too many schools fail to confront the racial, class, gender, language, and homophobic biases woven into our social fabric.

Years of classroom experience have convinced us that these shortcomings are intimately connected to low student achievement. The problems many schools have in teaching children to read, write, and think are, to a large extent, symptoms of the inequality that permeates our educational system. In fact, we would argue that unless our schools and classrooms are animated by broad visions of equity, democracy, and social justice, they will never be able to realize the widely proclaimed goal of raising educational achievement for all children.

Historically, efforts to expand the reach of public education or to democratize curriculum have been accompanied by extensions of the sorting and labeling mechanisms schools use to preserve pockets of privilege. (See for example the role play activity on the origins of tracking in *Rethinking Our Classrooms, Volume 1*, p. 117. The activity is also available at www.rethinkingschools.org/rsr.)

Today the standardized testing crusade threatens to play a similar role. It professes to raise the bar for all children, yet without dramatic increases in resources and radical improvements in teaching and learning inside classrooms, the testing crusade is more likely to create a new credentialing maze that continues to channel some students to lives of privilege and others to educational oblivion.

Teachers are often simultaneously perpetrators and victims in this process. They typically have little individual control over many of the factors that shape the conditions of schooling. But in their classrooms they often have a measure of autonomy to create a space that can profoundly affect the lives of young people. Teachers can create classrooms that are places of hope, where students and teachers gain glimpses of the kind of society we could live in, and where students learn the academic and critical skills needed to make it a reality.

This effort to rethink our classrooms must be both visionary and practical: visionary, because we need to go far beyond the prepackaged formulas and narrow agendas now being imposed on our schools and classrooms; and practical, because the work of reshaping educational practice and countering the agendas imposed from above requires daily, school-based efforts at learning, teaching, organizing, and educational activism by those with the most at stake — teachers, students, parents, and local communities.

We believe further that efforts at classroom transformation should grow from a common social and pedagogical vision that, taken as a whole, strives toward what we call a social justice classroom. In such a social justice classroom, curriculum and classroom practice must be:

- **Grounded in the lives of our students.** All good teaching begins with a respect for children, their innate curiosity and their capacity to learn. Curriculum should be rooted in children's needs and experiences. Whether we're teaching science, mathematics, English, or social studies, ultimately the class has to be about our students' lives as well as about a particular subject. Students should probe the ways their lives connect to the broader society, and are often limited by that society.

- **Critical.** The curriculum should equip students to "talk back" to the world. From an early age, students must learn to pose essential critical questions: Who makes decisions and who is left out? Who benefits and who suffers? Why is a given practice fair or unfair? What are its origins? What alternatives can we imagine? What is required to create change? Through critiques of advertising, cartoons, literature, legislative decisions, foreign policy choices, job structures, newspapers, movies, consumer culture, agricultural practices, and school life itself, students should have opportunities to question social reality. Wherever possible, student work should also move outside the classroom walls so that academic learning is linked to real-world issues and problems.

- **Multicultural, anti-bias, pro-justice.** A social justice curriculum must strive to include the lives of everyone in our society, and to examine critically their histories and interconnection. With some 40% of the students in public schools from communities of color, while more than 90% of the teachers are white, we need to address directly and constructively the racial, class, and gender dimensions of educational inequity and school failure. We need to move from what anti-racist educator Enid Lee calls the "soft stuff" to the "hard stuff." This means not only "celebrating our diversity," but also helping ourselves and our students understand why some differences translate into access to wealth and power, while others become a source of discrimination and injustice. To uncover the common ground that public schools in a multiracial society need in order to thrive, we need to face honestly the truths about our past and our present. There is already a backlash against the unfinished efforts of recent years to revise traditional versions of history, literature, and other subjects, and to include the experience and voices of people of color, women, gays and lesbians, and working people. Nevertheless, we need to push this effort further and deeper. We must resist attempts by state tests and standards to push multicultural curriculum reform to the margins.

◆ **Participatory, experiential.** Traditional classrooms often leave little room for student involvement and initiative. They encourage a passivity that is reinforced by fragmented, test-driven curriculum, and which discourages students from taking more responsibility for their own education. In a "rethought" classroom, concepts need to be experienced firsthand, not just read about or heard about. Through projects, role plays, simulations, mock trials, or experiments, students need to be mentally, and often physically, active. They need to be involved as much as possible in explicit discussions about the purposes and processes of their own education. Our classrooms also must provoke students to develop their democratic capacities: to question, to challenge, to make real decisions, to solve problems collectively.

◆ **Hopeful, joyful, kind, visionary.** The ways we organize classroom life should seek to make children feel significant and cared about — by the teacher and by each other. Unless students feel emotionally and physically safe, they won't share real thoughts and feelings; discussions will be artificial and dishonest. We need to design activities that help students learn to trust and care for each other. Classroom life should, to the greatest extent possible, prefigure the kind of democratic and just society we envision, and thus contribute to building that society.

◆ **Activist.** We want students to come to see themselves as truth-tellers and change-makers. If we ask children to critique the world but then fail to encourage them to act, our classrooms can degenerate into factories of cynicism. Part of a teacher's role is to suggest that ideas have real consequences and should be acted upon, and to offer students opportunities to do just that. Children can also draw inspiration from historical and contemporary efforts of people who struggled for justice. A critical curriculum should be a rainbow of resistance, reflecting the diversity of people from all cultures who acted to make a difference, many of whom did so at great sacrifice. Students should be allowed to learn about, and feel connected to, this legacy of defiance.

◆ **Academically rigorous.** A social justice classroom equips children not only to change the world, but also to navigate in the world that exists. Far from devaluing the vital academic skills young people need, a critical and activist curriculum speaks directly to the deeply rooted alienation that currently discourages millions of students from acquiring those skills. By addressing the social context and social relationships that help create school failure, critical classrooms seek to break the cycle of remedial tedium and replace it with more self-conscious, purposeful student activity.

A social justice classroom offers more to students than do traditional classrooms, and expects more from students. Critical teaching aims to inspire levels of academic performance significantly greater than those motivated or measured by grades and test scores. When children write for real audiences, read books and articles about issues that really matter, and discuss big ideas with compassion and intensity, "academics" start to breathe. Yes, we must help students "pass the tests," even as we help them critique the harmful impact of test-driven education. But only by systematically reconstructing how and what we teach do we have any hope of cracking the cynicism that lies so close to the heart of massive school failure, and of raising academic expectations and performance for all children.

◆ **Culturally sensitive.** Critical teaching requires that we admit we don't know it all. Each class presents new challenges to learn from our students, and demands that we be good researchers and good listeners. These days the demographic reality of schooling makes it likely that white teachers will enter classrooms filled with children of color. As African-American educator Lisa Delpit has written: "When teachers are teaching children who are different from themselves, they must call upon parents in a collaborative fashion if they are to learn who their students really are." They must also call upon the cultural diversity of their colleagues and on community resources for insights into the communities they seek to serve. What can be said about racial and cultural differences between teachers and students also holds true for class differences.

We know from our own experience that creating successful critical classrooms is not easy. It is difficult, demanding work that requires vision, support, and resources. Finding groups and networks of support is crucial for the long haul, as is the need to build alliances for equity beyond the class-room among parents, professional associations, teachers' unions, and com-munity groups. The success of our classroom efforts is ultimately tied to efforts at the district, state, and national levels to improve public education and to sustain the collective social obligations that a democratic system of public schooling implies.

We know too that there will be opposition from those who think criti-cal teaching for social justice is "too political," as if traditional teaching for the status quo were not equally "political" in its authoritarian practice, its unequal outcomes, and its endorsement of the established order.

Some colleagues will resist calls to take on greater responsibility for school failure. Others will succumb to corrosive cynicism or force of habit. At times, wrongheaded mandates will be imposed on us from above by bureaucrats or politicians. At other times the small steps we manage to take may seem painfully short of our grand visions, even isolated and utopian in the face of the broader social changes needed.

But the alternative to critical teaching for social justice is to surrender to a system that, left to its own logic, will never serve the common good. Critical classroom practice is an indispensable and much-neglected missing piece in the puzzle of school improvement. Without social justice teaching inside classrooms, even vital reforms in funding equity or school governance will have limited impact.

For all its flaws, public education exists because generations of people have fought to improve the future for themselves and their children. Whether public education continues to exist, and whether it rises to the challenges before it, remains an open question. How we as teachers respond will help determine the answer.

A classroom veteran once told younger colleagues that teachers had two choices: "We can teach for the society we live in, or we can teach for the one we want to see." Rethinking Schools is for those with the vision to reach for their dreams.

Untracking English

Linda Christensen

Aaron, a dancer in Jefferson High School's elite Jefferson Dancers, tapped his pencil against his desk as he spoke: "Schools are geared towards repeating society's pattern. Some people succeed; some people fail. Tracking makes it seem like the kids are at fault. My father is a doctor. My mother is a voracious reader who read to me and bought me books. What about the kids whose parents didn't have the time or couldn't afford that? I entered school ahead of the race. I ended up in all advanced classes. An 'aha' I came to is that everybody should have all opportunities open to them. Why figure out ahead of time for people what they're going to do with their lives?"

Aaron paused and looked around the room at his classmates in this junior Literature and U.S. History class before calling on Jim, who hadn't spoken during our discussion on tracking.

Jim drew a deep breath before speaking. His voice cracked with tears. "What I learned in school is that I'm not good enough. I was never in an advanced class. Schools are set up like beauty pageants — some of us were set up to fail. The way they treat us, they might as well say, 'You suck. Get lost. Get out of here.' Look, I've always been in bonehead English. Why wasn't I good enough to be in top classes? Haven't I written as good papers as you? Can't I talk about things as good as you?"

Jim's statement continues to haunt me years later as I teach a "low-tracked" class where students gleam like unpolished agates on Moonstone Beach. And Aaron's question, "Why figure out ahead of time for people what they're going to do with their lives?" should be placed at the top of every course guide that designates the test scores students need before they apply for an honors class.

Jefferson High School is located in the heart of Portland's predominately working-class African-American community. In the late 1970s, Jefferson became a performing arts magnet school in an effort to desegregate

Portland's schools. White students from around the city took advantage of Jefferson's outstanding dance, theater, television, and music programs.

Initially, magnet students could attend part-time — taking their academic classes at their home schools and their performing arts classes at Jefferson. But as the programs increased in popularity, Jefferson's administration required that magnet students attend the school full-time. This was when I noticed a shift in the racial composition of the honors classes. Increasingly, the honors classes became a track for the magnet students, while the neighborhood students were placed in the lower-track classes. In other words, in an effort to desegregate the school, the school became segregated at the classroom level.

The classes I taught at Jefferson — Literature and U.S. History, Contemporary Literature and Society, and Writing for Publication — were all untracked. I knew tracking was unjust, and I didn't want to perpetuate the myths about academic ability that tracking imparts. I also wanted to demonstrate that it was possible to teach a wide range of students in one class, to present a model for my school and district.

After ten years of teaching remedial English, I also knew I didn't want to teach one more low-tracked class. Even if my seniority allowed me the privilege of teaching advanced classes, morally, I couldn't teach them any longer either.

Tracking helps create and legitimate a social hierarchy within a school based on perceived differences in student ability. Students in higher tracks have access to college preparatory classes: algebra, geometry, calculus, chemistry, physics. But even in English and social studies, students participate in different educational experiences. Students in advanced classes read whole books from the canon, write papers analyzing literature, and complete library research which prepares them for college, while students in lower-track classes typically read "light bites" of literature and history — short stories or adolescent novels. Their writing, if they write, tends to remain in the narrative, personal storytelling mode rather than moving to the analytical.

Beyond the lack of preparation for academic tasks, the larger problem I witness is the embedded beliefs students carry with them when they leave these classrooms. Students in advanced classes come to believe they "earned" a privilege that is often given them based on race, class, or gender, while students in remedial classes come to feel they are incapable of completing more difficult work.

But I wonder what other messages students learn when they see majority white or wealthy students in advanced classes. Do they believe that those students are smarter than students of color or poor and working-class students? When we allow tracking — especially tracking which privileges one race, one class, or one gender over another — we unwittingly allow students to walk away with these and who knows what other assumptions.

At the same time, I recognize that untracking a school is a complicated business. Too many good intentions have been undermined by implementing a detracking policy without helping teachers reconstruct their ideas about students and curriculum. Dumping low-tracked students into advanced classes without changing strategies and content harms students and derails the possibility for change. It becomes all too easy to point at the drop-out and failure rates of underprepared students and say, "See, untracking doesn't work." To successfully untrack English classes, teachers must unmask the myths about student ability, redesign the curriculum, and change teaching strategies.

I created untracked classes because of the injustice I saw in students' education. I continued to teach untracked classes as long as I was at Jefferson because they are better classes — for the students and the teacher.

Looking for Each Student's Gifts

After teaching untracked classes for several years, I've come to believe that the notion of great differences in student capacity is false. One of the first obligations of a teacher in an untracked class is to look at student ability in a new light. Teachers must see the gifts that each student brings to class, not the deficits. The teacher must absolutely believe in the potential of the student, but even more essentially, the teacher must believe in the right of the student to have access to a rigorous education. And the teacher must convey those beliefs clearly to the student who may be working off years of failure and poor work habits. Many of the students who come from remedial or regular classes are bright. But the abilities they bring to class often go unrecognized because they aren't the skills traditional education has prized: reading and writing. I especially found this to be true of many African-American males who had been misplaced in special education. These students had amazing dexterity with verbal language and astute social/political insights, but too often their literacy skills were underdeveloped.

Because of the variation in students' scholastic histories, they come with distinct sets of skills, but not necessarily different sets of intellectual capacities. The students who typically perform well in class have better reading, writing, geographic, and math skills. They have better school work habits. They know how to study. They come to school on time. Sometimes they are voracious readers. They have written more essays and frequently know how to put together a well-organized paper. They are confident of their ability as students. They see teachers as allies and know how to use their teachers, and others, as resources. Often they have college-educated parents who can help them with homework and who are available in the evenings to make sure their work is completed. They have access to more information and materials — from computers and home libraries to transportation to city and college libraries. Their parents are not intimidated by these institutions and know how to use computer searches, librarians, and the school system to gain information. And because they travel through their school careers being rewarded for their performance, they are generally better behaved.

On the other hand, many lower-track students may still have problems with the basics in punctuation, spelling, sentence structure, and grammar. They may not know where to begin or end a sentence, much less a paragraph or an essay. Some have never read a complete book by their junior or senior year in high school. Some are not accustomed to the practice of homework. They are often intimidated when it comes to advanced classwork because they lack the skills necessary to perform the tasks — especially if they are assigned rather than taught. Unlike their high-achieving peers, they often don't view their teachers as resources and aren't as successful in using the school system for their benefit. Frequently, they are alienated or bored by the material in advanced classes and don't see the immediate relevance to their lives. Their parents may work one or more jobs and may not have the time, expertise, or materials to help or push their children at home. Over the years, I've noticed how much my training as an English teacher is called on with my two daughters' education, and I wonder how children without college-educated parents (or with parents who have to work the night shift) can compete.

But often the most creative students in my mixed-ability classes are the students who have not succeeded in school. Many previously low-tracked students have a great ear for dialogue and metaphor because their listening and speaking skills are more finely honed. These students tend to be playful, talkative, adept at role plays, debates, and class discussions. They are the risk-takers. Steven, for example, literally jumped into the middle of a debate. Once, in a unit on men and women in literature and society, he strode to the center of our circle and acted out how he believed women have a shopping-mall approach to men. Steven pretended he was a woman inspecting each man as if he were a piece of merchandise, then tossing him aside when someone better came along. Although he had difficulty writing an essay on the topic, his spontaneous "presentation" during discussion was well-argued and gave students a metaphoric framework for many of their debates on the topic.

Each group of students (as well as each individual student) presents its own problems. While most of the "advanced" students complete their classwork and homework on time, too often they write "safe" papers. Chris, a potential valedictorian, summed it up when he asked, "What do I have to do to get an A?" Not "what tools must I be capable of using," not "what knowledge will I need to understand literature, writing, society, or history," but "what must I get done." My goal is to shake these students out of their safety, to create a desire to write instead of a desire to complete the work, to awaken some passion for learning, to stop them from slurping up education without examining it.

I want them to walk around with note-pads, ready for their next poem, story, or essay, but I also want them to question themselves and the world. In fact, I want them to question the privilege that placed them into advanced or honors classes. I want the same for my low-skilled students, but additionally, I am challenged to harness their verbal dexterity onto paper and motivate them to work outside of class. And I also want to provoke them to examine the inequities that landed many of them in low-skilled classes in the first place.

Changing Misperceptions

One of the biggest lies about ending ability grouping is that low-tracked students benefit while "advanced" students languish. Parents and educators worry that the behavior of unruly, uninterested students will keep the teacher focused on classroom control rather than on teaching. As my student Ellie said when I discussed untracking with her high-tracked class, "We couldn't learn if those students were in our class." Chetan Patel wrote one of his college essays for University of Chicago — "A Lesson in Tolerance" — about his view of my class on the first day:

> Rowdy students hung off their seats as I walked into class the first day of my junior year. The desks were arranged in a circle around the classroom, almost every seat was occupied. I looked for a chair next to a friend, but found the only empty seat near a window. I sat and looked around the class. It included dancers, athletes, and the left-overs from Jefferson's dismantled Scholar's program. I was in the Scholar's program until its end, taking advantage of the small classes, countless field trips and advanced curriculum. Because of last year's budget cuts, the program was disassembled and students were left to face Jefferson's overcrowded and often crude classes. Outside the 30 students in the Scholar's program, I thought the rest of Jefferson's thousand students were completely ignorant. They spat in hallways, punched ceiling tiles, smoked on the street curb, and talked in slang. The Literature and U.S. History class I was in was supposed to be the best Jefferson had to offer. From the looks of it, Jefferson's best didn't seem like much.

While I don't want to underplay the challenge to maintain an orderly classroom so that all students can learn, too often the word "rowdy" is a code word for "lots of poor students or students of color" — as can be seen in Chetan's initial portrayal of the students who were not in the Scholar's program. When the expectations are clear and the assignments challenge students to think critically about the world and their place in it, students are not as likely to act out. Because low-tracked students, in general, have less patience for busy work and value grades less than honors students, they are more likely to complain loudly, and criticize the demeaning work and their teachers. They are more likely to turn their attention to disrupting the class. And they have lots of practice; they're good at it.

I can't entirely dismiss the fact that some classes are more boisterous — especially low-tracked classes where students do not believe that the work has any real meaning for their lives. Yes, untracked classes will probably be louder than honors classes. Yes, more students will arrive more academically unprepared than in an honors class. Yes, if the balance of the class is shifted too heavily in favor of low-tracked students, "discipline" may remain an issue. But well-balanced untracked classes will also be more inventive, more creative, and more honest. As Chetan wrote, "The following days, I began to talk with my neighbors and my opinion of the class changed entirely. I loved coming to second block and hearing everyone's clever stories.... My [former classmates] looked down on other students who I now thought of as equals."

Certainly, untracking honors English is not an easy sell for students — or their parents — who have been offered the privileges of honors programs that Chetan outlined earlier: small classes, frequent field trips, and advanced curriculum. They like their privileges and believe they've earned them, unlike the "rowdy students" Chetan met on the first day of my class. Parents and educators worry that top students end up playing teacher to their underprepared peers in an untracked class — and unfortunately this is sometimes true, but it shouldn't be. Turning advanced students into tutors occurs when the curriculum and methodology of a high-tracked class remain the same. It's the worst-case scenario that proponents of tracking use to scare us into maintaining the status quo. They assume that top students master the material quickly and must either tap their toes or play teacher while remedial students struggle to catch up. This situation places students, like Jim in the opening of this piece, who arrive feeling one-down educationally, at a further disadvantage, but it also takes time away from more skilled students who should be working at the edge of their ability instead of repeating what they already know. Adam, a senior in my untracked Contemporary Literature and Society class, wrote of his experience in this role:

> I was always the one the teacher looked at when someone else needed help. "Oh, Adam can help you." It's not the usual form of discrimination, but I realize now how much it bothered me when I was in grade school. "Well, so-and-so isn't a good student, he needs extra help. We'll make him partners with Adam. Adam won't mind spending his extra time explaining things to so-and-so."

If we turn the practice of students as teachers around and look more carefully at our students' gifts, then we acknowledge that all students can be teachers. As Jessica noted in her class evaluation:

> This is the first English class in three years where I have been around different students. All of us have been tracked into separate little migrating groups, forever stuck with each other. I think that having so many different thinking minds made it rich. All the experiences we shared were exciting and new. It made us debate things because most often we didn't agree with each other. But we listened and we all think a little bit differently now. Don't you wish the whole world could be like our class?

When there is real diversity in the class, students teach each other by sharing their strengths: Steven's improvisation on gender issues helped create a metaphor for students to discuss men and women in society and literature. Jessica's ability to capture the talk of the neighborhood provided her classmates with a model of how to use dialogue to build characters in their own writing. Kanaan's analysis of the teaching of language, and how it affected African-American students as they were learning to read and write, had a profound effect on his fellow students' understanding of how political the nature of language can be. Curtina's images in her poetry broke the barrier between the academy and the music scene. Joe's insight into how the politics of race reverberate in his neighborhood educated his peers who lived on the other side of town, in a way that no traditional book learning could have.

Students teach each other by telling the stories of their lives or debating issues from diverse perspectives. Scott, who drove to Jefferson every day from an almost all-white suburb, thought that racism had disappeared after the '60s. When Suntory wrote about the hour it took for police to respond after gunshots were fired into his house, Scott's education about race relations moved up a notch. So did DeShawn's when Alejandro spoke of crossing the border with his grandmother when he was six and acting as a translator for his parents.

Chetan learned quickly that his initial assessment of his peers was flawed and that he had a lot to learn from his classmates:

> The teacher, Ms. Christensen, spent five minutes silencing the side chatter.... It took almost an hour for her to go over the class expectations that seemed entirely too high for this group. Amid more side talk, Ms. Christensen expounded on the first assignment, "We're going to write profiles on each other." After a five-minute explanation of what a profile was, the class groaned. She partnered the students up and I got stuck with Ayanna Lashley, a short girl whose growing stomach contrasted with her tiny body... [A]s the bell rang, Ms. Christensen announced, "Bring your finished profile tomorrow."
>
> That night I wondered how bad the year was going to be. Expecting Ayanna to write a poor profile, I quickly scribbled a few notes on a piece of paper about her.
>
> The next day Ms. Christensen told us to read what we wrote. She asked for a volunteer and the all-too-eager Tony started us out. Ten readers later, I couldn't believe what I was hearing. I had never heard writing like this — writing this good. To my surprise, no one used a single slang word.... One by one, the class went around the circle, every person painting a perfect picture of their partner. My turn finally came and I nervously read my shameful piece. I slumped into my chair as my partner read hers. I frowned, not because her piece was bad (it was terrific), but because I had let myself and the class down....
>
> The students around me wrote in different, exciting styles instead of the bookish Scholars' type. My writing became dynamic and versatile, something my past efforts had failed to accomplish.
>
> At year's end, I realized how prejudiced I had been. I totally misjudged my fellow students and learned more making and sitting next to new friends. The class turned out to be my favorite at Jefferson, not because everyone suddenly changed their ways, but because I changed mine.

In fact, the writing was rougher, less polished than Chetan remembers. I know for sure that I spent more time teaching them to write portfolios.

Students began the year with rich lives, not rich writing skills. Chetan wrote his memories of the class after spending his junior and his senior year — by choice — in untracked classes. But he is right that he learned from the stories of classmates and from their writing styles. This notion of enlisting all students as teachers implies a major shift in the structure, content, and methodology of the class.

Changing the Curriculum

Successfully untracking means re-examining and changing the curriculum. Instead of constructing my curriculum around a parade of novels, I teach thematic units that emphasize the social/political underpinnings of my students' lives: the politics of language, the politics of literacy, men and women in society and literature, the politics of cartoons and mass media. In each unit I attempt to engage students in a dialogue, to teach them to find connections between their lives, literature, and society while at the same time remaining academically rigorous. "Essential" questions provide the focus for most units. In the politics of literacy section of sophomore English, I ask, "What is literacy? Can people who don't know how to read and write be literate?" There is no one text that answers those questions.

A variety of readings — essays, poetry, short stories — as well as role plays, discussions, improvisations, writing from our own lives, all serve as "texts." We read excerpts from Frederick Douglass's and Malcolm X's autobiographies. We read sections from Joe Kane's *Savages* where an old man leads Kane through the Amazon jungle, identifying and discussing the properties of each plant. Students conduct interviews with their parents or grandparents about ways they "read the world without words," and return with stories about fishing, hairstyling, and driving diesel trucks. The curriculum becomes a symphony or a church choir. Each text, each student's life, adds a "voice." The texts are interwoven, but the recurring refrain is made up of the students' stories and analyses — their voices, either in discussion or in read-arounds of their own pieces — hold the song together.

But let me state clearly, in case this sounds like all we do is sit around in a cafe-like atmosphere discussing politics and our lives: In all of these classes, the mainstay of the curriculum is rigorous reading and writing activities that prepare all students for the university or post-secondary institutions. The way these activities are taught, the undergirding of preparation for each reading and writing activity, and the follow-up differ from more traditional classes.

Years ago, when I taught my first untracked classes, I eliminated the canon from the curriculum altogether because I wanted students to hear the voices of women and people of color who are not traditionally represented. Students complained that *The Scarlet Letter* and *The Odyssey* weren't relevant to their lives. But I have come to see the value of maintaining some pieces from the canon so that students can understand literary allusions, read and critique the common curriculum, enter conversations that include these classics, and perceive how some themes do reverberate through the years. I also want them to look for the relevance that they might have missed. *Pygmalion* is the perfect example. On the surface, students may not see how a play set in England could teach them anything about their own lives, but a closer look reveals how the class issue of language that Shaw explored when it was first produced in London in 1914 is as relevant to their lives as it was to Eliza's.

Of course, some classics can also be used to hone students' critical reading skills as they investigate race, class, and gender issues in these books. Students need to ask the question, "Whose classics? Why these books and not others?" as anti-racist educator Enid Lee does in her *Rethinking Schools* interview, "Taking Multicultural, Anti-Racist Education Seriously": "[W]hen we say classical music, whose classical music are we talking about? European? Japanese? And what items are on the test? Whose culture do they reflect? Who is getting equal access to knowledge in the school? Whose perspective is heard, whose is ignored?"

For example, students might ask: Why teach Shakespeare, who wasn't even an American, in an American literature class, but not a play by the Pulitzer Prize-winning African-American August Wilson? If discussion of the issue of slavery is important, why read Mark Twain and not Toni Morrison or Frederick Douglass? These questions raise important issues as students become "literate."

Also, students who have not been prepared for honors classes must learn to negotiate texts like *Othello* or *The Scarlet Letter* that are not immediately accessible. They must develop the ability to work through frustrations and immediate impulses to dismiss these texts as irrelevant or too hard. They need to learn that all readers get confused, but they must also have enough opportunities to succeed with complex materials to embed the belief that if they struggle long enough, they will understand. Sometimes this means developing note-taking systems as well as study strategies, including learning when and where to find help.

The biggest shift in curriculum in most honors classes entails a more inclusive reading list. As my daughter Anna wrote when she was a senior at a school where advanced classes are predominantly white, "What student of color would want to come into a tracked honors class where all the work is by dead white men? The fact that writers of color are not a part of the curriculum pulls the welcome mat out from under their feet."

My explicit focus on the politics of language in my senior class, and on the study of education in my junior class, plays an additional role in untracking my classes. Because tracking has, to one degree or another, shaped students' academic self-concepts, especially for low-tracked students, taking a critical look at this process helps them rethink their potential. As Bill Bigelow wrote in an article on untracking the social studies classroom, "[T]he unequal system of education, of which tracking is an important part, needs a critical classroom examination so that students can expose and expel the voices of self-blame, and can overcome whatever doubts they have about their capacity for academic achievement."

Changing Reading Strategies

On the surface, a typical reason for not untracking classes is that lower-tracked students don't have the skills or the desire to work at more advanced levels, and will get left behind or slow down their more capable peers. But given the right strategies, these challenges to classroom success need not become barriers to untracking. Throughout the year, I teach students who lack skills to write more effectively. But the real challenge in untracked classes is the difference in students' reading ability. Perhaps the greatest roadblock for those of us who want to untrack classes is our students' inability to read difficult texts.

How do we continue to assign challenging literature when not all of our students are initially capable of reading it? Some of the readings I use with students are difficult — for all students. To "dumb down" the curriculum would deny capable students access to a rigorous curriculum, and to always give different assignments to students based on their reading levels would defeat the purpose of joining students together.

Over the years, I've developed strategies to help readers at various levels engage in the curriculum. For example, I begin the year with my "Unlearning the Myths" unit, where students critique cartoons and children's literature for race, class, and gender bias because I want students to learn how to read for silences in the literature. Whose voices are heard? Whose stories are told? Whose lives are marginalized? Who's the hero and who gets saved? I want students to develop a habit of reading for recurring patterns of domination and exclusion. And I want them to approach these questions with "texts" that feel accessible to all: cartoons and children's literature. (See Christensen's article "Unlearning the Myths That Bind Us," page 126, for more information on this unit.)

And, I admit we read fewer texts/novels in my class because I choose to read, discuss, and think about each piece more thoroughly. Any text we tackle is an investigation into both literature and society, chosen not because it's on some university's reading-for-college-preparation list, but rather because it allows us to examine our society and ourselves more fully. *The Color Purple*, for example, permits us to probe the relationships between men and women as well as to explore their roles in the world. In *A Pedagogy for Liberation*, Ira Shor's discussion of the "illuminating" course helped me shape my classes:

> [W]e want the 'illuminating' course to be serious and on the other hand it has to develop the habits of intellectual seriousness in a culture field that discourages students from being critical....The point is not to assign fewer books so that students will have time to memorize more of what they read. Learning is not a memory Olympics! The idea is to make critical reflection on society the fundamental activity. The idea is to avoid flying over the words in an heroic effort to reach the end of the reading list, flying over society

also in such a way as to avoid knowing how learning relates to reality. Simply shortening the syllabus is not the same thing as investing the pedagogy with a purpose.

Sometimes that "pedagogy with a purpose" is served best by using literature circles that give students a choice of novels at different reading levels within a thematic unit. Students in my junior class, for example, chose from a list of novels written by African Americans about the conditions of slavery: *Beloved*; *Kindred*; *I, Tituba, Black Witch of Salem*; *A Narrative of the Life of Frederick Douglass*; and *Middle Passage*. Because all students read literature dealing with slavery, they were able to discuss the connected issues, but inform each other with examples from various texts.

Sometimes I insist we all read the same material, especially when I try to teach certain reading, writing, critical literacy, or dialogue strategies. Literary tea parties, improvisations, dialogue journals, poetry, and interior monologues, as well as other tactics, teach students in any class how to read more critically. But in an untracked class, these methods equalize access to reading as well as push students to discuss content. Not every student in my class completes the readings by the due date, but they can still be involved in the discussion. Often the class talk entices nonreaders to read and provides a meaningful context for them to understand the text.

Literary Tea Party

Experienced readers don't balk at slow beginnings of novels. They are like swimmers who dive into cold water knowing there will be a delicious rush when they burst into a breast stroke or Australian crawl. But inexperienced readers panic and drown. There are too many names, the location is unfamiliar, they don't see the point. "What's this got to do with me?" They give up too soon — before the writer has grabbed them.

In a class discussion about reading, I once asked strong readers to talk about their habits. Renesa said, "Even if I don't like the first chapter, I keep reading. I know it will get better." Marvin, a poor reader, said if he didn't like the first few paragraphs, he couldn't keep reading. It tired him out just trying to remember the characters' names and long, descriptive passages bored him. Yet Marvin, like many poor readers, could memorize the lyrics to popular music and knew as much about rap artists as I know about most authors. The capacity was evident; the will and the belief that he could succeed were not. For nonreaders like Marvin, teachers must be willing to overcome years of resistance to reading as well as break well-developed nonreading coping strategies.

I use the Tea Party to entice poor readers into novels (or historical periods). The Tea Party is like a movie preview, presenting brief clips of the story line and characters to draw the audience in. For nonreaders or poor readers, this preview is essential, especially as they approach texts generally reserved for advanced classes. On the day we begin a new book, I bring cookies and juice for the party. I type out five roles for main characters in the book. I color code the cards for easy identification. For example, in Melba Patillo Beals' *Warriors Don't Cry,* all of the Melba cards are blue, Grandma's cards are yellow, and so on. I write a paragraph from the character's point of view to create intrigue and questions as well as to familiarize students with the characters before they begin reading. I write the role in first person, so students can more easily get into the character's head.

Dialogue Journals

The method I use most frequently to equalize access to articles, essays, stories, and novels in untracked classes is the dialogue journal. The purpose of the journal is to teach students to read closely. As Shor (op. cit.) emphasized, "The idea is to make critical reflection on society the fundamental activity." Instead of reading to consume the story line or just for literary elements, I encourage students to "talk back" to the author — to engage in a conversation with the book, but also to think about the same kind of questions we asked earlier when examining cartoons.

In the dialogue journal, students become the authors of their own questions about reading, instead of reading merely to answer my questions. Because their dialogue journals are the starting ground for class discussions, students usually bring questions or passages they are really interested in discussing with their classmates.

Depending on the book I might prompt students to keep track of specific kinds of information. For example, in the biographical novel *Thousand*

Pieces of Gold, I wanted to focus our discussion on immigration and history. I asked students to keep track of:

* Laws relating to the Chinese in the United States.
* Roles of women and men.
* Historical evidence — descriptions of camp conditions, what was happening in western states, etc.
* Relationships between racial groups.
* Similarities or differences in treatment of Chinese, Native Americans, African Americans.
* Good jumping off points to write poetry, interior monologues, narratives, essays.

At the beginning of class, I ask students to read over their dialogue journals and circle questions or passages they want the entire class to discuss. After students have assembled their contributions, I divide them into small groups and ask them to talk with each other using their questions/comments to initiate the conversation.

Each student poses a question, an observation, or a quote to the group, which they discuss before moving to the next person. Because small-group work requires students to share passages and questions, all students must continually go back to the text to read and reread for clarification — a technique that helps both the skilled and the unskilled reader.

Each group posts one or two questions and passages on the board. The class chooses one, and we begin the class talk. In an untracked class, this strategy keeps less-skilled readers involved in the conversation. Once they've rehearsed and reread in the small group, they are ready to jump into a discussion — and usually ready to argue. For some students, it pulls them back into the novel because they like being part of the class debates.

In my Literature and U.S. History class, one group returned to the full class discussion with the following question: Is Craig Lesley (author of the novel *River Song* [1990]) racist, sexist, or homophobic when he makes Mexican jokes, etc., or is he just trying to develop Danny's character? I took notes while the students discussed the question. The following selections are a partial snapshot of that discussion — my hand wasn't as fast their voices:

Angela: I think he's just trying to show what Danny is like.

Aaron: Okay, but then why does he have to keep bringing [racist remarks] up? Couldn't he just have him make those jokes during the first few chapters, then leave it alone? When he keeps doing it, it's an overkill. It seems like with the Native-American issues there is so much to cover, why spend time making jokes about Mexicans or male nurses?

Janice: Wouldn't he have to keep doing it if it's a characteristic? I mean he couldn't just do it for a few chapters then stop or else his character wouldn't be consistent.

Aaron: Yeah. I hadn't thought of that.

Sarah: I think he's trying to make a point about the Native-American culture, that since they are consistently being put down —alcoholism, lazy — that they put other people down, other racial groups.

Aiden: I think he's just trying to make it realistic. That's how people talk, they make fun of others.

Jim: Maybe he's trying to make us think about the racism, that's why he puts in so many — and against so many groups.

Aaron: But couldn't he do that and then have someone make a comment about it — like Pudge? When Danny makes a joke, couldn't she say, "Hey, that's not funny. Think about how people talk about Indians"?

Janice: Yeah. Because people do that in real life, too — stop someone when they're telling a racist joke.

This questioning method puts students in charge of the discussion rather than the teacher. It validates their questions. This is vital as we work toward a pedagogy of untracking. Sometimes in large group discussions when the teacher discusses symbolism or a well-read student remarks on the imagery in a passage, less-skilled readers are too intimidated to ask the simple questions — which may often be more socially relevant. With dialogue journals, these students have an opportunity to figure out confusions with this small group before taking a point to the large group.

Again, students learn from each other by challenging each other's assumptions and listening to other opinions. Writing about the use of dialogue journals and the class discussions that stemmed from them, Claire wrote: "I got ideas I wouldn't have thought of, interpretations I would not have considered. When I really thought about all of it, I acquired some new skills from [my classmates]." Mira said that her notes made it easier to write an essay because she had page numbers and passages to review. And Tracy said, "Writing dialogue journals made me slow down to read."

Improvisations

The Tea Party sets the stage for the novel and helps students get into the book, and the dialogue journal and group work provide opportunities for rich discussions, but sometimes the story drags or the language is inaccessible for some students. Able readers create images while they are reading, but poor readers often struggle so much with word meanings that they don't visualize the story. In working with untracked students, it is essential to get them to "see" the book and improvisations help do just that. Improvisations — or acting out scenes from the work — can also make a "classic" work more relevant by pushing students to create a contemporary version of the scene.

The play *Pygmalion*, for example, has phrasing and vocabulary that leave poor readers confused. I use improvisations to bring the work to life, to make the meaning of the piece clearer by staging it. I divide students into small groups, give each group a provocative part and ask them to create a scene that will help the class understand what took place in that particular section of the play. In small groups, students discuss the scene. As I move from group to group, I catch snatches of questions: What is going on? Who is Freddie? And then moving to higher level discussions: Why does Eliza throw the slipper at Higgins? Why doesn't she fight back when he calls her a "squashed cabbage leaf?"

As the groups reread their scenes, discuss the content, and act out the text, they provide new understandings to confused students. In *Pygmalion*, Goldie and Antonia rewrote the slipper scene in modern Jefferson language. Steffanie and Licy worked with the original script on the bath scene. After performing each scene, students stay in character "on stage" as the class questions them. Although I usually begin by modeling the kinds of questions I want students to ask, they quickly take over. To Higgins, one student asked, "Why do you feel like you can talk about Eliza in that way?" Another student asked Eliza's father, "Don't you care about your daughter?

Aren't you just selling her? Isn't that like prostitution?"

Disagreements about the interpretation of a scene lead to engaged dialogue about character motivation, author's intent, and society. Often, students go back to the original text to "prove" their point to the class. One year Mark's statement, "Henry didn't love Eliza, he considered her a professional equal," kept the class debating for an hour. In another class, Licy questioned whether Eliza's life improved with her new knowledge or if it brought her misery. Her reading and questioning of the play got at the politics of language. But as she questioned, she also talked about growing up in a Spanish-speaking home, and the difficulty of moving between the English-only world of school and the Spanish-only world of home — offering the class insights that would likely be rare in a more homogenous high-tracked class.

The improvisations help poor and able readers understand the work more deeply and critically. The improvs bring the story to life. We see and hear the story. But additionally, as we question the "actors," we also search for character motivation, for social influence. We read the story from the inside out. For poor readers, improvs provide a pause to bring them back to the table if they've failed to connect with the work or if they experience difficulty reading the piece on their own.

Interior Monologues and Poetry

When writing interior monologues and poems from a literary or historical character's point of view, students examine why characters act the way they do or capture the character's feelings at a critical moment. The writing puts students inside the literature. My students who come "up" from lower-tracked classes are often quite poetic in their responses. Interior monologues and point-of-view poems allow all students — regardless of their previous academic levels — to succeed and achieve greater insight.

Prior to writing interior monologues, students brainstorm strong "meditation" points of various characters. I share models from previous years so students understand what I want. There is no right answer in these exercises. As I tell students, "The only way you can do this wrong is to not do it." Jenelle Yarbrough wrote from Janie's point of view after she married Joe in Zora Neale Hurston's *Their Eyes Were Watching God*:

> I am only a vision to them. I am an object. I'm loved by the curious eyes of a man or hated by the envious eyes of a woman. I will never know the love of everyone's caring and generous hearts. I keep silent because I'm told beauty speaks louder than words. Well, if my beauty speaks so loud, why can't anybody hear my heart crying for someone to love me for the reasons God intended them to and not the reasons of a mirror?

We share the pieces out loud the following day and use the students' monologues as a springboard for our discussion. For example, after Jenelle read her piece, we talked about how Janie's position as the Mayor's wife separates her from the townspeople.

The poetry that students write from literature can generate unusual and important insights. In one exercise, I ask students to draw a metaphor about a character in the book. After students draw, I ask them to explain their drawing to the class, then write a poem which extends the metaphor. Jessica Rawlins drew a bottle of perfume and wrote her poem about Shug Avery from *The Color Purple:*

> I am Shug,
> I am the sweet breath
> every man holds onto at night.
> I am the lingering scent
> that stays
> to bring memories
> of violets
> and lily kisses.
> I am the sugar perfume
> that comes on strong,
> burns the senses,
> then vanishes.
> Leaving nothing
> but the life of a stolen thought.

These poems sometimes become the raw outline of a metaphorical essay about the character. Again, the poetry balances the fulcrum of achievement in an untracked class, because students from lower-track classes sometimes engage in more word play or music. But also, the poetry and the drawing allow for students who process information in different ways to share their strengths.

Filtering reading through improvisations, dialogue journals, interior monologue, poetry, and class discussions "slows" the class down. We don't "cover" as many novels as we did before. But students learn to think more deeply. They discover how to dig beneath the surface, how to make connections between texts, their own lives, and society.

In class evaluations students let me know in no uncertain terms that the units they enjoyed and learned the most from were the units we spent more time on. The units they enjoyed the least were the ones where I "bombarded [them] with readings" which I didn't give them time to digest.

The common element in each of the reading and writing strategies I've presented is students working together in a community to make meaning and to make change. Students often mistakenly assume that it's cheating to work in a group. Yet most adults know that the while certain aspects of projects must be completed individually, a community of thoughtful people makes any endeavor stronger. In my own work, the teachers who comprise the local and national Rethinking Schools groups, my Writing Project colleagues, and the teacher-leaders from every high school in our district have been invaluable to my growth as a teacher. Their insights, critiques, reflection, and especially our points of disagreement, make my teaching, writing, and community work stronger.

Courage in the Face of Anger

Tracking perpetuates systems of inequality that condemn students not only to unequal education, but to unequal opportunities once they leave school. In examining data regarding the placement of students of color in advanced or honors English classes (and even more drastically in math) in the Portland Public Schools, it is clear that inequalities exist.

But untracking schools is not easy. It can be mandated by an administration — but that alone won't ensure success. Teachers must be an integral part of the process; they must have time to meet together, teach each other strategies, and prepare materials for a more diverse audience. Parents — representative of the entire student population — must be involved in creating a successful program to bring quality education to a broader range of students. But without the vision and the experience of a successful untracked class, parents — especially the parents of high-tracked students — might be uneasy partners, as Chetan's initial reaction to the loss of his privileges suggests.

Years after my students discussed the social impact of tracking, schools continue to be "beauty pageants" where some students learn they're "not good enough," where they become tracked for life. In addition to making a case against the injustice of tracking, we need to create not only a vision for an education that serves all children, we need models that demonstrate untracked classrooms can work. We can't just wish tracking away. There are too many barriers and too much resistance on too many levels. Now is the time for the language arts community to prove that justice and quality education are possible.

References

Bigelow, Bill. "Getting Off the Track: Stories from an Untracked Classroom," in Bigelow, et al., *Rethinking Our Classrooms, Volume 1: Teaching for Equity and Justice*. Milwaukee, WI: Rethinking Schools, 1994, pp. 58-65.

Butler, Octavia. *Kindred*. Garden City, NY: Doubleday, 1979.

Condé, Maryse. *I, Tituba, Black Witch of Salem*. Charlottesville, VA: University Press of Virginia, 1992.

Douglass, Frederick. *Narrative of the Life of Frederick Douglass: An American Slave*. Cambridge, MA: Belknap Press of Harvard University, 1960.

Hurston, Zora Neale. *Their Eyes Were Watching God*. Urbana, IL: University of Illinois Press, 1991.

Johnson, Charles. *Middle Passage*. New York: Scribner, 1998.

Kane, Joe. *Savages*. New York: Knopf, 1995.

Lee, Enid. "Taking Multicultural, Anti-Racist Education Seriously," in Bigelow, et al., *Rethinking Our Classrooms, Volume 1*, op. cit., pp. 19-22.

Lesley, Craig. *River Song*. New York: Dell, 1990.

Malcolm X. *The Autobiography of Malcolm X*. New York: Ballantine, 1992.

McCunn, Ruthanne. *Thousand Pieces of Gold: A Biographical Novel*. San Francisco: Design Enterprises of San Francisco, 1981.

Morrison, Toni. *Beloved*. New York: Penguin, 1998.

Shaw, George Bernard. *Pygmalion: A Play in Five Acts*. Harmondsworth, England: Penguin, 1914.

Shor, Ira and Freire, Paulo. A Pedagogy for Liberation: Dialogues on Transforming Education. South Hadley, MA: Bergin & Garvey, 1987.
Walker, Alice. The Color Purple. New York: Washington Square, 1982.

For Further Reading
Owen, David. None of the Above: Behind the Myth of Scholastic Aptitude. Boston: Houghton Mifflin, 1985.
Rodriguez, Richard. "Achievement of Desire," in Colombo, Gary, (Ed.), Rereading America: Cultural Contexts for Critical Thinking and Writing. Boston: Bedford, 1998.
Smitherman, Geneva. Talkin' and Testifyin': The Language of Black America. Detroit: Wayne State University Press, 1986.
Tatum, Beverly. 'Why Are All the Black Kids Sitting Together in the Cafeteria?' and Other Conversations About Race. New York: Basic Books, 1997.

Unsung Heroes

Howard Zinn

A high school student recently confronted me: "I read in your book *A People's History of the United States* about the massacres of Indians, the long history of racism, the persistence of poverty in the richest country in the world, the senseless wars. How can I keep from being thoroughly alienated and depressed?"

It's a question I've heard many times before. Another question often put to me by students is: Don't we need our national idols? You are taking down all our national heroes — the Founding Fathers, Andrew Jackson, Abraham Lincoln, Theodore Roosevelt, Woodrow Wilson, John F. Kennedy.

Granted, it is good to have historical figures we can admire and emulate. But why hold up as models the 55 rich white men who drafted the Constitution as a way of establishing a government that would protect the interests of their class — slaveholders, merchants, bondholders, land speculators?

Why not recall the humanitarianism of William Penn, an early colonist who made peace with the Delaware Indians instead of warring on them, as other colonial leaders were doing?

Why not John Woolman, who in the years before the Revolution refused to pay taxes to support the British wars, and who spoke out against slavery?

Why not Capt. Daniel Shays, veteran of the Revolutionary War, who led a revolt of poor farmers in Western Massachusetts against the oppressive taxes levied by the rich who controlled the Massachusetts Legislature?

Why go along with the hero-worship, so universal in our history textbooks, of Andrew Jackson, the slaveowner, the killer of Indians? Jackson was the architect of the Trail of Tears, which resulted in the deaths of 4,000 of 16,000 Cherokees who were kicked off their land in Georgia and sent into exile in Oklahoma.

Why not replace him as national icon with John Ross, a Cherokee chief who resisted the dispossession of his people, and whose wife died on the Trail of Tears? Or the Seminole leader Osceola, imprisoned and finally killed for leading a guerrilla campaign against the removal of the Indians?

And while we're at it, should not the Lincoln Memorial be joined by a memorial to Frederick Douglass, who better represented the struggle against slavery? It was that crusade of black and white abolitionists, growing into a great national movement, that pushed a reluctant Lincoln into finally issuing a halfhearted Emancipation Proclamation, and persuaded Congress to pass the Thirteenth, Fourteenth, and Fifteenth amendments.

Take another presidential hero, Theodore Roosevelt, who is always near the top of the tiresome lists of Our Greatest Presidents. There he is on Mount Rushmore, as a permanent reminder of our historical amnesia about his racism, his militarism, his love of war.

Why not replace him as hero — granted, removing him from Mount Rushmore will take some doing — with Mark Twain? Roosevelt, remember, had congratulated an American general who in 1906 ordered the massacre of 600 men, women, and children on a Philippine island. As vice president of the Anti-Imperialist League, Twain denounced this and continued to point out the cruelties committed in the Philippine war under the slogan, "My country, right or wrong."

As for Woodrow Wilson, another honored figure in the pantheon of American liberalism, shouldn't we remind his admirers that he insisted on racial segregation in federal buildings, that he bombarded the Mexican coast, sent an occupation army into Haiti and the Dominican Republic, brought our country into the hell of World War I, and put anti-war protesters in prison?

Should we not bring forward as a national hero Emma Goldman, one of those Wilson sent to prison, or Helen Keller, who fearlessly spoke out against the war?

And enough worship of John F. Kennedy, a Cold Warrior who began the covert war in Indochina, went along with the planned invasion of Cuba, and was slow to act against racial segregation in the South.

Should we not replace the portraits of our presidents, which too often take up all the space on our classroom walls, with the likenesses of grass-roots heroes like Fannie Lou Hamer, the Mississippi sharecropper? Hamer was evicted from her farm and tortured in prison after she joined the Civil Rights Movement, but she became an eloquent voice for freedom. Or with Ella Baker, whose wise counsel and support guided the young black people who joined the Student Nonviolent Coordinating Committee, the militant edge of the Civil Rights Movement in the Deep South?

In the year 1992, the quincentennial of the arrival of Columbus in this hemisphere, there were meetings all over the country to celebrate him, but also, for the first time, to challenge the customary exaltation of the Great Discoverer. I was at a symposium in New Jersey where I pointed to the terrible crimes against the indigenous people of Hispaniola committed by Columbus and his fellow explorers. Afterward, the other man on the plat-form, who was chairman of the New Jersey Columbus Day celebration, said to me: "You don't understand — we Italian Americans need our heroes." Yes, I understood the desire for heroes, I said, but why choose a murderer and kidnapper for such an honor? Why not choose Joe DiMaggio, or Toscanini, or Fiorello LaGuardia, or Sacco and Vanzetti? (The man was not persuaded.)

The same misguided values that have made slaveholders, Indian-killers, and militarists the heroes of our history books still operate today. We have heard Sen. John McCain, Republican of Arizona, repeatedly referred to as a war hero. Yes, we must sympathize with McCain's ordeal as a war prisoner in Vietnam, where he endured cruelties. But must we call someone a hero who participated in the invasion of a far-off country and dropped bombs on men, women, and children?

I have come across only one voice in the mainstream press daring to dissent from the general admiration for McCain — that of the poet, novel-ist, and Boston Globe columnist James Carroll. Carroll contrasted the hero-ism of McCain, the warrior, to that of Philip Berrigan, who went to prison dozens of times for protesting the war in Vietnam and the dangerous nuclear arsenal maintained by the U.S. government. Carroll wrote: "Berri-gan, in jail, is the truly free man, while McCain remains imprisoned in an unexamined sense of martial honor."

Our country is full of heroic people who are not presidents or military leaders or Wall Street wizards, but who are doing something to keep alive the spirit of resistance to injustice and war.

I think of Kathy Kelly and all those other people from Voices in the Wilderness who, in defiance of federal law, have traveled to Iraq more than a dozen times to bring food and medicine to people suffering under U.S.-imposed sanctions.

I think also of the thousands of students on more than 100 college campuses across the country who have protested their universities' connection with sweatshop-produced apparel.

I think of the four McDonald sisters in Minneapolis, all nuns, who have gone to jail repeatedly for protesting against the Alliant Corporation's production of land mines.

I think, too, of the thousands of people who have traveled to Fort Benning, Georgia, to demand the closing of the murderous School of the Americas.

I think of the West Coast longshoremen who participated in an eight-hour work stoppage to protest the death sentence levied against Mumia Abu-Jamal.

And so many more.

We all know individuals — most of them unsung, unrecognized — who have, often in the most modest ways, spoken out or acted on their beliefs for a more egalitarian, more just, peace-loving society.

To ward off alienation and gloom, it is only necessary to remember the unremembered heroes of the past, and to look around us for the unnoticed heroes of the present.

Teaching About Unsung Heroes

Bill Bigelow

Schools are identity factories. They teach students who "we" are. And as Howard Zinn points out in his essay "Unsung Heroes" (see p. 33), too often the curricular "we" are the great slaveholders, plunderers, imperialists, and captains of industry of yesteryear.

Thus when we teach about the genocide Columbus launched against the Taínos, or Washington's scorched-earth war on the Iroquois, or even Abraham Lincoln's promise in his first inaugural address to support a constitutional amendment making slavery permanent in Southern states, some students may experience this new information as a personal loss. In part, as Zinn suggests, this is because they've been denied a more honorable past with which to identify — one that acknowledges racism and exploitation, but also highlights courageous initiatives for social equality and justice.

One of the best and most diverse collections of writing I have received from my sophomore U.S. history students was generated from a project aimed to get students to appreciate those "other Americans." From time to time over the years, I've had students do research on people in history who worked for justice. But these were often tedious exercises and, despite my coaxing and pleading, the student writing ended up sounding eerily encyclopedia-like.

An idea to revise this assignment came to me while reading Stephen O'Connor's curricular memoir, *Will My Name Be Shouted Out?*, about his experiences teaching writing to junior high school students in New York City. O'Connor was captivated by the monologues in August Wilson's play *Fences*. He read some of these aloud to his students and offered them a wide-open prompt: "Write a monologue in which a parent tells his or her life story to a child."

It struck me that I might get much more passionate, imaginative writing about the lives of social justice activists if I offered students a similar assignment. Instead of asking them to stand outside their research subjects and write in the third person, I invited them to attempt to become those individuals at the ends of their lives. Students could construct their papers as meditations about their individuals' accomplishments and possibly their regrets. They might narrate parts of their lives to a child, a younger colleague, or even to a reporter.

I first decided to launch this project out of a unit I do that looks at the sometimes tense relationship between the abolitionist movement and the women's rights movement in the years before and right after the Civil War. I framed it as the "Racial and Gender Justice Project: People Who Made Change." Because this would likely be the only time during the year that I would structure an entire research project around the lives of individual social justice activists, I wanted to give students an opportunity to learn about people throughout U.S. history, not simply during the decades between the 1830s and 1860s. I was aware that this presented something of a problem, as students wouldn't yet have the historical context to fully appreciate the work of, say, Dolores Huerta or Emma Goldman. But their reading would alert them to themes and events that we would cover later, and I could fill in some of the blank spots in their knowledge as they completed their research.

I remember, in an earlier year, writing up and assigning a choice-list of activists for students to research. I reviewed them in class one by one, talking briefly about their work and accomplishments. Can you spell b-o-r-i-n-g? This time I decided to write up short first-person roles for students to "try on" in class and to meet each other in character. I wasn't very scientific in the choices of activists that I offered students — in fact some, like Bessie Smith, fell a bit awkwardly into the "activist" category. I tried for racial and gender diversity; I also tried to mix the famous with the not-so famous, mostly concentrating on people who worked in social movements. (If the activists were too "unsung," students would have difficulty finding out enough about them to complete the writing.) My list was unavoidably idiosyncratic and missed lots of worthy individuals. However, in the end, if none of the people I included excited students, they could propose alternatives.

I wanted the roles I wrote up to be short and provocative. The point was not to do the assignment for students but to lure them into the activists' lives. Because my students are mostly white — and within this group (my only U.S. History class that year) overwhelmingly male — I wanted to make sure that at least several of the social justice activists were white men. It was important that the young white men in class know that people who look like they do have not only been the slaveowners and land-grabbers, they have also been part of a rainbow of resistance in U.S. history. Here are a couple of typical roles:

- **John Brown:** People have called me crazy because I, a white man, gave up my life in the cause to free black slaves. I fought in what was called "bloody Kansas" to make sure that Kansas did not enter the United States as a slave state. And it's true, I killed people there. But it was a just cause, and I took no pleasure in killing. I'm most famous for leading the attack on the U.S. arsenal at Harper's Ferry, Virginia. In one sense my mission failed, because we were captured and I was executed. But I am convinced that my actions hastened the day of freedom for black slaves.

- **Fannie Lou Hamer:** I was the youngest of 20 children. After I married, I was a sharecropper in Mississippi for 18 years. I risked my life when I registered to vote in 1962. I'd had enough of poverty. I'd had enough of racism. I began to organize for our rights, by working with SNCC, the Student Nonviolent Coordinating Committee. In the summer of 1964, I traveled to the Democratic National Convention where I was a representative of the Mississippi Freedom Democratic Party, which we'd created because the regular Democratic Party wouldn't allow blacks to participate. I sang "Go Tell It on the Mountain," and asked the now-famous question: "Is this America?"

In class, I briefly described the project and distributed a card with one role description to each student. I gave them a few minutes to trade cards if they felt like it, but I emphasized that ultimately they weren't stuck researching the person on the card they drew; they would be able to choose someone else if they liked. I wanted these students-as-historical-activists to meet each other and learn a bit about each other's life work. Once they'd settled on an individual, I distributed "Hello, My Name Is...." stickers and had them write down and wear their names prominently, so other students would be able to easily see who was who. Finally, I gave each of them a "Racial and Gender Justice Hunt" sheet. The assignment gave students tasks like: "Find someone in the group who has spent time in jail for their activities or beliefs (or would have if they'd been caught). What happened?" I required them to use a different person in their answers to each question, so they needed to keep circulating among other class members to complete the assignment. This was a delightful activity, filled with laughter and energy.

The following day we circled-up to review some of the questions and talk over what they had learned about the different individuals. Before we headed for the library to begin research, I gave the students an assignment sheet:

> Choose an individual who stood up for racial or gender justice. Perhaps this individual worked to end slavery, for women's right to own property or to vote, for farmworkers' rights, or to integrate schools in the South. You needn't agree with everything this person stood for, or agree with how he or she went about working for change. The only requirements are that the person tried to make this a better place to live and also significantly affected society. You may choose an individual (or group) who attended the "getting to know you" gathering we did in class, or come up with one of your own. If you choose one on your own, check with me first.

I told them that they were each going to be writing about their individual in the first person, but I didn't want to describe the full assignment until they had read and collected stories.

For their library and outside-of-class research, I gave students written research guidelines:

> Find out as much about your individual as you can. Try to answer the following questions — and be sure to look for specific stories from their lives:
> 1. What significant events in this person's life shaped their social commitment? What happened in their life to make them willing to take the risks they took?
> 2. What did the person want to accomplish or change?
> 3. What did they accomplish?
> 4. What methods did this person use to try to effect change?

5. What, if anything, about their life reminds you of something in your life? Is there anything in their life that you relate to, or that is similar to feelings or experiences you've had?
6. What meaning does this person's life have for today?
7. Find at least three quotes from the individual that you agree with or think are somehow significant.

I told them that they would need to turn in full answers to these questions with their final write-up.

Not surprisingly, some students had an easier time than others. The student doing Elaine Brown, one-time leader of the Black Panther Party, had trouble finding anything on her life and, unfortunately, didn't have the energy to read the entirety of Brown's excellent book, A *Taste of Power*, and so moved on to Elizabeth Cady Stanton. But by and large students were able to discover lots about their activists.

Grandma T. and Other Stories

I've found that it's always better to show students what I'm looking for, rather than just tell them. So I save student papers from year to year to use as examples. My student Wakisha Weekly virtually became Sojourner Truth in a paper she had written for me in a previous year. I read it to the class to demonstrate the kind of intimacy, detail, and voice that I hoped students would strive for. She structured it as a conversation between a dying Sojourner Truth and her granddaughter. It opened:

"Grandma T, how are you?"
"Oh, I am fine, baby doll. As fine as you can be in a hospital bed with all of these tubes."
"Are you going to die, Grandma?"
"I'm not going to die, honey. I'm going home like a shooting star."
"Can you tell me a story, Grandma?"

Wakisha's "Grandma T" tells her granddaughter about life as a slave, being sold when her master died and of life with successive owners. She talks of her escape and her conversion:

"Later in my life is when I felt a powerful force. It was God all around me. God gave me the name Sojourner and told me to move to New York and to speak to people. I called it preaching. I often put people in tears. The better educated didn't like me because I was so good at what I did, and I loved speaking out to people. I can't read a book, but I can read the people."

"You don't know how to read, Grandma?"

"No, I was never taught. Slaves didn't go to school or to college to be educated. The masters thought you were there just to work for them."

"But Grandma, I love to read, and I am really good at it."

"That's good, baby. And part of the reason you can read and go to school is because women didn't like to be put down by the men and wanted to work, earn money, and even go to school. So we stood up for ourselves."

"Who is we, Grandma T?"

Wakisha used the granddaughter's questions to pull her narrative along. In response to questions and comments, Grandma T. continued to tell the history, weaving her personal story with movement history — both the abolitionist and women's rights movements.

After hearing Wakisha's piece, students and I talked about what they liked about it and what made the writing both interesting and informative. We followed by brainstorming ways that we could write about the lives of our racial and gender justice activists. They came up with excellent ideas, including: students going to a nursing home to interview someone for a class project; a letter to a loved one, saying what you never got to say during your life; two lifelong friends walking and talking about the activities they participated in together.

I didn't want students to run simply with the first thing that came into their heads, so for homework I asked them to write two different introductions to their piece. We began these in class and the next day they brought them in and read them to one another in pairs. I asked people to nominate exemplary openings that they heard so that these could be shared with the entire class and would broaden our sampling of possible approaches.

What students ultimately produced sounded nothing like an encyclopedia. Andy wrote a story about "Nicholas," a former member of the Massachusetts 54th, the first regiment of black soldiers in American history. Drawing largely on letters in the book *A Grand Army of Black Men* (edited by Edwin S. Redkey), Andy set his piece in a facility for seniors, many years after the Civil War. Nicholas is sitting with his regular breakfast companion, Susan, who asks him at long last about the part of his ear that is missing. "To know about my ear, I would have to tell you a story," he says, and launches into a richly detailed tale about his decision to volunteer for the 54th and his experiences fighting in South Carolina.

Tyler's Marcus Garvey lies on his deathbed wondering whether or not he did enough for racial equality. He flashes back to his impoverished Jamaican childhood: "Though we had close to no money, we had heart, and each other."

Jennifer patterned her story about Rosa Parks on Wakisha's Grandma T. In an interior monologue, Jeff's Malcolm X reflected on how he changed, and what he feared and hoped for, while sitting in a hotel room the day before his final speech at the Audubon Ballroom. Jonathan wrote an unusual and complex piece that began on the day Leonard Peltier was released from prison — a day that is still in the future. His daughter tells the story of how she became an activist for Native-American rights after listening to her father narrate a videotape-letter to her about why he can't be with her as she grows up.

Gina wrote an utterly authentic-feeling story about two young children who visit César Chávez for a class project. In her story, Chávez narrates episodes from La Causa:

> "The fight was not over. In 1968, I fasted — that means I didn't eat anything — for 25 days. A different time I fasted for 24 days, and again I fasted, this time for 36 days. You know how hungry you can get when you miss breakfast or lunch — but imagine missing 36 breakfasts, lunches, and dinners."
>
> "But Mr. Chávez, didn't you ever fight? Like punch them or anything?" Richard asked.
>
> "No, no! Violence isn't right. Everything can be done without hurting somebody else. You can always show people your side with words or pictures or actions. Hurting somebody to make your point is wrong, and it never needs to be done. We never punched anyone, even if they punched us first. We just stayed at our place and showed them that they couldn't stop us."

"That's really neat, Mr. Chávez! I'm gonna do that," Linda said determinedly.

"I'm Gonna Do That"

In a myth-shattering history curriculum where heroes are regularly yanked from their pedestals, it's vital that we alert students to currents of generosity, solidarity, democracy, anti-racism, and social equality in the nation's past — and present. We don't need to make these up. They are there. Yes, we need to carefully analyze movements for change and acknowledge their shortcomings, the times they manifested those very characteristics that they sought to oppose in the larger society. And yes, we need to engage students in thinking about the relationship between strategies and aims, because not all activism is equally effective, and some can actually be counterproductive.

But the curriculum that demands perfection will be filled with blank pages. As Howard Zinn emphasizes, there are countless individuals who have worked "to keep alive the spirit of resistance to injustice and war." Let's work concretely toward a curriculum of hope. Let's give students the opportunity to conclude: "I'm gonna do that."

The Truth About Helen Keller

Ruth Shagoury Hubbard

It's time to start telling the truth about Helen Keller. The "Helen Keller story" that is stamped in our collective consciousness freezes her in childhood. We remember her most vividly at age seven when her teacher, Annie Sullivan, connected her to language through a magical moment at the water pump. We learned little of her life beyond her teen years, except that she worked on behalf of the handicapped.

But there is much more to Helen Keller's history than a brilliant deaf and blind woman who surmounted incredible obstacles. Helen Keller worked throughout her long life to achieve social change; she was an integral part of many important social movements in the 20th century. She was a socialist who believed she was able to overcome many of the difficulties in her life because of her class privilege — a privilege not shared by most of her blind or deaf contemporaries. "I owed my success partly to the advantages of my birth and environment," she said. "I have learned that the power to rise is not within the reach of everyone."

More than an icon of American "can-do," Helen Keller was a tireless advocate of the poor and disenfranchised. Her life story could serve as a fascinating example for children, but most picture books about Helen Keller are woefully silent about her life's work.

Covert Censorship: Promoting the Individual

"The world is moved not only by the mighty stories of heroes, but also by the aggregate of the tiny pushes of each honest worker." — Helen Keller

In the last decade, there has been a surge in literature for children that depicts people who have worked for social change. On a recent search for nonfiction picture books that tell the stories of those involved in social activism, I found scores of books — beautifully illustrated multicultural texts. Initially, I was delighted to be able to share these books with kids in my neighborhood and school. But as my collection grew, so did my frustration.

One problem with many of the books is that they stressed the individual, rather than the larger social movements in which the individuals worked. In his critique of popular portrayals of the Rosa Parks story, educator and author Herb Kohl argues convincingly that her role in the Montgomery bus strike is framed again and again as that of a poor, tired seamstress acting out of personal frustration rather than as a community leader in an organized struggle against racism. (See "The Politics of Children's Literature," in *Rethinking Our Classrooms, Volume 1*, p. 37.)

Picture books frame the stories of many other key community leaders and social activists in similar ways. Activist and educator Patrick Shannon's careful analysis of the underlying social message of books for young readers highlights this important finding: "Regardless of the genre type, the authors of these books promoted concern for self-development, personal emotions, self-reliance, privacy, and competition rather than concern for social development, service to community, cooperation toward shared goals, community, and mutual prosperity."

I first became interested in the activist work of Helen Keller a few years ago when I read James Loewen's *Lies My Teacher Told Me: Everything Your American History Textbook Got Wrong*. Loewen concludes that the way that Helen Keller's life story is turned into a "bland maxim" is lying by omission. When I turned to the many picture books written about her, I was discouraged to discover that books for young children retain that bland flavor, negating the power of her life work and the lessons people learned from it. Here is a woman who worked throughout her long life as a radical advocate for the poor, but she is depicted as a kind of saintly role model for people with handicaps.

The Image of Helen Keller in Picture Books

For the purposes of this investigation, I chose six picture books published from 1965 through 1997, which are the most readily available from bookstores and websites. Four of the six covers depict the famous moment at the well where Annie, her teacher, spells "water" into Helen's hand. This clichéd moment is the climax of each book, just as it is in the biographical movies. To most people, Helen remains frozen in time in her childhood.

According to these picture books, she is remembered for two things after she grew up: her "courage" and her "work with the blind and deaf."

Young Helen Keller, Woman of Courage by Anne Benjamin (Troll, 1991) is typical. The first 29 pages bring us to Helen, age 12, who can read and write "and even speak." The last page, page 30, sums up the remaining 66 years of her life:

> When Helen was 20, she did something that many people thought was impossible. She went to college. Annie went with her to help her study. Helen spent her life helping blind and deaf people. She gave speeches and wrote many books.
>
> Helen Keller died on June 1, 1968. But people all over the world still remember her courageous, helpful life.

But courage to do what? The statements that sum up her "courageous accomplishments" are ambiguous and confusing. "She gave speeches and wrote books." What were they about? What did she do that was so courageous?

None of the children's books I reviewed mentioned that in 1909 Helen Keller became a socialist and a suffragist — movements that framed most of her writing. "I felt the tide of opportunity rising and longed for a voice that would be equal to the urge sweeping me out into the world," she wrote.

Nor do those books tell readers that Helen Keller's publishing options dwindled because she wrote passionately for women's voting rights and against war and corporate domination. In order to promote the social justice she believed in, she decided she would take lessons to improve her speaking voice so that she could publicly speak out against injustice. This was true courage. Even after three years of daily work, her voice was uneven and difficult to control. Though she was embarrassed by her speaking voice and terrified of the crowds, Helen Keller boldly went on the lecture circuit. She later wrote that it felt as if she were going to her own hanging: "Terror invaded my flesh, my mind froze, my heart stopped beating. I kept repeating, 'What shall I do? What shall I do to calm this tumult within me?'"

The picture books omit the courage that took Helen Keller farther away from her home to visit poverty-stricken neighborhoods in New York City, where she learned firsthand about the horror of the crowded, unhealthy living conditions in tenement buildings. Outraged over the child labor practices she encountered, she educated herself about union organizing and the violence that organizers and strikers faced. She wrote angry articles about the Ludlow Massacre where, in an attempt to break a miners' strike, the Colorado National Guard shot 13 people and burned alive 11 children and two women.

The Ludlow Mine belonged to the powerful millionaire John D. Rockefeller, who paid the wages of the National Guard. When newspapers hesitated to publish her articles, Helen Keller spoke out publicly against Rockefeller: "I have followed, step by step, the developments in Colorado, where women and children have been ruthlessly slaughtered. Mr. Rockefeller is a monster of capitalism," she declared. "He gives charity in the same breath he permits the helpless workmen, their wives, and children to be shot down."

Helen Keller was not afraid to ask tough, "impolite" questions: "Why in this land of great wealth is there great poverty?" she wrote in 1912. "Why [do] children toil in the mills while thousands of men cannot get work, why [do] women who do nothing have thousands of dollars a year to spend?"

This courage to speak out for what she believed in is also ignored in the picture book *Helen Keller: Courage in the Dark* by Johanna Hurwith (Random House, 1997). Here, her achievements are summed up on the final page:

> Helen's story has been retold over and over. She has been the subject of books, plays, films, and television programs. The United States Postal Service has dedicated a stamp to her. And an organization with her name works to help blind people.
>
> Helen Keller's life was filled with silence and darkness. But she had the courage and determination to light her days.

This is courage at its blandest — and most passive. Notice that Helen herself is simply an icon — a "subject" of the media, the name behind an organization, and of course, best of all, an image on a stamp!

What a contrast to Helen Keller's own commitment to an active, productive life. When she wrote her autobiography in 1929, Keller declared: "I resolved that whatever role I did play in life, it would not be a passive one." Children don't learn that Helen Keller not only supported organizations to support blind people, she supported radical unions like the Industrial Workers of the World, becoming a "Wobbly" herself. Nor do they learn of her support for civil-rights organizations like the National Association for the Advancement of Colored People. W. E. B. DuBois printed news of her financial donations and the text of her letter of support in the organization's publication: "Ashamed in my very soul, I behold in my beloved south-land the tears of those oppressed, those who must bring up their sons and daughters in bondage to be servants, because others have their fields and vineyards, and on the side of the oppressor is power," she wrote.

During a recent search, the two best-selling picture books on Helen Keller listed at Amazon.com were *A Picture Book of Helen Keller* by David Adler (Scott Foresman, 1992) and *A Girl Named Helen Keller* by Margo Lundell (Cartwheel, 1995). The theme of passive courage is at the center of both these books as well.

At least in Lundell's book, Helen is credited with some action. After focusing on her childhood for 42 of the book's 44 pages, the author sums up Helen Keller's life with the following list:

> In her life, Helen wrote 5 books.
> She traveled many places.
> She met kings and presidents.
> She spoke to groups of people around the world.
> Most of the work she did was to help people who were blind or deaf.
> She was a warm and caring person.
> People loved her in return.
> The life of Helen Keller brought hope to many.

Helen Keller herself would probably be horrified by this vague and misleading representation of her life's work. She spoke to groups of people around the world, yes, but Lundell doesn't hint that she said things like: "The future of America rests on the leaders of 80 million working men and women and their children. To end the war and capitalism, all you need to do is straighten up and fold your arms." Lundell is equally vague about the content of her books, neglecting to mention essays such as "How I Became a Socialist" or books she wrote such as *Out of the Dark: Essays, Letters, and Addresses on Physical and Social Vision*.

Lundell's synopsis of Keller's accomplishments focuses on the famous people — "kings and presidents" — whom she met in her life. But at the core of her commitment was her work for political change with blue-collar workers, child laborers, and the oppressed, taking part in rallies, marches, meeting with friends to talk politics and to strategize. "I have never felt separated from my fellow men by the silent dark," she wrote. "Any sense of isolation is impossible since the doors of my heart were thrown open and the world came in." She showed that connection to her fellow workers in her actions again and again.

One fascinating example occurred in 1919, when Keller starred in *Deliverance*, a silent movie about her life. Helen supported the Actors Equity Union's strike by refusing to cross the picket line to attend the opening — and by joining a protest march with the striking actors.

Adler's *A Picture Book of Helen Keller* is the best-selling illustrated biography of Helen Keller for young readers. Like the other books I reviewed, this one focuses almost solely on her life before graduating from Radcliffe. The two important adult episodes Adler includes are her visits to blind soldiers during World War II and her work for the American Foundation for the Blind. The book ignores her phenomenal and productive life work as a writer and social activist. On the last page of the book, Adler sums up her work:

> Helen Keller couldn't see or hear, but for more than 80 years, she had always been busy. She read and wrote books. She learned how to swim and even how to ride a bicycle. She did many things well. But most of all, Helen Keller brought hope and love to millions of handicapped people.

Adler has space to note that Helen Keller learned to swim and ride a bicycle, but not to state that she helped found the American Civil Liberties Union or take on the medical establishment to improve health care for infants. The inadequacy of the information in these books for children is staggering. Her life of hard work is reduced to the phrase "she had always been busy."

Children could also learn from Helen Keller's compassion and recommitment to pacifism after her visit to Hiroshima and Nagasaki in 1948.

Deeply moved by the people she met and what they described to her, she wrote that the experience "scorched a deep scar" in her soul and that she was more than ever determined to fight against "the demons of atomic warfare…and for peace."

What's Wrong with This Story?

"So long as I confine my activities to social service and the blind, they compliment me extravagantly, calling me 'archpriestess of the sightless,' 'wonder woman,' and 'a modern miracle,'" Helen wrote to her friend Robert LaFollette, an early pacifist who ran for president as a third-party Progressive candidate in 1924. "But when it comes to a discussion of poverty, and I maintain that it is the result of wrong economics — that the industrial system under which we live is at the root of much of the physical deafness and blindness in the world — that is a different matter!"

While she was alive, Helen Keller fought against the media's tendency to put her on a pedestal as a "model" sweet, good-natured, handicapped person who overcame adversity. The American Foundation for the Blind depended on her as spokesperson, but some of its leaders were horrified by her activism. As Robert Irwin, the executive director of the foundation, wrote to one of the trustees: "Helen Keller's habit of playing around with Communists and near-Communists has long been a source of embarrassment to her conservative friends. Please advise!"

In the years since her death, her lifelong work as a social justice activist has continued to be swept under the rug. As her biographer Dorothy Herrmann concludes:

> Missing from her curriculum vitae are her militant socialism and the fact that she once had to be protected by six policemen from an admiring crowd of 2,000 people in New York after delivering a fiery speech protesting America's entry into World War I. The war, she told her audience, to thunderous applause, was a capitalist ploy to further enslave the workers. As in her lifetime, Helen Keller's public image remains one of an angelic, sexless, deaf-blind woman who is smelling a rose as she holds a Braille book open on her lap.

But why is her activism so consistently left out of the picture book versions of her life stories? Perhaps because the mythical Helen Keller creates a politically conservative moral lesson that stresses the ability of the individual to overcome personal adversity in a fair world: "Society is fine the way it is. Look at Helen Keller! Even though she was deaf and blind, she worked hard — with a smile on her face — and overcame her disabilities. She even met kings, queens, and presidents, and is remembered for helping other handicapped people. So what do you have to complain about in this great nation of ours?"

This demeaning view of Helen Keller keeps her in her place. She never gets to be an adult; rather she is framed as a grown-up child who overcame her handicap. Like other people with disabilities, Helen Keller must not be defined by her blindness or her deafness. She saw herself as a free and self-reliant person — as she wrote, "a human being with a mind of my own."

It's time to move beyond the distorted and dangerous Helen Keller myth, repeated in picture book after picture book. It's time to stop lying to children and to go beyond Keller's childhood drama and share the remarkable story of her adult life and work. What finer lesson could children learn than the rewards of the kind of engaged life that Helen Keller lived as she worked with others toward a vision of a more just world?

For Further Reading

Bigelow, Bill, et al. *Rethinking Our Classrooms, Volume 1: Teaching for Equity and Justice*. Milwaukee, WI: Rethinking Schools, 1994.

Herrman, Dorothy. *Helen Keller: A Life*. Chicago: University of Chicago Press, 1989. (A fine recent biography that covers her adult life as well as her famous childhood.)

Keller, Helen. *Out of the Dark: Essays, Letters, and Addresses on Physical and Social Vision*. Garden City, NY: Doubleday, 1913.

Keller, Helen. *Midstream: My Later Life*. Garden City, NY: Doubleday, 1929. (Helen Keller's fascinating autobiography gives readers a taste of her writing voice, her passionate beliefs, and her social convictions.)

Lawlor, Laurie. *Helen Keller: Rebellious Spirit*. New York: Holiday House, 2001. (A new biography for adolescents with excellent photographs to document Keller's life.)

Loewen, James. *Lies My Teacher Told Me: Everything Your American History Textbook Got Wrong*. Carmichael, CA: Touchstone, 1996.

Shannon, Patrick. *Becoming Political*. Portsmouth, NH: Heinemann, 1998.

Acting for Justice

Linda Christensen

When my niece Kelly was seven years old, she developed odd tics — blinking her eyes rapidly, jerking her arms, then her legs, then convulsing her entire body. Grunts followed the tics. She attempted to make them sound like hiccups. At school she stood alone at recess; during lunch she ate alone. Kids tormented her, mimicking her sounds and movements. When her tics and noises distracted the class, her teachers placed her desk in the hallway. Some days they sent her to the principal's office. When Kelly was in 8th grade, my sister discovered that her condition had a name — Tourette's Syndrome.

How did this affect Kelly? She hated going to school. She feigned illness. Some days when she was unable to endure the teasing and isolation, she ran home. Eventually she dropped out of high school and spent years regaining the dignity that students and teachers stripped her of when she was a child.

Kelly is not alone in her history. While most children don't have a medical condition that causes their isolation, too many children learn that their race, class, or language can set them up as targets in our society.

Unfortunately, many people experience acts of injustice daily. Sometimes these injustices occur in the form of an unkind comment about a person's weight, facial features, hair, or clothes. But often these injustices target people because of their race, language, or religion. Too often injustice moves beyond words. People are denied housing, jobs, fair wages, or decent education. As both history and daily news have informed us: People are physically abused — sometimes even killed — because of these differences.

But kids don't have to be cruel; in fact, part of our roles as teachers and administrators in schools should be to intervene when children hurt others, but more importantly, our job is to educate them to disrupt unjust behavior.

We can accomplish this by teaching about people who worked for change — Frederick Douglass, Lucretia Mott, John Brown, Rosa Parks,

Dolores Huerta, and other larger-than-life heroes who struggled to end slavery and injustice — so students have role models. We can teach them about the Abolitionist and Civil Rights movements, so students learn how to collaborate with others for change. But we also need to stop them from teasing a child who does not speak English as a first language or help them to stand up for the overweight girl in Algebra.

Warriors Don't Cry

I developed this "Acting for Justice" unit for students to "practice" behaving as allies. In the past few years, I connected this "acting for justice" lesson to literature or history that demonstrated both ally behavior and purposeful organizing for change. Although this activity can stand alone, I use it when I teach Melba Patillo Beals' autobiography *Warriors Don't Cry*. The book tells the story of Beals' days as one of the "Little Rock Nine" who struggled to integrate Central High School in Arkansas. The story is an insider's view of integration — the large and the small story of how people fight for change.

As students read the book, I ask them to keep track of people who act as allies for the Little Rock Nine. And they do — from the NAACP leaders who fought for integration, to the white woman who led Elizabeth Eckford to safety on the first day of integration, to Melba's white classmate Link, who called her nightly to let her know which halls to avoid and who helped her escape torture on numerous occasions.

We also read an interview with James Farmer, one of the founders of CORE, the Congress of Racial Equality. In the interview, Farmer discusses some of CORE's early activities in the 1940s using Gandhi's nonviolent strategies to integrate Jack Spratt's, a Chicago restaurant. Students love the white customers who aren't part of the sit-in, but who realize what is happening and act as spontaneous allies, refusing to leave their seats or eat. They chuckle at the ingenuity of the allies' answer when they, too, are asked to "eat and get out." They answer, "Well, madam, we don't think it would be polite for us to begin eating our food before our friends here have also been served." As we read the interview, I ask students to answer the restaurant personnel as if they are CORE members. "The restaurant says they will serve the blacks in the basement. How do you answer them?"

The students yell: "No. We won't be served in the basement."

I come back at them with the restaurant's next proposal. "The restaurant says they will serve the blacks at the two booths in the back of the restaurant. How do you answer them?"

The students yell: "No. We won't be served in the back of the restaurant."

Creating Scenes

Once students have steeped in historical and literary descriptions of ally behavior, I ask them to create a chart on their paper with four categories:

- Ally
- Target
- Perpetrator
- Bystander

First, they categorize the historical/literary characters from *Warriors Don't Cry:* Link and Grandma India were allies, Melba was a target, many white students and teachers were perpetrators, Danny was both an ally and a bystander. Once students are clear about the categories, I ask them to brainstorm a list from their own lives. When have they acted as allies? Were they ever targets? Perpetrators? Bystanders? (See Tom McKenna's "Confronting Racism, Promoting Respect," p. 315.)

When I first started using this activity, I developed "scenes" for students to act out because I wanted to get at injustices that I wasn't sure they would cover. Over the years, I discovered that it was far more powerful for students to write from their own experiences. When I taught this unit to a sophomore class, I was astounded at how many students confessed to being perpetrators, targets, and bystanders, and how few acted as allies. One student offered that he was a "jackass" in middle school and regularly tormented other students. Many talked about making fun of younger, weaker students. Sometimes their abuse was physical. Few students had stories of acting as an ally. In our discussion, it was clear that students didn't feel good about their participation or their lack of intervention, but they didn't feel powerful enough to stop the racist, homophobic, or belittling behavior and comments.

After students make their lists, I encourage a handful of students to share their incidents. Mario, an African-American sophomore, talked about store clerks following him because they thought he might steal clothes. Adam, an African-American student, discussed how the counselor automatically placed him in a "regular" English class without checking his test scores. Michelle shared the story of acting as an ally for several special-education students who were teased by a group of boys.

Once a few students share in the large group, I ask students to write the story of the injustice and encourage them to include a description of where the story took place, a description of the people involved, and what was said during the incident. They might also include how they felt about the act and whether or not they were changed because of the discrimination.

After students write their first drafts, I divide them into small groups to share their stories. Power relations in the classroom get played out in small groups. The more popular or assertive students sometimes silence or rudely ignore their peers when they tell their stories. I've observed students file their nails, flip through a magazine, or complete an algebra assignment while one of their group members reads. Besides modeling how I want them to act, I create written tasks for students to perform while they listen to their classmates in order to break students of these "silencing" behaviors. After each story is read, students write on the following prompts to focus their attention on the storyteller:

- Explain what can be learned from the piece.
- Ask the writer questions to get more details.
- Share any similar experiences from your life.
- If no one intervened to stop the discrimination in real life, discuss how someone could have "acted for justice" in the incident.

Group members choose one story from their group to act out, then assign character roles and decide how to stage the story. Because this is an improvisation, they don't need to write down lines, but I do encourage them to practice. I tell them to make sure at least one person in their group acts as an ally to interrupt the discriminatory behavior — even if that didn't happen in real life. They can add details, characters, and props to make their scene come to life. Typically, students share and select a scene during one 50-minute period, then gather for about 15 to 20 minutes the next day to rehearse their scene.

Over the years, I've learned to be an advocate during this part of the activity. I circle the class listening to as many stories as I can. Sometimes the most forceful stories come from students who don't have "power" in the classroom: limited English speakers, shy students, and chronic non-attending students. Their stories might be pushed aside by more talkative or popular students if I don't intervene. For example, one popular girl wanted to act out the story of how her best friend stole her boyfriend — not exactly the kind of "social injustice" story I had in mind. When I asked about the other stories, I discovered Sabine's:

> I came to this school as a 9th grader. I didn't arrive in the United States until August. I studied and practiced my English, but it wasn't too good. I was afraid to come to school. In my PE class, girls made fun of me because I'm Muslim and I wear a scarf. They also made fun of my English. I would go home from school and cry. But one girl stood by me in class. She wouldn't let the other students tease me.

I told the group that Sabine's story would be a better improvisation than the boyfriend-stealing story. In other words, sometimes I intervene in the classroom on behalf of the silenced.

Sharing Our Stories

After students have an opportunity to rehearse, I bring the large group back together and arrange the desks or chairs in "theater" style. Before we begin I say: "You might feel uncomfortable in your roles as you act as either people who discriminate or as the victims, and laughter is often a way that we release our discomfort. However, that doesn't mean that we think discrimination is funny."

As each group improvises its story, the rest of the class watches and takes notes to capture any great lines or words to use in the interior monologue they will write from one of the character's points of view.

After each group presents its scene, students talk about the incident. Sometimes it helps for the "actors" to stay on stage, so that the audience can ask them questions: "How did you feel when Stella called you a name?

What caused you to disrupt the injustice? How did you feel afterwards?" When Jennifer Wiandt, a language arts teacher at Cleveland High School in Portland, Oregon taught this lesson, she added the question: "Who had power in the situation?" Students in her class discussed how older students, popular students, and teachers have power.

When Sabine's group acted out her incident of injustice, I asked: "Who would have been Sabine's ally in PE?" Two girls raised their hands. Then I asked, "Who would act as an ally now?" All of the students raised their hands.

After all groups have performed, I ask students to write an interior monologue from one character's point of view. An interior monologue captures the thoughts and feelings of a character as they are engaged in a situation. They may write from a character they portrayed or observed, or from their own original story.

As students read their monologues to the rest of the class, they often excavate the emotional territory these pieces triggered. How do people feel when they are laughed at? Excluded? How do they feel when they gather the courage to stand up for someone else, when they fight back against ignorance and hate? Why didn't some of us act even when we felt immoral standing by as a witness to injustice? Who gets hurt? As I mentioned earlier, I was surprised at how many of my students shared instances when they tormented others. I was equally surprised at how few intervened to help when someone was hurt. But I also learned that students felt conflicted and unhappy about their roles in hurting others.

One student, a biracial girl who hid her African-American identity from the class, told me in private that she cried after watching the cruelty of her classmates in middle school, but she was so afraid that they'd turn on her that she never helped anyone out. She was light enough to pass, and she'd heard friends tell jokes about African Americans, so she hid her racial heritage. "They had teased me about my facial hair. I was afraid that if I helped the boy they were teasing that they would remember my hair or find out I was part black and start laughing at me again."

Students need the tools to confront injustice; they need to hear our approval that intervention is not only appropriate and acceptable to their peers, but heroic. Acting in solidarity with others is a learned habit. Elena, a sophomore, wrote about her experience tormenting a fellow student:

> In a classroom of 32 fifth graders only one was singled out. His name was Lee. The only thing that made him different from the rest was the fact that he was smart, walked on the balls of his feet, wore a rat's tail, and did a funny thing with his hands when he got happy.…I'm sure if we could all go back in time none of us would make fun of his unique ways.
>
> Was it the rat tail that singled him out or the fact we were all oblivious to people's feelings? Or could it have been that we were all looking for a cheap laugh even if it was at someone's expense?
>
> Sure I admit it. I was one of those individuals who made fun of him. Worst of all, I was the one who did most of the nit-picking. I was the original class clown, the one who would get the class roaring. I made fun of him not to boost my self-esteem, but to get a cheap laugh. It was almost like a job to attend to.
>
> By the time I realized this was an individual's feelings I was juggling in my hands, it was too late. At this point he would break down on the first insult that came his way. The way the tears rolled down a 10-year-old boy's face made me think twice about what I'd done. I backed off him after that, but when it came to other kids making fun of him, I stood by myself knowing what they were doing was wrong.

In the introduction to *The Power in Our Hands* (Monthly Review Press, 1988), Bill Bigelow and Norm Diamond write that to "teach is to be a warrior against cynicism and despair." Our classrooms provide spaces for us to help students become warriors against cynicism and despair by acting for justice.

One Teacher's Journey

Bob Peterson

I t's November and a student brings in a flyer about a canned food drive during the upcoming holiday season. The traditional teacher affirms the student's interest — "That's nice and I'm glad you care about other people" — but doesn't view the food drive as a potential classroom activity.

The progressive teacher sees the food drive as an opportunity to build on students' seemingly innate sympathy for the downtrodden, and, after a class discussion, has children bring in cans of food. They count them, categorize them, and write about how they feel.

The critical teacher does the same as the progressive teacher — but more. The critical teacher also uses the food drive as the basis for a discussion about poverty and hunger. How much poverty and hunger is there in our neighborhood? Our country? Our world? Why is there poverty and hunger? What is the role of the government in making sure people have enough to eat? Why isn't it doing more? What can we do in addition to giving some food?

Participating in a food drive isn't essential to critical teaching. But engaging children in reflective dialogue is.

Unfortunately, a lack of reflective dialogue is all too common in American schools. Less than one percent of instructional time in high school is devoted to discussion that requires some kind of response involving reasoning or an opinion from students, according to researcher John Goodlad in his study of American schooling. A similar atmosphere dominates all too many elementary classrooms, where worksheets and mindless tasks fill up children's time.

Divisions between traditional, progressive, and critical teaching are often artificial and many teachers use techniques common to all three. As I attempt to improve my teaching and build what I call a "social-justice classroom," however, I have found it essential to draw less on traditional methods and more on the other two.

Lots of literature has been written on progressive methods — the process approach to writing, whole language, activity-based mathematics, and so forth. But there is little written about critical/social-justice approaches to teaching, especially for elementary teachers. What follows is an outline of lessons that I have learned as I have tried, sometimes more successfully than others, to incorporate my goal of critical/social-justice teaching into my classroom practice over the past 15 years. The outline includes five characteristics essential to a critical/social-justice classroom:

- ◆ A curriculum grounded in the lives of our students.
- ◆ Dialogue.
- ◆ A questioning/problem-posing approach.
- ◆ An emphasis on critiquing bias and attitudes.
- ◆ The teaching of activism for social justice.

In addition, a well-organized class based on collaboration and student participation is a prerequisite for implementing such a program. I'd also like to add that such "characteristics" are actually goals — never quite reached by even the best teachers, but always sought by all good teachers.

Curriculum Grounded in the Lives of Our Students

A teacher cannot build a community of learners unless the voices and lives of the students are an integral part of the curriculum. Children, of course, talk about their lives constantly. The challenge is for teachers to make connections between what the students talk about, the curriculum, and the broader society.

I start the year with a six-week unit on the children's families and backgrounds. To begin the unit I have students place their birth dates on the class timeline — which covers nearly 600 years (an inch representing a year), and runs above the blackboard and stretches around two walls. Students write their names and birth dates on 3x5 cards and tie the cards with yarn to the hole in the timeline that corresponds to their year of birth. On the second day we place their parents' birth dates on the timeline, on the third day those of their grandparents or great-grandparents. Throughout the year, students add dates that come up in our study of history, literature, science, and current events. The timeline provides students with a visual representation of time, history, and sequence, while fostering the understanding that our lives and history are interrelated.

The weekly writing homework assignment during this family background unit consists of children collecting information about their families — how they were named, stories of family trips, favorite jokes, an incident when they were young, a description of their neighborhood. Students share these writings with each other and at times with the whole class. They use these assignments as rough drafts for autobiographies, which are eventually bound and published. The assignments also inspire classroom discussion and further study.

For example, one of my students, Faviola Perez, wrote a poem about her neighborhood, which led to discussions about violence and what we might do about it.

MY STREET AT NIGHT

My mom says, "Time to go to bed."
The streets at night
are horrible
I can't sleep!
Cars are passing
making noise
sirens screaming
people fighting
suffering!
Suddenly the noise goes away
I go to sleep
I start dreaming
I dream about people
shaking hands
caring
caring about our planet
I wake up
and say
Will the world be
like this some day?

In the discussion that followed, many students shared similar fears and gave examples of how family members or friends had been victims of violence. Others offered ways to prevent violence. "We shouldn't buy team jackets," said one student. "The police should keep all the criminals in jail forever," was another suggestion.

Needless to say, the students don't have a uniform response, and I use their comments and stories to foster discussion. When necessary or appropriate, I interject questions that might help the students deepen or reconsider their views. I also try to draw connections between such problems and issues of conflict that I witness daily in the class. When a student talks about a killing over a mundane argument or a piece of clothing, for instance, I ask how these conflicts differ from some of those in our school and on our playground, and how we might solve them.

Focusing on problems in writing and discussion acknowledges the seriousness of a child's problem; it also fosters community because the students recognize that we share common concerns. Ultimately, it can help students to re-examine how their personal problems connect to the broader society. Throughout the year I try to integrate an examination of children's lives and their community into all sections of the curriculum. In reading groups, for example, children relate both contemporary and classic children's books to their own lives. In one activity I have students divide their paper vertically. On one side they copy an interesting sentence from a book they are reading; on the other side they write how that reminds them of something in their own lives. The students then share and discuss their reflections.

In math, students learn about percentages, fractions, graphing, and basic math through using numbers to examine their own lives. For example, my fifth-grade class keeps logs of the time that they spend watching television. They graph these data, and analyze them in terms of fractions and percentages. As part of our school's nine-week, schoolwide theme called "We Send Messages When We Communicate," they survey all the classes in the school to see how many households have various kinds of communication equipment, from telephones to computers to VCRs.

Such activities are interesting and worthwhile but not necessarily critical. I try to take the activity a step further — not only to affirm what's going on in the children's lives, but to help them question if watching television is always in their best interests. As we've looked at television viewing, for instance, we've found that some of our students could save over 1,000 hours a year by moderating their TV watching.

"I can't believe I waste so much time watching TV," one girl stated during a discussion.

"You're not wasting it. You're learning what they want you to buy!" said one boy sarcastically.

Similar discussions have helped children become more conscious of the impact of television on their lives and minds, and even have led a few to reduce the number of hours they watched.

One problem, however, that I have encountered in "giving voice" to students is that the voices that dominate are sometimes those of the more aggressive boys or those students who are more academically skilled. I try to overcome this problem by using structures that encourage broader participation. During writing workshop, for example, I give timed "free writes" where children write about anything they want for a set period of time. Afterward they immediately share their writing with another student of their choice. Students then nominate classmates to share with the entire class, which often has the effect of positive peer pressure on those who don't normally participate in class. By hearing their own voices, by having other students listen to what they have to say, children become more self-confident in expressing their own ideas, and feel more a part of the classroom community.

Dialogue

The basic premise of traditional teaching is that children come to school as empty vessels needing to be filled with information. "Knowledge" is something produced elsewhere, whether by the teacher or the textbook company, and then transferred to the student. This approach dominates most schools. "Reform" usually means finding more effective ways for children to remember more "stuff" or more efficient ways to measure what "stuff" the students have memorized.

I agree that children need to know bunches of "stuff." I cringe any time one of my fifth graders confuses a basic fact like the name of our city or country. But I also know that the vast bulk of "stuff" memorized by children in school is quickly forgotten, and that the "empty vessel" premise is large-ly responsible for the boring, lecture-based instruction that dominates too many classrooms.

The curricular "stuff" that I want the children to learn will be best remembered if it relates to what they already know, if they have some input into what "stuff" is actually studied, and if it is studied through activities rather than just listening. All three approaches depend on dialogue and making students an integral part of their own learning.

To initiate dialogue I may use a song, poem, story, news article, photo, or cartoon. These dialogue "triggers" are useful for both classroom and small-group discussion. I often use them as starting points in social studies, writing, or math lessons. I have a song, word, poster, and quotation of the week which, whenever possible, are related to our curriculum topics.

For example, during the study of the American Underground Railroad, I use the song "New Underground Railroad," written by Gerry Tenney and sung by Holly Near and Ronnie Gilbert. The song compares the Under-ground Railroad of the mid-1800s in the United States to that of the movement to save Jews during World War II and to the sanctuary move-ment to help "illegal" Salvadoran refugees in the 1980s. One student from El Salvador connected immediately to the song. She explained to the class the problems of violence and poverty that her family had faced because of war in El Salvador. This one song raised many more questions, for example: Why did the Nazis kill people? What is anti-Semitism? Who runs El Salvador? Why has the United States sent guns to El Salvador? Why have people from El Salvador been forced to come to the United States secretly?

Another trigger that I use is overhead transparencies made from provocative newspaper or magazine photographs. For example, for a poetry lesson during writing workshop, I've used a *New York Times* photograph taken during a winter cold spell that shows piles of snow-covered blankets and cardboard on park benches near the White House. Many students ini-tially think the piles are trash. When I tell them that they are homeless people who were snowed upon while asleep, many students get angry. The discussions range from their own experiences seeing homeless people in the community to suggestions of what should be done by the president.

"That's not fair," one student responded.

"Clinton said he'd take care of the homeless people if he got elected and look what he's done," said a second student, referring to the then-president. "Nothing."

"I didn't vote for him," said a third. "Us kids never get to do anything, but I know that if we were in charge of the world we'd do a better job."

"Like what?" I asked.

"Well, on a day that cold he should have opened up the White House and let them in," responded one student. "If I were president, that's what I'd do."

One of my students, Jade Williams, later wrote a poem:

HOMELESS

I walk to the park
I see homeless people laying
on a bench I feel sad
to see people sleeping outside
nowhere to go I felt
to help them let them stay
in a hotel
give them things
until they get
a job and
a house to stay
and let them
pay me back
with their love

A Questioning/Problem-Posing Approach

Lucy Calkins, director of the Teachers College Writing Project at Columbia University, argued that teachers must allow student viewpoints to be part of the classroom curriculum. "We can't give children rich lives, but we can give them the lens to appreciate the richness that is already there in their lives," she wrote in her book *Living Between the Lines*.

But even that approach is not enough. We should also help students probe the ways their lives are both connected to and limited by society.

This is best done if students and teachers jointly pose substantive, challenging questions for the class to try and answer.

Any time a student poses a particularly thoughtful or curious question in my class we write it down in the spiral notebook labeled "Questions We Have" that hangs on the board in front of the room. It might be during a discussion, at the beginning of a day, or during a reflection on another student's writing. Not every question is investigated and thoroughly discussed, but even the posing of the question helps students to consider alternative ways of looking at an issue.

In a reading-group discussion, for example, the question arose of how it must have felt for fugitive slaves and free African Americans to fear walking down the street in the North during the time of slavery. One student said: "I sort of know how they must have felt."

Others immediately express their doubts. But then she explained. "The slaves, especially fugitive slaves, weren't free because they couldn't walk the streets without fear of the slave masters, but today are we free?" she asked. "Because we can't walk the streets without fear of gangs, violence, crazy people, drunks, and drive-bys."

In reading groups students pose questions from the literature that we read. For example, while reading *Sidewalk Story* by Sharon Bell Mathis, a children's novel in which the main protagonist, a young girl, struggles to keep her best friend from being evicted, my students have asked questions about the ethics of eviction, failure to pay rent, homelessness, discrimination, and the value of material possessions over friendship. "Is it better to have friends or money?" one student asked, which formed the basis of a lengthy discussion in the reading circle.

Other questions that students have raised in our "Questions We Have" book include:
- Who tells the television what to put on?
- Why do geese fly together in an angle?
- Who invented slavery?
- Did ministers or priests have slaves?
- How many presidents owned slaves? (For more on this question see "Write the Truth," p. 115.)

- Why haven't we had a woman president?
- Why are the faces of the presidents on our money?
- How do horses sweat?
- If we are free, why do we have to come to school?
- When did photography start?
- Why are people homeless?
- What runs faster, a cheetah or an ostrich?
- Did any adults die in the 1913 massacre of 73 children in Calumet County, Michigan? (in reference to the Woody Guthrie song about a tragedy that grew out of a labor struggle).

Some questions are answered by students working together using reference materials in the classroom or school library. (For example: Cheetahs can run at up to 65 miles an hour while ostriches run at only 40 mph.) Other questions are subjects of group discussion; still others we work on in small groups.

For example, the question "What is the difference between the master/slave relationship and parent/child relationship?" developed one afternoon when a child complained that his parent wouldn't allow him out in the evening for school story hour. A girl responded that we might as well all be slaves, and a third student posed the question. After a brief group discussion, I had children work in groups of three or four and they continued the debate. They made two lists, one of similarities and one of differences, between the master/slave relationship and the parent/child relationship. They discussed the question in the small groups, then a spokesperson from each group reported to the class.

In this way I learned more about my students' lives. Also, the activity forced the students to reflect on what we had been studying in our unit on slavery and the Underground Railroad: When one student said, "Yeah, it's different because masters whipped slaves and my mom doesn't whip me," another student responded by saying, "All masters didn't whip their slaves." When another student said that their mothers love them and masters didn't love their slaves, another girl gave the example of the slave character Izzie in the movie *Half Free, Half Slave*, which the class had watched: Izzie got special privileges because she was the master's girlfriend. Another girl responded that that wasn't an example of love; she was just being used.

In this discussion, students pooled their information and generated their own understanding of history, challenging crude generalizations typical of children this age. Students also started evaluating what was fair and just in their own lives. It was clear to all that the treatment of slaves was unjust. Not so clear was to what extent and how children should be disciplined by their parents. "That's abuse!" one student remarked after hearing about how one child was punished. "No, it's not. That's how my mom treats me whenever I do something bad," responded another.

While no "answers" were found, the posing of this question by a student, and my facilitating its discussion, added both to kids' understanding of history and to their sense of the complexity of evaluating what is fair and just in contemporary society.

Emphasis on Critiquing Bias

Raising questions about bias in ideas and materials — from children's books to school texts, fairy tales, news reports, song lyrics, and cartoons — is another key component of a social justice classroom. I tell my fifth graders it's important to examine "the messages that are trying to take over your brain" and that it's up to them to sort out which ones they should believe and which ones promote fairness and justice in our world.

To recognize that different perspectives exist in history and society is the first step toward critiquing materials and evaluating what perspectives they represent or leave out. Ultimately it helps children see that they, too, can have their own values and perspectives independent of what they last read or heard.

We start by examining perspective and voice. "Whose point of view are we hearing?" I ask. One poem that is good to initiate such a discussion is Paul Fleischman's dialogue poem, "Honeybees," from *Joyful Noise: Poems for Two Voices* (HarperTrophy, 1995). The poem is read simultaneously by two people, one describing the life of a bee from the perspective of a worker, and one from the perspective of a queen. Children love to perform the poem and often want to write their own. They begin to understand how to look at things from different perspectives. They also start to identify with certain perspectives.

After hearing the song of the week, "My Country 'Tis of Thee My People Are Dying" by Buffy Sainte-Marie, one of my students wrote a dialogue poem between a Native American and a U.S. soldier about smallpox-infected blankets the U.S. government traded for land. In another instance, as part of a class activity when pairs of students were writing dialogue poems between a master and a slave, two girls wrote one between a field slave and a house slave, further deepening the class's understanding about the complexity of slavery. During writing workshop six weeks later, three boys decided to write a "Triple Dialogue Poem" that included the slave, a slave master, and an abolitionist.

Students need to know that children's books and school textbooks contain biases and omissions. I find the concept of "stereotypes" and "omissions" important to enhance children's understanding of such biases. This emphasis on critique is also an excellent way to integrate math into social studies. Students, for example, can tally numbers of instances certain people, viewpoints, or groups are presented in a text or in mass media. One year my students compared the times famous women and famous men were mentioned in the fifth-grade history text. Some of the boys suggested that men were mentioned far more frequently because women must not have done much throughout history. To help facilitate the discussion, I provided background resources for the students, including biographies of famous women. This not only helped students better understand the nature of "omission," but also generated interest in reading biographies of women.

In another activity I had students tally the number of men and women by occupation as depicted in magazine and/or TV advertisements. By comparing their findings to the population as a whole, various forms of bias were uncovered, not only in how the media portray the population, but in the structure of jobs that helps segregate women into occupations such as office worker or waitress. Another interesting activity is having students tally the number of biographies in the school library and analyze them by race, gender, and occupation.

One of my favorite activities involves comparing books. I stumbled on this activity one year when my class read a story about inventions in a reading textbook published by Scott Foresman Co. The story stated that the traffic light was invented by an anonymous policeman. Actually it was invented by the African-American scientist Garrett A. Morgan. I gave my students a short piece from an African-American history book and we compared it with the Scott Foresman book. We talked about which story we should believe and how one might verify which was accurate. After checking out another book about inventions, the students realized that the school text was wrong.

The Teaching of Activism for Social Justice

The underlying theme in my classroom is that the quest for social justice is a never-ending struggle in our nation and world; that the vast majority of people have benefited by this struggle; that we must understand this struggle; and that we must make decisions about whether to be involved in it.

I weave the various disciplines around this theme. When I read poetry and literature to the children I often use books that raise issues about social justice and, when possible, that have young people working for social justice as protagonists. In math, we look at everything from the distribution of wealth in the world to the percentage of women in different occupations. The class songs and posters of the week also emphasize social struggles from around the world. I also have each student make what I call a "people's textbook" — a three-ring binder in which they put handouts and some of their own work, particularly interviews that they've conducted. There are sections for geography, history, current events, songs, poetry, and mass media. I also have a gallery of freedom fighters on the wall — posters of people we have studied in social studies and current events.

In addition to studying movements for social justice of the past, students discuss current problems and possible solutions. One way I do this is by having students role-play examples of discrimination and how they might respond.

I start with kids dramatizing historical incidents such as Sojourner Truth's successful attempt to integrate street cars in Washington, D.C. after the Civil War, and Rosa Parks' role in the Montgomery, Alabama, bus boycott. We brainstorm contemporary problems where people might face discrimination, drawing on our current events studies and interviews children have done with family members and friends about types of discrimination of which they are aware.

One day in the spring of 1993, my class was dramatizing contemporary examples. Working in small groups, the students chose a type of discrimination — such as not being allowed to rent a house because one receives welfare, or not getting a job because one is a woman — and developed a short dramatization. Afterward, the kids led a discussion about the type of discrimination they acted out.

After a few dramatizations, it was Gilberto, Juan, and Carlos' turn. It was a housing discrimination example — but with a twist. Gilberto and Juan acted the part of two gay men attempting to rent an apartment, and Carlos was the landlord who refused to rent to them. I was surprised, in part because in previous brainstorming sessions on discrimination none of my students had mentioned discrimination against gay people. Further, as is often unfortunately the case with fifth graders, in the past my students had shown they were prone to uncritically accept anti-gay slurs and stereotypes. But here, on their own initiative, were Gilberto, Juan, and Carlos transferring our class discussion of housing discrimination based on race to that of sexual orientation.

The dramatization caused an initial chorus of laughs and jeers. But, I noticed, the students also listened attentively. Afterwards, I asked the class what type of discrimination had been modeled.

"Gayism," one student, Elvis, yelled out.

It was a new word to me, but it got the point across. The class then went on to discuss "gayism." Most of the kids who spoke agreed that it was a form of discrimination. During the discussion, one student mentioned a march on Washington a week earlier demanding gay rights. (Interestingly, Gilberto, Juan, and Carlos said they were unaware of the march.)

Elvis, who coined the term "gayism," then said: "Yeah, my cousin is one of those lesi… lesi…"

"Lesbians," I said, completing his sentence.

"Yeah, lesbian," he said. He then added enthusiastically, "And she went to Washington to march for her rights."

"That's just like when Dr. King made his dream speech at the march in Washington," another student added.

Before long the class moved on to a new role play. But the "gayism" dramatization lingered in my memory. I was pleased that the class had been able to move beyond the typical discussions around gay issues — which had in the past seemed to center on my explaining why students shouldn't call each other "faggot." More fundamentally, however, the incident reminded me of the inherent link between the classroom and society, not only in terms of how society influences the children who are in our classrooms for six hours a day, but also in terms of how broader movements for social reform affect daily classroom life.

It's important not only to study these progressive social movements and to dramatize current social problems, but to encourage students to take thoughtful action. By doing this they see themselves as actors in the world, not just things to be acted upon.

Sometimes the opportunity to act for justice comes from our curriculum. One year when I was working at an elementary school, my students' reaction to biases and omissions in our textbooks led to student activism. Around Thanksgiving time I showed my students an excellent filmstrip called "Unlearning Native American Stereotypes" produced by the Council on Interracial Books for Children. It's narrated by Native-American children who visit a public library and become outraged at the various stereotypes of Indians in the books. That year my kids seemed particularly angry about what they had learned. They came the next day talking about how their siblings in first grade had come home with construction paper headdresses with feathers. "That's a stereotype," my kids proudly proclaimed.

"What did you do about it?" I asked.

"I ripped it up," "I slugged him," came the chorus of responses.

After further discussion, they decided there were more productive things they could do than hit their siblings. They scoured the school library for books with Indian stereotypes and found few. So they decided to investigate the first-grade room. Two of the students wrote a letter to the teacher asking permission to enter the room. They found a picture of an Indian next to letter "I" in the alphabet strip on the wall, a red-skinned person wearing feathers, the only human image among the collection of "things" representing the letters. They came back excited, declaring that they had "found a stereotype that everybody sees every day!" They decided they wanted to teach the first graders about stereotypes. I was skeptical, but agreed, and after much rehearsal they entered the first-grade classroom to give their lesson. Returning to my classroom, they expressed frustration that the first-graders didn't listen as well as they had hoped, but nonetheless thought it had gone well. Later the two students, Paco Resendez and Faviola Alvarez, wrote in our school newspaper:

> We have been studying stereotypes of Native Americans. What is a stereotype? It's when somebody says something that's not true about another group of people. For example, it is a stereotype if you think all Indians wear feathers or say "HOW!" Or if you think that all girls are delicate. Why? Because some girls are strong.

Another excellent way to help students learn about activism is by example — to expose them to people in the community who are fighting for social justice. I regularly have social activists visit and talk with children in my classes. I also explain the activities that I'm personally involved in, as examples of what might be done. I tell students they can write letters, circulate petitions, and talk to other classes and children about their concerns. My students have gone with me to marches that demanded that - Martin Luther King Jr.'s birthday be made a national holiday and that there be an end to the nuclear arms race. They came with me with me to an anti-white-supremacist rally in downtown Milwaukee, where we joined with thousands of people of every ethnicity to protest the "white power" rantings of a handful of racists on the courthouse steps. Two of my students testified before the City Council, asking that a Jobs With Peace referendum be placed on the ballot. Another time students at our school testified with parents in front of the City Council that money should be allocated to rebuild our school playground.

If we neglect to include an activist component in our curricula, we cut students off from the possibility of social change. We model apathy as a response to the world's problems.

Such apathy is not OK. At a time when cynicism and hopelessness increasingly dominate our youth, helping students understand the world and their relationship to it by encouraging social action may be one of the few antidotes. Schools are a prime place where this can take place. Teachers are a key element in it happening. Teaching for social justice is a necessary priority in the new century.

PART 2

Taking Bias Seriously

Ebonics and Culturally Responsive Instruction

Lisa Delpit

The "Ebonics Debate" has created much more heat than light for most of the country. For teachers trying to determine what implications there might be for classroom practice, enlightenment has been a completely non-existent commodity.

I have been asked often enough, "What do you think about Ebonics? Are you for it or against it?" My answer must be neither. I can be neither for Ebonics nor against Ebonics any more than I can be for or against air. It exists. It is the language spoken by many of our African-American children. It is the language they heard as their mothers nursed them and changed their diapers and played peek-a-boo with them. It is the language through which they first encountered love, nurturance and joy.

On the other hand, most teachers of those African-American children who have been least well-served by educational systems believe that their students' life chances will be further hampered if they do not learn Standard English. In the stratified society in which we live, they are absolutely correct. While having access to the politically mandated language form will not, by any means, guarantee economic success (witness the growing numbers of unemployed African Americans holding doctorates), not having access will almost certainly guarantee failure.

So what must teachers do? Should they spend their time relentlessly "correcting" their Ebonics-speaking children's language so that it might conform to what we have learned to refer to as Standard English? Despite good intentions, constant correction seldom has the desired effect. Such correction increases cognitive monitoring of speech, thereby making talking difficult.

To illustrate, I have frequently taught a relatively simple new "dialect" to classes of preservice teachers. In this dialect, the phonetic element "iz" is added after the first consonant or consonant cluster in each syllable of a word. (Maybe becomes *miz-ay-biz-ee* and apple, *iz-ap-piz-le*.) After a bit of drill and practice, the students are asked to tell a partner in "iz" language why they decided to become teachers. Most only haltingly attempt a few words before lapsing into either silence or into Standard English. During a follow-up discussion, all students invariably speak of the impossibility of attempting to apply rules while trying to formulate and express a thought. Forcing speakers to monitor their language typically produces silence.

Correction may also affect students' attitudes toward their teachers. In a recent research project, middle-school, inner-city students were interviewed about their attitudes toward their teachers and school. One young woman complained bitterly: "Mrs. ___ always be interrupting to make you 'talk correct' and stuff. She be butting into your conversations when you not even talking to her! She need to mind her own business." Clearly this student will be unlikely to follow the teacher's directives or to want to imitate her speech style.

Group Identity

Issues of group identity may also affect students' oral production of a different dialect. Researcher Sharon Nelson-Barber, in a study of phonologic aspects of Pima Indian language, found that in first through third grades, the children's English most approximated the standard dialect of their teachers. But surprisingly, by fourth grade, when one might assume growing competence in standard forms, their language moved significantly toward the local dialect. These fourth graders had the *competence* to express themselves in a more standard form, but chose, consciously or unconsciously, to use the language of those in their local environments.

Nelson-Barber believes that by age eight or nine, these children became aware of their group membership and its importance to their well-being, and this realization was reflected in their language.[1] They may also have become increasingly aware of the schools' negative attitude toward their community and found it necessary — through choice of linguistic form — to decide with which camp to identify.

What should teachers do about helping students acquire an additional oral form? First, they should recognize that the linguistic form a student brings to school is intimately connected with loved ones, community, and personal identity. To suggest that this form is "wrong," or even worse, ignorant, is to suggest that something is wrong with the student and his or her family. To denigrate your language is, then, in African-American terms, to "talk about your mama." Anyone who knows anything about African-American culture knows the consequences of that speech act!

On the other hand, it is equally important to understand that students who do not have access to the politically popular dialect form in this country are less likely to succeed economically than their peers who do. How can both realities be embraced in classroom instruction?

It is possible and desirable to make the actual study of language diversity a part of the curriculum for all students. For younger children, discussions about the differences in the ways television characters from different cultural groups speak can provide a starting point. A collection of the many children's books written in the dialects of various cultural groups also can provide a wonderful basis for learning about linguistic diversity,[2] as can audiotaped stories narrated by individuals from different cultures, including taping books read by members of the children's home communities. Mrs. Pat, a teacher chronicled by Stanford University researcher Shirley Brice Heath, had her students become language "detectives," interviewing a variety of individuals and listening to the radio and television to discover the differences and similarities in the ways people talked.[3] Children can learn that there are many ways of saying the same thing, and that certain contexts suggest particular kinds of linguistic performances.

Some teachers have groups of students create bilingual dictionaries of their own language form and Standard English. Both the students and the teacher become engaged in identifying terms and deciding upon the best translations. These can be done as generational dictionaries too, given the proliferation of "youth culture" terms growing out of the Ebonics-influenced tendency for the continual regeneration of vocabulary. Contrastive grammatical structures can be studied similarly, but, of course, as Oakland, California's policy suggests, teachers must be aware of the grammatical structure of Ebonics before they can launch into this complex study.

Other teachers have had students become involved with standard forms through various kinds of role-play. For example, memorizing parts for drama productions will allow students to practice and "get the feel" of speaking Standard English while not under the threat of correction. A master teacher of African-American children in Oakland, Carrie Secret, has used this technique and extended it so that students videotaped their practice performances and self-critiqued them as to the appropriate use of Standard English. (But I must add that Carrie's use of drama and oration goes much beyond acquiring Standard English. She inspires pride and community connections which are truly wondrous to behold.) The use of self-critique of recorded forms may prove even more useful than I initially realized. California State University–Hayward professor Etta Hollins has reported that just by leaving a tape recorder on during an informal class period and playing it back with no comment, students began to code-switch — moving between Standard English and Ebonics — more effectively. It appears that they may have not realized which language form they were using until they heard themselves speak on tape.

Young students can create puppet shows or role-play cartoon characters — many "superheroes" speak almost hypercorrect Standard English! Playing a role eliminates the possibility of implying that the *child's* language is inadequate and suggests, instead, that different language forms are appropriate in different contexts. Some teachers in New York City have had their students produce a news show every day for the rest of the school. The students take on the personae of famous newscasters, keeping in character as they develop and read their news reports. Discussions ensue about whether Tom Brokaw would have said it that way, again taking the focus off the child's speech.

Discourse Style and Language Use

Although most educators think of Black Language as primarily differing in grammar and syntax, there are other differences in oral language of which teachers should be aware in a multicultural context, particularly in discourse style and language use. Harvard University researcher Sarah Michaels and other researchers identified differences in children's narratives at "sharing time."[4] They found that there was a tendency among young white children to tell "topic-centered" narratives — stories focused on one event — and a tendency among black youngsters, especially girls, to tell "episodic" narratives — stories that include shifting scenes and are typically longer.

While these differences are interesting in themselves, what is of greater significance is adults' responses to the differences. C. B. Cazden reported on a subsequent project in which a white adult was taped reading the oral narratives of both black and white first graders, with all syntax dialectal markers removed.[5] Adults were asked to listen to the stories and comment about the children's likelihood of success in school.

The researchers were surprised by the differential responses given by black and white adults. In responding to the retelling of a black child's story, the white adults were uniformly negative, making such comments as "terrible story, incoherent" and "[n]ot a story at all in the sense of describing something that happened." Asked to judge this child's academic competence, all of the white adults rated her below the children who told "topic-centered" stories. Most of these adults also predicted difficulties for this child's future school career, such as, "This child might have trouble reading," that she exhibited "language problems that affect school achievement," and they theorized that "family problems" or "emotional problems" might hamper her academic progress.

The black adults had very different reactions. They found this child's story "well formed, easy to understand, and interesting, with lots of detail and description." Even though all five of these adults mentioned the "shifts" and "associations" or "nonlinear" quality of the story, they did not find these features distracting. Three of the black adults selected the story as the best of the five they had heard, and all but one judged the child as exceptionally bright, highly verbal, and successful in school.[6]

This is not a story about racism, but one about cultural familiarity. However, when differences in narrative style produce differences in interpretation of competence, the pedagogical implications are evident. If children who produce stories based in differing discourse styles are expected to have trouble reading, and are viewed as having language, family, or emotional problems, as in the case quoted by Cazden, they are unlikely to be viewed as ready for the same challenging instruction awarded students whose language patterns more closely parallel the teacher's.

Learning to Read

Most teachers are particularly concerned about how speaking Ebonics might affect learning to read. There is little evidence that speaking another mutually intelligible language form, per se, negatively affects one's ability to learn to read.[7] For commonsensical proof, one need only reflect on non-Standard-English-speaking Africans who, though enslaved, not only taught themselves to read English, but did so under threat of severe punishment or death.

But children who speak Ebonics do have a more difficult time becoming proficient readers. Why? In part, appropriate instructional methodologies are frequently not adopted. There is ample evidence that children who do not come to school with knowledge about letters, sounds, and symbols need to experience some explicit instruction in these areas in order to become independent readers. Another explanation is that, where teachers' assessments of competence are influenced by the language children speak, teachers may develop low expectations for certain students and subsequently teach them less.[8] A third explanation rests in teachers' confusing the teaching of reading with the teaching of a new language form.

Reading researcher Patricia Cunningham found that teachers across the United States were more likely to correct reading miscues that were "dialect" related ("Here go a table" for "Here is a table") than those that were "nondialect" related ("Here is a dog" for "There is a dog").[9] Seventy-eight percent of the former types of miscues were corrected, compared with only 27% of the latter. He concludes that the teachers were acting out of ignorance, not realizing that "here go" and "here is" represent the same meaning in some black children's language.

In my observations of many classrooms, however, I have come to conclude that even when teachers recognize the similarity of meaning, they are likely to correct Ebonics-related miscues. Consider a typical example:

Text: Yesterday I washed my brother's clothes.

Student's rendition: Yesterday I wash my bruvver close.

The subsequent exchange between student and teacher sounds something like this:

T: Wait, let's go back. What's that word again? [Points at *washed*.]

S: Wash.

T: No. Look at it again. What letters do you see at the end? You see "e-d." Do you remember what we say when we see those letters on the end of the word?

S: "ed."

T: OK, but in this case we say "washed." Can you say that?

S: Wash*ed*.

T: Good. Now read it again.

S: Yesterday I wash*ed* my bruvver…

T: Wait a minute, what's that word again? [Points to *brother*.]

S: Bruvver.

T: No. Look at these letters in the middle. [Points to *brother*.] Remember to read what you see. Do you remember how we say that sound? Put your tongue between your teeth and say "th"….

The lesson continues in such a fashion, the teacher proceeding to correct the student's Ebonics-influenced pronunciations and grammar, while ignoring that fact that the student had to have comprehended the sentence in order to translate it into her own language. Such instruction occurs daily and blocks reading development in a number of ways. First, because children become better readers by having the opportunity to read, the overcorrection exhibited in this lesson means that this child will be less likely to become a fluent reader than other children who are not interrupted so consistently. Second, a complete focus on code and pronunciation blocks children's understanding that reading is essentially a meaning-making process. This child, who understands the text, is led to believe that she is doing something wrong. She is encouraged to think of reading not as something you do to get a message, but something you pronounce. Third, constant corrections by the teacher are likely to cause this student and others like her to resist reading and to resent the teacher.

Language researcher Robert Berdan reports that, after observing the kind of teaching routine described above in a number of settings, he incorporated the teacher behaviors into a reading instruction exercise that he used with students in a college class.[10] He put together sundry rules from a number of American social and regional dialects to create what he called the "language of Atlantis." Students were then called upon to read aloud in this dialect they did not know. When they made errors he interrupted them, using some of the same statements/comments he had heard elementary school teachers routinely make to their students. He concludes:

> The results were rather shocking. By the time these PhD candidates in English or linguistics had read 10-20 words, I could make them sound totally illiterate....The first thing that goes is sentence intonation: They sound like they are reading a list from the telephone book. Comment on their pronunciation a bit more, and they begin to subvocalize, rehearsing pronunciations for themselves before they dare to say them out loud. They begin to guess at pronunciations....They switch letters around for no reason. They stumble; they repeat. In short, when I attack them for their failure to conform to my demands for Atlantis English pronunciations, they sound very much like the worst of the second graders in any of the classrooms I have observed.
>
> They also begin to fidget. They wad up their papers, bite their fingernails, whisper, and some finally refuse to continue. They do all the things that children do while they are busily failing to learn to read.

The moral of this story is to not confuse learning a new language form with reading comprehension. To do so will only confuse the child, leading her away from those intuitive understandings about language that will promote reading development, and toward a school career of resistance and a lifetime of avoiding reading.

Unlike unplanned oral language or public reading, writing lends itself to editing. While conversational talk is spontaneous and must be responsive to an immediate context, writing is a mediated process which may be written and rewritten any number of times before being introduced to public scrutiny. Consequently, writing is more amenable to rule application — one may first write freely to get one's thoughts down, and then edit to hone the message and apply specific spelling, syntactical, or punctuation rules. My college students who had such difficulty talking in the "iz" dialect found writing it, with the rules displayed before them, a relatively easy task.

What Teachers Must Do

To conclude, the teacher's job is to provide access to the national "standard," as well as to understand the language the children speak sufficiently to celebrate its beauty. The verbal adroitness, the cogent and quick wit, the brilliant use of metaphor, the facility in rhythm and rhyme evident in the language of Jesse Jackson, Whoopi Goldberg, Toni Morrison, Henry Louis Gates, Tupac Shakur, and Maya Angelou, as well as in that of many inner-city black students, may all be drawn upon to facilitate school learning. The teacher must know how to effectively teach reading and writing to students whose culture and language differ from that of the school, and must understand how and why students decide to add another language form to their repertoire. All we can do is provide students with access to additional language forms. Inevitably, each speaker will make his or her own decision about what to say in any context.

But I must end with a caveat that we keep in mind a simple truth: Despite our necessary efforts to provide access to Standard English, such access will not make any of our students more intelligent. It will not teach them math or science or geography — or, for that matter, compassion, courage, or responsibility. Let us not become so overly concerned with the language *form* that we ignore academic and moral *content*. Access to the standard language may be necessary, but it is definitely *not* sufficient to produce intelligent, competent caretakers of the future.

---

[1] Nelson-Barber, S. "Phonologic Variations of Pima English," in R. St. Clair and W. Leap (Eds.), *Language Renewal Among American Indian Tribes: Issues, Problems and Prospects*. Rosslyn, VA: National Clearinghouse for Bilingual Education, 1982.

[2] Some of these books include Lucille Clifton, *All Us Come 'Cross the Water* (New York: Holt, Rinehart, and Winston, 1973); Paul Green (aided by Abbe Abbott), *I Am Eskimo — Aknik My Name* (Juneau, AK: Alaska Northwest Publishing, 1959); Howard Jacobs and Jim Rice, *Once Upon a Bayou* (New Orleans, LA: Phideaux Publications, 1983); Tim Elder, *Santa's Cajun Christmas Adventure* (Baton Rouge, LA: Little Cajun Books, 1981); and a series of biographies produced by Yukon-Koyukkuk School District of Alaska and published by Hancock House Publishers in North Vancouver, BC, Canada.

[3] Heath, Shirley Brice. *Ways with Words*. Cambridge, England: Cambridge University Press, 1983.

[4] Michaels, S. and Cazden, C. B. "Teacher-Child Collaboration on Oral Preparation for Literacy," in B. Schieffer (Ed.), *Acquisition of Literacy: Ethnographic Perspectives*. Norwood, NJ: Ablex, 1986.

[5] Cazden, C. B. *Classroom Discourse*. Portsmouth, NH: Heinemann, 1988.

[6] *Ibid*.

[7] Sims, R. "Dialect and Reading: Toward Redefining the Issues," in J. Langer and M.T. Smith-Burke (Eds.), *Reader Meets Author: Bridging the Gap*. Newark, DE: International Reading Asssociation, 1982.

[8] *Ibid*.

[9] Cunningham, Patricia M. "Teachers' Correction Responses to Black-Dialect Miscues Which Are Nonmeaning-changing," *Reading Research Quarterly 12* (1976-77).

[10] Berdan, Robert. "Knowledge into Practice: Delivering Research to Teachers," in M. F. Whiteman (Ed.), *Reactions to Ann Arbor: Vernacular Black English and Education*. Arlington, VA: Center for Applied Linguistics, 1980.

Once Upon a Genocide: Columbus in Children's Literature

Bill Bigelow

Children's biographies of Christopher Columbus function as primers on racism and colonialism. They teach youngsters to accept the right of white people to rule over people of color, of powerful nations to dominate weaker nations. And because the Columbus myth is so pervasive — Columbus's "discovery" is probably the only historical episode with which all my students are familiar — it inhibits children from developing democratic, multicultural, and anti-racist attitudes.

Almost without exception, children's biographies of Columbus depict the journey to the New World as a "great adventure" led by "probably the greatest sailor of his time." It's a story of courage and superhuman tenacity. Columbus is depicted as brave, smart, and determined.

But behind this romanticized portrayal is a gruesome reality. For Columbus, land was real estate and it didn't matter that other people were already living there; if he "discovered" it, he took it. If he needed guides or translators, he kidnapped them. If his men wanted women, he captured sex slaves. If the indigenous people resisted, he countered with vicious attack dogs, hangings, and mutilations.

On his second voyage, desperate to show his royal patrons a return on their investment, Columbus rounded up some 1,500 Taíno Indians on the island of Hispaniola and chose 500 as slaves to be sold in Spain. Slavery did not show a profit as almost all the slaves died en route to Spain or soon after their arrival. Nonetheless, he wrote, "Let us in the name of the Holy Trinity go on sending all the slaves that can be sold."

Columbus decided to concentrate on the search for gold. He ordered every Indian on Hispaniola 14 years and older to deliver a regular quota of gold. Those who failed had their hands chopped off. In two years of the Columbus regime, perhaps a quarter of a million people died.

This article examines eight children's biographies of Columbus,[1] comparing the books with the historical record and analyzing how these accounts may influence young readers.

Portrait of Columbus

Why did Columbus want to sail west to get to the Indies? The answer offered to children in today's books hasn't changed much since I was in fourth grade. I remember my teacher, Mrs. O'Neill, asking our class this question. As usual, I didn't have a clue, but up went Jimmy Martin's hand. "Why do men want to go to the moon?" he said triumphantly. Mrs. O'Neill was delighted and told us all how smart Jimmy was because he answered a question with a question. In other words: just because — because he was curious, because he loved adventure, because he wanted to prove he could do it — just because. And for years I accepted this explanation (and envied Jimmy Martin).

In reality, Columbus wanted to become rich. It was no easy task convincing Queen Isabella and King Ferdinand to finance this highly questionable journey to the Indies, partly because his terms were outrageous. Columbus demanded 10% of all the wealth returned to Europe along the new trade route to Asia (where Columbus thought he was headed) — that's 10% of the riches brought back by everyone, not just by himself. And he wanted this guaranteed forever, for him, for his children, for their children, in perpetuity. He demanded that he be granted the titles "Viceroy" and "Admiral of the Ocean Sea." He was to be governor of all new territories found; the "Admiral" title was hereditary and would give him a share in proceeds from naval booty.

As for Queen Isabella and King Ferdinand, curiosity, adventure, and "exploration" were the last things on their minds. They wanted the tremendous profits that could be secured by finding a western passage to the Indies.

The books acknowledge — and even endorse — Columbus's demands and readily admit that securing "gold and spices" was an objective of the enterprise. "Of course [Columbus] wanted a lot! What was wrong with that?" James de Kay's *Meet Christopher Columbus* tells second graders. But this quest for wealth is downplayed in favor of adventure. "Exploration" meant going to "strange cities" where "many wonderful things" could be seen. [de Kay] Travel was exciting: Columbus "felt the heady call of the open sea. 'I love the taste of salt spray in my face,' he told a friend, 'and the feel of a deck rising and falling under my feet....'" [Monchieri]

According to these eight biographies, a major reason Columbus wanted to sail west was because of his deep faith in God. Columbus thought "that the Lord had chosen him to sail west across the sea to find the riches of the East for himself and to carry the Christian faith to the heathens. His name was Christopher. Had not the Lord chosen his namesake, Saint Christopher, to carry the Christ Child across the dark water of a river?" [D'Aulaire]

Religion, curiosity, adventure — all those motives are given preference in the Columbus biographies. But each of these supposed motives pales before the Spanish empire's quest for wealth and power. In burying these more fundamental material forces, the Columbus books encourage students to misunderstand the roots of today's foreign policy exploits. Thus students are more likely to accept platitudes — "We're involved in the Middle East for freedom and democracy" — than to look for less altruistic explanations.

The Kind and Noble Columbus

None of the biographies I evaluated — all still on the shelves of school and public libraries and widely available — disputes the ugly facts about Columbus and the Spanish conquest of the Caribbean. Yet the sad irony is that all encourage children to root for Columbus and empathize with him, using phrases such as "It was lucky that Christopher Columbus was born where he was or he might never have gone to sea," [Fritz] or "There once was a boy who loved the salty sea." [D'Aulaire] Some of the books, particularly those for younger readers, refer to Columbus affectionately, using his first name. Unlike the people he will later exterminate, Columbus is treated as a real human being, one with thoughts and feelings: "When Christopher Columbus was a child, he always wanted to be like Saint Christopher. He wanted to sail to faraway places and spread the word of Christianity." [Osborne]

The series title of Robert Young's *Christopher Columbus and His Voyage to the New World* sums up the stance of most biographies: "Let's Celebrate."

The books cheer Columbus on toward the Indies. Each step on the road to "discovery" is told from his point of view. When Columbus is delayed, this is the "most unhappy part of his great adventure." [de Kay] Every successful step is rewarded with exclamation marks: "Yes, [the Queen] would help Columbus!" [Osborne] "After all these years, Columbus would get his ships!" [de Kay]

Columbus's devout Christianity is a theme in all the books — and is never questioned. The most insistent of these — and the worst of the lot in almost every respect — is Sean J. Dolan's *Christopher Columbus: The Intrepid Mariner*. By the second page in Dolan's reverent volume, we're reading about Columbus's attachment to his leather-bound Bible. Dolan is constantly dipping us into the Admiral's thoughts. Usually these meditations run deep and pious: "[He] believed that the awe-inspiring beauty that surrounded him could only be the handiwork of the one true God, and he felt secure in his Lord and Savior's protection. 'If only my crewmen shared my belief,' Columbus thought." And this is only on the third page — Dolan's narrative goes on like this for 114 more. The reader is practically strangled by Columbus's halo.

Jean Fritz's *Where Do You Think You're Going, Christopher Columbus?* is the only book somewhat skeptical about religion as a motive. Fritz tells her readers that Queen Isabella "was such an enthusiastic Christian that she insisted everyone in Spain be a Christian too.... Indeed, she was so religious that if she even found Christians who were not sincere Christians, she had them burned at the stake. (Choir boys sang during the burnings so Isabella wouldn't have to hear the screams.)"

This is pretty strong stuff, but the implied critique would likely be lost on upper elementary students, the book's targeted readers.

The close association between God and Columbus in all the books, with the possible exception of Fritz's, discourages children from criticizing Columbus. "Columbus marveled at how God had arranged everything for the best," the D'Aulaires write. Well, if God arranged everything, who are we, the insignificant readers, to question?

No book even hints that the Indians believed in their own God or gods who also watched over and cared about them. The Columbus expedition may be the first encounter between two peoples — Us and Them — where children will learn that "God is on our side."

Evils? Blame the Workers

Columbus's journey across the Atlantic was not easy, according to most of the books, because his crew was such a wretched bunch. The sailors were stupid, superstitious, cowardly, and sometimes scheming. Columbus, on the other hand, is portrayed as brave, wise, and godly. These characterizations, repeated frequently in many of the books, protect the Columbus myth. Anything bad that happens, like murder and slavery, can always be blamed on the men. Columbus, the leader, is pure of heart.

Taken together, the books' portrayals serve as a kind of anti-working class, pro-boss polemic: "Soon [Columbus] rose above his shipmates, for he was clever and capable and could make others carry out his orders." [D'Aulaire] Evidently, ordinary seamen are not "clever and capable," and thus are good merely for carrying out the instructions of others. "Soon [Columbus] forgot that he was only the son of a humble weaver," the D'Aulaires write, as if a background as a worker were a source of shame. The books encourage children to identify with Columbus's hardships, even though his men worked and slept in horrible conditions while the future Admiral slept under a canopy bed in his private cabin. The lives of those who labored for Columbus are either ignored or held in contempt.

The 'Discovery'

At the core of the Columbus myth — and repeated by all eight books — is the notion that Columbus "discovered" America. Indeed, it's almost as if the same writer churned out one ever-so-slightly different version after another.

De Kay describes the scene this way in *Meet Christopher Columbus:*

The sailors rowed Columbus to the shore. He stepped on the beach. He got on his knees and said a prayer of thanks.

Columbus named the island San Salvador. He said it now belonged to Ferdinand and Isabella.

He tried to talk to the people on San Salvador. But they could not understand him.

Of course he couldn't understand them, either. But de Kay attributes the inability to understand solely to the Indians. Is it these Indians' implied ignorance that justifies heavily armed men coming onto their land and claiming it in the name of a kingdom thousands of miles away? In *Christopher Columbus and His Voyage to the New World,* Robert Young doesn't even tell his young readers of the people on these islands. Young's Columbus found "lands" but no people: In illustrations we see only palm trees and empty beaches.

Why don't any of the books ask students to think about the assumptions that underpinned this land grab? Naively, I kept waiting for some book to insert just a trace of doubt: "Why do you think Columbus felt he could claim land for Spain when there were already people living there?" or "Columbus doesn't write in his journal why he felt entitled to steal other people's property. What do you think?"

This scene of Columbus's first encounter with the Indians — read in school by virtually every child — is a powerful metaphor about relations between different countries and races. It is a lesson not just about the world 500 years ago, but about the world today: Clothed, armed, Christian white men from a more technologically "advanced" nation arrive in a land peopled by darker-skinned, naked, unarmed, non-Christians — and take over. Because no book indicates which characteristic of either group necessitates or excuses this kind of bullying, students are left alone to puzzle it out: Might makes right. Whites should rule over people who aren't white. Christians should control non-Christians. "Advanced" nations should dominate "backward" nations. Each and every answer a student might glean from the books' text and images invariably justifies colonialism and racism.

In Columbus's New World "adventures," the lives of the Indians are a kind of "muzak" — insignificant background noise. Only one book, *Where Do You Think You're Going, Christopher Columbus?*, tries to imagine what the Indians might have been thinking about the arrival of the Spaniards. Still, the point here seems more to gently poke fun at Columbus and crew than to seriously consider the Indians' point of view: "[I]f the Spaniards were surprised to see naked natives, the natives were even more surprised to see dressed Spaniards. All that cloth over their bodies! What were they trying to hide? Tails, perhaps?" Jean Fritz's interior monologue for the Indians makes fun of the explorers but in the process trivializes the Indians' concerns.

Not a single Columbus biography ever asks children: "What might the Indians have thought about the actions of Columbus and his men?"

The silent Indians in Columbus stories have a contemporary consequence. The message is that white people in "developed" societies have consciousness and voice, but Third World people are thoughtless and voiceless objects. The books rehearse students in a way of looking at the world that begins from the assumption: They are not like us. A corollary is that we are more competent to determine the conditions of their lives: their social and economic systems, their political alliances, and so on. Interventions in Iraq and Vietnam, subversion of the government headed by Salvador Allende in Chile, the invasions of Grenada and Panama, the attempted overthrow by proxy of the Nicaraguan and Angolan governments: Our right to decide what's best for *them* is basic to the conduct of this nation's foreign policy. As most children's first exposure to "foreign policy," the Columbus myth helps condition young people to accept the unequal distribution of power in the world.

Theft, Slavery, and Murder

Columbus's genocidal policies toward the Indians were initiated during his second journey. The three books aimed at children in early elementary grades, Gleiter and Thompson's *Christopher Columbus*, de Kay's *Meet Christopher Columbus*, and Young's *Christopher Columbus and His Voyage to the New World*, all conveniently stop the story after his first journey. The Columbus myth can take root in young minds without the complications of the slavery and mass murder to come.

After his first trip, Columbus returned to a hero's welcome in Spain. He also arrived telling all kinds of lies about gold mines and spices and unlimited amounts of wealth. The admiral needed royal backing for a second trip, and had to convince his sponsors that the islands contained more than parrots and naked natives.

During his second voyage, in February of 1495, Columbus launched the slave raids against the Taínos of Hispaniola. Four of the eight books I reviewed — the ones aimed at older children — admit that Columbus took Indians as slaves. [Monchieri, Fritz, Osborne, and Dolan.] Their critique, however, is muted. No account tells children what slavery meant for its victims. One of the books, Monchieri's *Christopher Columbus*, says that taking slaves was "a great failing of Columbus.... He saw nothing wrong with enslaving the American Indians and making them work for Spanish masters.... Missionaries protested against this policy, but they were not listened to." End of discussion.

Mary Pope Osborne in *Christopher Columbus: Admiral of the Ocean Sea* writes that "this terrible treatment of the Indians was Columbus's real downfall." Still, Osborne is unable to offer even this minimal critique of the admiral without at the same time justifying his actions: "Since Columbus felt despair and disappointment about not finding gold in the Indies, he decided to be like the African explorers and try to sell these Indians as slaves." Neither book ever describes the character of slave life — or slave death.

The other two biographies offer Columbus's justifications for taking slaves: "African explorers were always sending Africans back to Spanish slave markets, Columbus told himself. Besides, the natives were all heathens. It wasn't as if he were selling Christians into slavery." [Fritz] Dolan at one point blames it all on the men: "Given the attitude of the men at large, however, [Columbus] had little choice but to give his approval to the slaving sorties."

Imagine, if you will, Nazi war crimes described in this way — nothing about the suffering of the victims, tepid criticism of the perpetrators, the horrendous crimes explained by the rationalizations of Hitler and his generals. How long would these books last in our schools?

From the beginning, locating gold was Columbus's primary objective. In one passage, not included in any of the children's books, Columbus wrote: "Gold is a wonderful thing! Whoever owns it is lord of all he wants. With gold it is even possible to open for souls the way to paradise." Two of the eight authors, Fritz and Dolan, describe Columbus's system for attempting to extract gold from the Indians. Dolan writes that Columbus instituted "a system of forced tribute: each Indian was to provide a certain amount of gold each year. Penalties for failure to comply with this rule included flogging, enslavement, or death." Nothing here about cutting people's hands off, which is what Columbus did, but still it's pretty explicit. Fritz writes simply that Indians who didn't deliver enough gold "were punished." She concludes that "between 1494 and 1496 one-third of the native population of Hispaniola was killed, sold, or scared away." The passive voice in Fritz's version — "was killed, sold, or scared away" — protects the perpetrators: Exactly who caused these deaths?

More significantly, these accounts fail to recognize the Indians' humanity. The books' descriptions are clinical and factual, like those of a coroner. What kind of suffering must these people have gone through? How did it feel to have their civilization completely destroyed in just a few years? What of the children who watched their parents butchered by the Spanish gold-seekers? These books show no passion or outrage — at Columbus or at the social and economic system he represented. This devastation happened to several hundred thousand human beings, maybe more. Why don't the writers of these books get angry?

I find the most "honest" books about Columbus's enterprise — those that admit slavery and other crimes — the most distressing. They lay out the facts, describe the deaths, and then move on to the next paragraph with no look back. These books foster a callousness toward human suffering — or is it simply a callousness toward people of color? Apparently students are supposed to value bravery, cunning, and perseverance over a people's right to life and self determination.

Contempt for Native Resistance

Given that Columbus biographies scarcely consider Indians as human beings, it's not surprising that native resistance to the Spaniards' atrocities is either barely acknowledged or treated with hostility. Gleiter and Thompson's *Christopher Columbus* notes that in future trips Columbus "fought with the natives." In a single sentence, Lino Monchieri writes: "The Indians became rebellious because [Columbus] compelled them to hand over their gold." At least here the author credits the Indians with what might be a legitimate cause for revolt, though offers no further details. Mary Pope Osborne buries the cause of resistance in non-explanatory, victimless prose: "But the settlers had run into trouble with the Indians, and there had been a lot of fighting."

Some writers choose to portray Indian resistance not as self-defense, but as originating from the indigenous people's inherently violent nature. In *Meet Christopher Columbus*, "unfriendly Indians" surprise the innocent Spaniards: "Suddenly more than 50 Indians jumped out from behind the trees. They had bows and arrows. They attacked the men. The men fought back." Thus, Indian resistance to the Spaniards' invasion and land grab is not termed "freedom fighting," but instead is considered "unfriendly." The violence of the Spaniards is described as self-defense. Note that in this quote, the Spaniards are "men" and the Indians are, well, just Indians.

The books which bother to differentiate between groups of Indians single out the Caribs for special contempt. Caribs are presented as cannibals, even though no historical evidence exists to corroborate such a claim. The Caribs lived on islands "so wild and steep, it seemed as if the waterfalls came tumbling out of the clouds. The Indians who lived there were wild too. They were cannibals who ate their enemies." [D'Aulaire]

In Dolan's *Christopher Columbus: The Intrepid Mariner*, Columbus sends an armed contingent to "explore" the island that today is St. Croix. Because Caribs attack the Spaniards, Dolan considers this resistance sufficient to label the Caribs as ferocious. In fact, according to the eyewitness account of Dr. Diego Alvarez Chanca, the Indians attacked only when the Spaniards trapped them in a cove. In today's parlance, the Caribs were "radicals" and "extremists" — in other words, they tenaciously defended their land and freedom.

The books condition young people to reject the right of the oppressed to rebel. We have a right to own their land, and they should not protest — at least not violently. Those who do resist will be slapped with a pejorative descriptor — cannibal, savage, communist, militant, radical, hard-liner, extremist — and subdued. The Columbus biographies implicitly lead students to have contempt for contemporary movements for social justice.

Obviously, they leave children ill-prepared to respect current Indian struggles for land and fishing rights.

Columbus's Legacy

I expected each book to end with at least some reflection on the meaning of Columbus's voyages. None did. In fact, only one book, *Meet Christopher Columbus,* even suggests that today's world has anything to do with Columbus: Thanks to the Admiral, "Thousands of people crossed the ocean to America. This 'new world' became new countries: the United States, Canada, Mexico, Brazil, and many others."

It's much simpler for the authors to ignore both short and long term consequences of Columbus's enterprise. Instead of linking the nature of Columbus's Spain to 20th century America, each book functions as a kind of secular Book of Genesis: In the beginning there was Columbus — he was good and so are we.

This is a grave omission. In addition to the genocide of native peoples in the Caribbean, the most immediate effect of Columbus's voyages was the initiation of the Atlantic slave trade between Africa and America.

Colonialism and slavery: this was the "new world" Columbus did not so much discover as help to invent. In the emerging commercial ethos of his society, human beings were commodities whose value was measured largely in monetary terms. The natural environment was likewise cherished not for its beauty but for the wealth that could be extracted. Columbus's enterprise and the plunder that ensued contributed mightily to the growth of the nascent mercantile capitalism of Europe. His lasting contribution was to augment a social order that confronts the world in commercial terms — how much is it worth? — and which appreciates markets rather than cultures.

Asking 'Why?'

Why are Columbus biographies characterized by such bias and omission? I doubt any writers, publishers, or teachers consciously set out to poison the minds of the young. The Columbus story teaches important values, some would argue. Here was a young man who, despite tremendous adversity, maintained and finally achieved his objectives. Fear and narrow-mindedness kept others from that which he finally accomplished.

But in the Columbus biographies, these decent values intermingle seamlessly with deep biases against working class people, people of color, and Third World nations. The blindness of writers and educators to these biases is simply an indication of how pervasive they are in the broader society. The seeds of imperialism, exploitation, and racism were planted with Columbus's first transatlantic enterprise — and these seeds have taken root.

Without doubt, ours is a very different world than Spanish America in the 15th and 16th centuries, but there is a lingering inheritance: the tendency for powerful groups to value profit over humanity; racial and cultural differences used to justify exploitation and inequality; vast disparities in living conditions for different social classes; economically and militarily strong nations attempting to control the fates of weaker nations. Hence, life amidst injustice in today's United States inures many of us to the injustice of 500 years earlier. Characteristics that appear to someone as natural and inevitable in the 21st century will likely appear as natural and inevitable in the descriptions of the world five centuries ago.

The Biographies' Pedagogy

The Columbus stories encourage passive reading, and never pose questions for children to think about. Did Columbus have a right to claim Indian land in the name of the Spanish crown? Were those Indians who resisted violently justified in doing so? Why does the United States commemorate a Columbus Day instead of a Genocide Day? The narratives require readers merely to listen, not to think. The text is everything, the reader nothing. Not only are young readers conditioned to accept social hierarchy — colonialism and racism — they are also rehearsed in an authoritarian mode of learning.

By implication, in this review essay I suggest the outlines of a more truthful history of Columbus and the "discovery" of America. First, the indigenous peoples of America must be accorded the status of full human beings with inalienable rights to self-determination. The tale of "discovery" needs to be told from their perspective as well as from the Europeans'. Although there is little documentation of how the Indians inter-preted the Spaniards' arrival and conquest, readers could be encouraged to think about these events from the native point of view. Columbus's in-terior monologue should not be the only set of thoughts represented in the story.

A more accurate tale of Columbus would not simply probe his personal history but would also analyze the social and economic system he repre-sented. And children might be asked to think about how today's world was shaped by the events of 1492. Above all, young readers must be invited to think and critique, not simply required to passively absorb others' historical interpretations.

Until we create humane and truthful materials, teachers may decide to boycott the entire Columbus canon. The problem with this approach is that the distortions and inadequacies characterizing this literature are also found in other children's books.

A better solution is to equip students to read critically these and other stories   inviting children to become detectives, investigating their biog-raphies, novels, and textbooks for bias. In fact, because the Columbus books are so bad, they make perfect classroom resources to learn how to read for social as well as for literal meaning. After students have been intro-duced to a critical history of Columbus, they could probe materials for accu-racy. Do the books lie outright? What is omitted from the accounts that would be necessary for a more complete understanding of Columbus and his encounters with native cultures? What motives are ascribed to Columbus, and how do those compare with the actual objectives of the admiral and the Spanish monarchs? Whom does the book "root" for, and how is this accomplished? What role do illustrations play in shaping the view of Columbus? Why do the books tell the story as they do? Who in our society benefits and who is hurt by these presentations?

Teachers could assign children to write their own Columbus biogra-phies — and some of these could be told from Indians' points of view. Or youngsters might take issues from their own lives suggested by the European invasion of America — fighting, fairness, stealing, racism — and write sto-ries drawn from these themes.

Significantly, to invite students to question the injustices embedded in text material is implicitly to invite them to question the injustices embedded in the society itself. Isn't it about time we used the Columbus myth to allow students to begin discovering the truth?

For Further Reading

Bigelow, Bill and Peterson, Bob (Eds.). *Rethinking Columbus: The Next 500 Years.* Milwaukee, WI: Rethinking Schools, 1998.

Zinn, Howard. *A People's History of the United States.* New York: Harper and Row, 1980.

Sale, Kirkpatrick. *The Conquest of Paradise: Christopher Columbus and the Columbian Legacy.* New York: Knopf, 1990.

Davidson, Basil. *The African Slave Trade: Precolonial History 1450-1850.* Boston: Little, Brown, 1961.

---

[1] Books reviewed in this article and their intended grade level:

Christopher Columbus and His Voyage to the New World (Let's Celebrate Series) by Robert Young. Silver Press, 1990, 32 pp. (2nd grade)

Meet Christopher Columbus by James T. de Kay, Random House, 1989, 72 pp. (2nd grade)

Christopher Columbus (Great Tales Series) by Jan Gleiter and Kathleen Thompson, Ideals, 1995, 32 pp. (3rd grade)

Columbus by Ingri and Edgar Parin D'Aulaire, Doubleday, 1987, 59 pp. (5th grade)

Where do you think you're going, Christopher Columbus? by Jean Fritz, G.P. Putnam's Sons, 1997, 80 pp. (Upper elementary)

Christopher Columbus by Lino Monchieri (trans. by Mary Lee Grisanti), Silver Burdett, 1985, 62 pp. (Upper elementary)

Christopher Columbus: Admiral of the Ocean Sea by Mary Pope Osborne, Dell, 1997, 90 pp. (Upper elementary/middle school)

Christopher Columbus: The Intrepid Mariner (Great Lives Series) by Sean J. Dolan, Fawcett Columbine, 1989, 117 pp. (Middle school)

Arranged Marriages, Rearranged Ideas

Stan Karp

Jihana was one of my favorite students. By the time she was a senior, we had been together for three years, first in a sophomore English class and then through two years of journalism electives where students produced school publications and learned desktop publishing.

Jihana's bright-eyed intelligence and can-do enthusiasm made her a teacher's dream. Her daily greeting in our busy journalism office was, "Hi, Mr. Karp, what needs to be done?" I used to joke that she'd get straight A's until the end of her senior year when I'd have to fail her so she couldn't graduate and leave. It was corny, but she always laughed.

Jihana was one of a growing number of Bengali students in my Paterson, New Jersey high school. Along with increasing numbers of Latin-American, Caribbean, Middle-Eastern, Central-European, and other immigrants, these new communities had transformed the school in the 20 years I'd been there as a teacher. What had once been a predominantly white, then later a primarily black and Latino student population was now thoroughly international. The teaching staff, however, remained mostly white, with a limited number of teachers of color.

Increasingly, some of my best students each year were young Bengali women. Some, like Jihana, covered their heads with scarves in keeping with Muslim tradition. A few wore the full veil. Others wore no special dress. Many seemed reserved and studious. Others gradually adopted the more assertive, outgoing styles of the citywise teens around them.

An Arranged Marriage

By the time Jihana was a senior it was natural for me to ask, during one of the many extra periods she spent in the journalism office, what her post-graduation plans were. She said she wanted to go to college, perhaps to study medicine, and was considering several schools. But, she added, a lot depended on whether she had to get married.

I knew enough about Jihana, and about the Bengali community, to know that she wasn't referring to a premature wedding prompted by an unplanned pregnancy, but to the possibility of an arranged marriage. Jihana made it pretty clear that she wasn't ready to get married. She was anxious to go to college and to move out of a household where she felt she had too many cleaning chores and child-care duties and not enough personal freedom. She said the outcome partly depended on what happened with her sister, who was several years older and also a candidate for marriage, and on whether her family decided to send them both back to Bangladesh in the summer for possible matches.

I listened sympathetically and made schoolteacher noises about how smart I thought she was and how I hoped she'd get the opportunity to attend college. Unsure of just what my role, as a white, male, high school teacher, could possibly be in this situation, I halfheartedly offered to speak to her family about her college potential if she thought it would help. Jihana smiled politely and said she'd keep me posted.

I went home thinking about Jihana's situation. I was upset, even angered by the thought that this young woman's promising prospects and educational future could be sidetracked by a cultural practice that seemed to me hopelessly unreasonable and unfair. No matter how I tried to come to terms with it, the custom of arranged marriages was completely alien to my own sensibilities and to my expectations for my students. I kept thinking of how my own high-school-aged daughter, raised at home and at least nominally at school to think in terms of gender equality and independence, would laugh in my face if I ever sat her down and tried to tell her my plans for her marital future.

I also thought, and not for the first time, about what my responsibilities were as a public school teacher, and how I should manage this mix of my own strongly held personal opinions, concern for my students' well-being, and respect for the cultural differences that were increasingly evident in my school community.

As both a political activist and a classroom teacher, I'd wrestled with these issues often. On the one hand, I'd come to believe that effective class-room teaching, especially in schools with a history of failure and pervasive student alienation, was inherently "political," in the sense that it had to take the social context of schooling and of students' lives as a primary point of departure. I tried to encourage students to "talk back" to the world we studied, and, wherever possible, to take action in response to ideas and issues. These premises informed any number of choices I made daily about curriculum, classroom organization, and how to channel in particular direc-tions the "oppositional energy" I found in most teenagers. It also meant I frequently tried to take real situations in my students' lives, both in and out of school, as starting points for research, writing, and class discussion.

At the same time, I know it is neither appropriate nor fair for teachers to restrict the curriculum to only those views and ideas that they personally agree with. Since teachers have power over students, it's especially neces-sary to be sensitive to issues of intimidation, the rights of dissent, personal privacy, and freedom of choice. In some ways, the closer issues hit to home, as in Jihana's situation, the more careful teachers must be, particularly where racial, cultural, and class differences are involved.

At first glance, Jihana's problem seemed personal and private, not read-ily the stuff of classroom discussion. It had social roots and cultural dimen-sions like other student concerns that had become the subject of class assignments or research. But it seemed to call for an individual, personal response on my part, rather than a pedagogical one, and I had real trouble imagining what that response should be.

Reluctant to Intervene

As a rule, I have generally been reluctant to intervene at home when it comes to handling personal and family issues with my teenage students. Though I've always supported parents' participation in their children's education, for me this usually has meant support for parent participation in governance and policymaking processes, or finding ways to include parent and family experience in my curriculum.

But when personal (as opposed to strictly academic) problems arise with secondary-age students, I've always hesitated to "call home" too quickly. Most of the 15- to 18-year-olds I deal with are emerging adults who've been semi-independent to varying degrees for years: holding down jobs, assuming family responsibilities, traveling the world, dealing with the courts and immigration authorities, and even coping with parenthood themselves. Others come from difficult family situations that are not always supportive or, not infrequently, may even be the source of the problems they choose to share with me. In the normal course of a year, it's not unusual for me to deal with teenagers who are wrestling with everything from homelessness, pregnancy, and sexual identity to depression, domestic violence, and drug abuse.

When my students bring such issues to me, I've always felt that my first allegiance was to them, to listen sympathetically and to offer whatever advice or access to services I could manage, and not, primarily, to act as a surrogate for, or even mediator with, parental authority. Yes, there have been occasions when my judgment, or the legal responsibilities that are periodically spelled out in nervous memos from central office, compel me to pick up the phone or make a home visit. But in general I take my signal about whether home intervention on my part makes sense from my students, and most of the time it doesn't. There have also been times when I've passed on information about where to get birth control or other kinds of counseling services (for example, for gay teens) that I knew might not be fully endorsed at home.

In Jihana's case I tried to imagine what I could possibly say to her family about the situation: "Hi, I'm Jihana's teacher, and as a politically progressive, pro-feminist, privileged white male, I think your plans for Jihana are a medieval abomination."

I don't think so.

But the more I thought about it, the more I realized that the problem wasn't finding more diplomatic ways to voice my opinions; the problem was figuring out the dividing line between responding to the needs of my students and interfering inappropriately with "other people's children."

I also thought about another student I had some ten years earlier, Rafia, who faced this same situation. Rafia was the youngest of four daughters in a Bengali family. Smart, sophisticated beyond her years, and ambitious, Rafia was anxious to go to college despite her family's objections. As I encouraged her and helped her fill out applications during her junior and senior years, it was Rafia who first made me aware that many Bengali families did not think girls should go to college, and that she and her sisters were facing, with varying degrees of dread, the prospect of arranged marriages.

I was horrified at the idea, and said so. In fact, as I recall, my main re-action consisted of expressing my outrage that women were oppressed this way in her culture. I told her I didn't think anyone had the right to tell her who to marry, and that it was much more important for her future to go to college than to please her parents. I even suggested that it was more impor-tant to choose college than to avoid a break with her family, and that, even if they got upset, they would probably get over it. I somewhat flippantly told her she could stay at my house for a while if she decided to run away.

Learning a Lesson

When Jihana's story jogged my memory, it was with more than a little embarrassment that I recalled how my reaction to Rafia had been foolish, and not a little arrogant. At the time I had acted as if the most important response to Rafia's dilemma was to show her that not everyone was as "backward" as her parents, and that there were swell, "enlightened" folks like myself who believed in her right to shape her own future and educa-tion. In effect I was showing off the "superior" values and "advanced" thinking of "progressive Western culture," especially of radicals like myself, and contrasting it to the "underdeveloped practices" of her own communi-ty, which I encouraged her to reject. I had also reacted as if what I thought and how I felt about the issues raised by her predicament were of para-mount importance, and should be the point of departure for my response.

Looking back, it seemed that the problem wasn't that I was wrong to oppose the custom of arranged marriages or to make my opinions known, but that I did it in a way that was essentially self-serving, and as a practical matter, not very helpful. I had basically denounced what I, as an outsider, saw as "deficient" in her culture and encouraged her to turn her back on it. While my sympathies may have been well-meant, my advice was culturally insensitive and wildly impractical. And it probably just reinforced Rafia's sense of alienation and being trapped.

Fortunately, Rafia was sharp enough to appreciate my personal support and ignore my advice. Instead of running away or openly breaking with her family, she steadfastly argued for her chance to attend college while continuing to excel in school. Eventually, she got her father's permission to go to college (though she was forced to study engineering instead of the humanities she preferred). The experience had stayed with me over the years, and now that a similar situation had arisen, I was anxious to do better by Jihana.

A couple of weeks passed after our first conversation, and it became clear that nothing decisive would happen with Jihana's situation until the summer came. Still looking for a way to lend support, one day I suggested to Jihana that she consider writing a story about arranged marriages for our student magazine. I mentioned briefly my experience with Rafia and asked how the growing community of female Bengali students in the high school felt about this and related issues. Instead of dwelling on my own opinions, I tried to emphasize that she wasn't the only one facing these issues, and that she could perform a service for both Bengali students and the rest of the school by focusing on a set of concerns that had gotten little attention.

Jihana seemed interested but hesitant. She was a good writer but generally took less ambitious assignments, like covering school news or activities. She expressed some concern that her family would be offended if they found out, and that, in the tightly-knit Bengali community, it might be hard to keep it a secret even if she published a piece anonymously. I asked her to think it over and told her she could get credit for writing the article even if she decided in the end not to publish it. I also told her, as I told all my students, that we could consider the implications or consequences of going public later, but she should write what she really thought and not censor herself in advance.

I was hoping to use the tremendous potential that writing has, not only to help students express their ideas and feelings but also to help them develop the skills, and sometimes the distance, needed to analyze complicated topics and clarify issues. While I hoped Jihana would eventually publish, it seemed valuable to have her organize and express her thoughts for her own purposes as well. After a few days, and after double-checking that she wouldn't have to publish the piece if she wasn't comfortable, she agreed. She asked for help making an outline, so we arranged a story conference.

A Broader Context

When we started discussing how to organize the article, Jihana said she wanted to deal first with stereotypes and misconceptions that Westerners had about Muslims. She said she wanted to put the issue of arranged marriages in a broader context of Muslim culture, which had a variety of customs and practices that she felt were misunderstood. Muslim women were not "slaves," she said, and not everyone did things the same way. When it came to marriage, there was a range of practices, and in many cases, Muslim women did have choices and varying degrees of input into the decision.

This led to a discussion of women and marriage customs in general, and how women have faced oppression and male supremacy in all cultures. We also talked about the generational conflict between young Bengalis (and other younger immigrants) raised in the United States, and their parents, rooted in more traditional "old country" customs, and how this exacerbated the struggle over marriage practices. Jihana told me stories about families that had been torn apart by these differences, as well as others where parents and children had found common ground and happy endings.

As we talked, several things started to become clear. By locating the issue of arranged marriages inside the broader issue of woman's rights, which cuts across all cultures and countries, it became easier for Jihana to address the topic without "stigmatizing" her own community. If Bengali women had to wrestle with arranged marriages and male dominance, the supposedly more "liberated" sexual culture of the United States presented women with its own set of problems: higher levels of sexual assault, single teenage parenthood, divorce, and domestic violence. Generational conflict between old ways and new also cut across cultures and made the issue seem more universal, again allowing it to be addressed in a context that didn't demonize one particular group.

Finally, it was clear that speaking on behalf of Bengali women, instead of just against the practice of arranged marriages, tended to make Jihana feel more empowered than isolated. She was still determined to question the imposition of marital arrangements against the woman's will, but would do so in the context of defending Muslim culture against stereotypes and as part of a critique of women's oppression as a whole. Added to the protection she felt from not having to publish her work if she chose not to, assuming this positive stance on behalf of herself and her peers seemed to give her the safe space she needed from which to address these difficult issues. By the end of our conversation, she seemed ready to go.

Within a week or two, Jihana was back with her article. "Do Muslim women have any rights?" she began.

> Do they make their own decisions? Are they allowed to think? Are they prisoners in their own homes? There are many stereotypes held by Westerners about the position and role of Muslim women....These notions are based upon the lack of knowledge Westerners have of Islam.
>
> Women, regardless of their culture or society, have suffered tremendously over inequality and have had to fight for a firm place in their society. During the Roman civilization, a woman was considered to be a slave. The Greeks bought and sold their women as merchandise rather than accept them as human beings. Early Christianity regarded their women as "temptresses," responsible for the fall of Adam.
>
> In Pre-Islamic times, as well as in certain places today, a female child is thought of as a cause for unhappiness and grief. Baby girls were sometimes buried alive after birth. But gaps in wealth, education, and justice between men and women can be found everywhere and just can't be explained by religion.

Jihana went on to discuss "some issues about the rights of a Muslim woman [that] stem from the issue of marriage." She wrote about the varying degrees of choice women may have in different families, the generational conflict, the problems associated with patterns of marriage in the United States. ("Some Muslim families say that while the Westerners seem to be 'more free,' their society is not working too well.") She cited examples to show that, "as in all marriages, whether arranged or not, some work and some do not."

Though many of the Bengali students Jihana spoke to declined to be quoted by name, she did find one senior who "extremely disagrees with arranged marriages" and who thought "all Muslim women should be given an opportunity and the privilege to choose the person that they want to spend the rest of their lives with."

After exploring the issues from several sides, Jihana came to a balancing act that suggested her own personal struggle:

> Arranged marriages and other Muslim customs of life, like the covering of the body and not dating, may seem to be burdensome to women of most Western cultures, but for Muslim women it's their way of life. We were brought up to follow and believe that these practices were the right ways of life. It is up to us as individuals to see that we follow what is expected of us....The Muslim religion, in my opinion, can include double standards....In many cases males are allowed to do certain things that females can't....For example, when a male does get married without his parents' permission, it is OK, but if a female does the same thing it is not OK. This is so because in the Holy Koran it states that a woman has to follow certain things. For example, it is a woman's duty and obligation to bring up her children according to the ways of Islam. She has to look after the family and has absolute control over domestic affairs. She must wear a covering cloak when meeting adult men outside her family. She is her husband's helpmate. Islam recognizes the leadership of a man over a woman, but that does not mean domination.
>
> In conclusion, women should have the freedom and right to do something they're interested in doing or accomplishing. They should go forward with their education if they want to continue it, with the help and support to do so. Women can cook and clean, but they could also do more.

At bottom, Jihana's "balancing act" was an affirmative statement about her place and her rights in her community. And though writing the article didn't resolve her dilemma, it did, I think, support her in her efforts to speak up for herself, and offered a way for her to develop some useful perspectives on her situation. It also helped focus attention on issues that she and her Bengali peers were wrestling with inside the school community.

New Pride

Though Jihana had originally balked at the idea of publication, by the time she was done she used the computer skills she'd learned in class to create a two-page layout for our magazine with her article, her byline, and her picture under the title, "Muslim Women: Where Do We Belong?" She seemed proud of it, and so was I, especially as I reflected on what I'd learned myself.

Switching the focus from my own reactions to my student's point of view, and developing a deeper appreciation of the need to deal with issues of cultural difference with more humility and care, had led me to a more effective and more appropriate response. I was still just as opposed as ever to arranged marriages, and still saw contradictions in Jihana's balancing act about the codes of Islam. But because I hadn't begun with an attack on the cultural norms of her community, I had managed to find a way that, to some degree at least, both supported and empowered her.

As it turned out, Jihana's willingness to raise such issues was not limited to our magazine. One morning in the spring, I found her working feverishly in the journalism office on a list of "Bengali Concerns" for the next Student Government Association meeting. The list had a tone familiar from earlier days of student activism, but it had specifics I'd never seen before. It read:

1. How come there aren't more Bengali SGA members?
2. There is a lack of Bengali students involved in school activities. We need more participation and more representation of the Bengali people.
3. We need Bengali-speaking guidance counselors and teachers.
4. We need Bengali mentors.
5. How come the history teachers never teach about Bangladesh and its culture when they teach world history?
6. Why isn't there Bengali student representation when the school presents a panel of students to represent the school?
7. How come all the newsletters that go home from the school are either in Spanish or in English? How come you can't send letters home that are in Bengali? That way the parents will know what is going on in their children's school. The lack of communication with the Bengali parents is a reason why many don't attend the Home-School Council meetings.

New Steps for Jihana

Around the same time that these concerns were being presented to the student government, preparations were underway for an assembly presentation of Bengali dance and traditional dress. Like many other schools, my high school was still in the relatively superficial stages of addressing multicultural issues, and tended toward food festivals and holiday celebrations. But the assembly program tapped the energy of many Bengali students, and Jihana had gotten involved. One afternoon, soon after our magazine had appeared, she came to the journalism office and asked if I could fax a copy of her article to a reporter from a local newspaper. She said she'd been interviewed in connection with the upcoming assembly program, but had left some things out. "I was trying to explain myself to the reporter and couldn't get the words out right," she said. "I told him I had written an article explaining what I thought, and it was all in there. I promised to send it to him." The article she had been hesitant to write and reluctant to publish had become a personal position statement.

As we headed into the last weeks of the school year, I occasionally asked Jihana if there were any new developments. There weren't any on the marriage front, but she did get accepted to several colleges and began to make plans to attend a state university. When we parted at year's end, I made her promise to let me know how things turned out.

About a month later, I returned from a trip to find a slightly ambiguous message. Jihana had called to say hello and to invite me to a wedding. Taken aback, and fearing that this might be her way of letting me know that marriage had won out over college, I called her at home. She was in good spirits and busy getting ready to move into the dorms on her new campus. The invitation was to her sister's wedding, Jihana explained, and if I could come I'd get a chance to see some more of how Bengali marriage customs worked. Unfortunately, I wasn't able to attend, but Jihana promised to show me the proceedings on videotape.

In September Jihana started college classes. A few weeks later, I got a note describing her new life. "College is OK," she wrote, "not that great as everyone said it would be. Maybe it is just me. I never realized how difficult my classes would be and so large in lectures!! I am taking an Arabic class so that I can be trilingual!

"I have to go home every weekend, but I don't mind," she wrote. "I have a new status in my family; everyone respects me more, and I also don't have to do any more housework. Isn't that great??!!"

I had to agree that it was.

The names of students in this article have been changed.

Presidents and Slaves: Helping Students Find the Truth

Bob Peterson

During a lesson about George Washington and the American Revolution, I explained to my fifth graders that Washington owned 317 slaves. One student added that Thomas Jefferson also was a slave owner. And then, in part to be funny and in part expressing anger — over vote fraud involving African Americans in the then-recent 2000 election and the U.S. Supreme Court's subsequent delivery of the presidency to George W. Bush — one of my students shouted: "Bush is a slave owner, too!"

"No, Bush doesn't own slaves," I calmly explained. "Slavery was finally ended in this country in 1865."

Short exchanges such as this often pass quickly and we move onto another topic. But this time one student asked: "Well, which presidents were slave owners?"

She had me stumped. "That's a good question," I said. "I don't know."

Thus began a combined social studies, math, and language arts project in which I learned along with my students, and which culminated in a fascinating exchange between my students and the publishers of their U.S. history textbook.

After I admitted that I had no clue exactly which presidents owned slaves, I threw the challenge back to the students. "How can we find out?" I asked.

"Look in a history book," said one. "Check the Internet," added another.

I realized that I had entered one of those "teachable moments" when students show genuine interest in exploring a particular topic. Yet I had few materials about presidents and slaves, and no immediate idea of how to engage 25 students on the subject.

I also recognized that this was a great opportunity to create my own curriculum, which might help students look critically at texts while encouraging their active participation in doing meaningful research. Such an approach stands in sharp contrast to the "memorize the presidents" instruction that I suffered through growing up, and which too many students probably still endure. I seized the opportunity.

First, I had a student write down the question — "Which presidents were slave owners?" — in our class notebook, "Questions We Have." I then suggested that a few students form an "action research group," which in my classroom means an ad hoc group of interested students researching a topic and then doing something with what they learn. I asked for volunteers willing to work during recess. Several boys raised their hands, surprising me because I would have guessed that some of them would have much preferred going outside to staying indoors researching.

Action Research by Students

At recess time, Raul and Edwin were immediately in my face. "When are we going to start the action research on the slave presidents?" they demanded. I told them to look in the back of our school dictionaries for a list of U.S. presidents while I got out some large construction paper.

The dictionaries, like our social studies text, had little pictures of each president with some basic information. "Why doesn't it show Clinton?" Edwin commented. "He's been president forever."

I think, yeah, Clinton's been president four-fifths of this 10-year-old's life. But I kept that thought to myself and instead replied "The book is old."

"Why don't they just tell whether they have slaves here in this list of presidents?" asked Edwin. "They tell other things about presidents."

"Good question," I said. "Why do you think they don't tell?"

"I don't know, probably because they don't know themselves."

"Maybe so," I responded. "Here's what I'd like you to do. Since slavery was abolished when Lincoln was president, and since he was the 16th president, draw 16 lines equal distance from each other and list all the presidents from Washington to Lincoln, and then a yes-and-no column so we can check off whether they owned slaves."

I was soon to find out that filling in those columns was easier said than done.

When my students and I began investigating which presidents owned slaves, our attempts focused on traditional history textbooks and student-friendly websites from the White House and the Smithsonian Institution. These efforts turned up virtually nothing.

We then pursued two different sources of information: history books written for adults and more in-depth websites.

I brought in two books that were somewhat helpful: James Loewen's *Lies My Teacher Told Me* (Simon and Schuster, 1995) and Kenneth O'Reilly's *Nixon's Piano: Presidents and Racial Politics from Washington to Clinton* (Free Press, 1995). By using the indexes and reading the text out loud, we uncovered facts about some of the presidents.

We also used the web search engines Google and AltaVista and searched on the words "presidents" and "slavery." We soon learned we had to be more specific and include the president's name and "slavery" — for example, "President George Washington" and "slavery." Some results were student-friendly, such as the mention of Washington's slaves (and some of their escapes) at www.mountvernon.org/education/slavery. There was also a bill of sale for a slave signed by Dolly Madison, the wife of president James Madison (for a link to the document see www.rethinkingschools.org/rsr).

Many websites had a large amount of text and were beyond the reading level of many of my students. So I cut and pasted long articles into word processing documents so we could search for the word "slave" to see if there was any specific mention of slave ownership.

In their research, students often asked, "How do we know this is true? Our history books aren't telling the truth, why should we think this does?"

I explained the difference between primary and secondary sources and how a primary source — like a bill of sale or original list of slaves — was pretty solid evidence. To help ensure accuracy, the students decided that if we used secondary sources, we needed to find at least two different citations.

Bits and Pieces of Information

In the next several days the students, with my help, looked at various sources. We checked our school's children's books about presidents, our social studies textbook, a 1975 *World Book Encyclopedia,* and a CD-ROM encyclopedia. We found nothing about presidents as slave owners.

I had a hunch about which presidents owned slaves, based on what I knew in general about the presidents, but I wanted "proof" before we put a check in the "yes" box. And though my students wanted to add a third column — explaining how many slaves each slave-owning president had — that proved impossible. Even when we did find information about which presidents owned slaves, the numbers changed depending on how many slaves had been bought, sold, born, or died.

In our research, most of the information dealt with presidential attitudes and policies toward slavery. It was difficult to find specific information on which presidents owned slaves. To help the investigation, I checked out a few books for them from our local university library.

Overall, our best resource was the Internet. The best sites required adult help to find and evaluate, and I became so engrossed in the project that I spent a considerable amount of time at home surfing the web. The "student-friendly" websites with information about presidents — such as the White House's gallery of presidents (www.whitehouse.gov/history/presidents) — don't mention that Washington and Jefferson enslaved African Americans. Other popular sites with the same glaring lack of information are the Smithsonian Institution (http://educate.si.edu/president) and the National Museum of American History (http://www.americanhistory.si.edu/presidency).

As we did the research, I regularly asked, "Why do you think this doesn't mention that the president owned slaves?" Students' responses varied including "They're stupid," "They don't want us kids to know the truth," "They think we're too young to know," and "They don't know themselves." (Given more time, we might have explored this matter further, looking at who produces textbooks and why they might not include information about presidents' attitudes about racism and slavery.)

During our research, my students and I found bits and pieces of information about presidents and slavery. But we never found that one magic resource, be it book or website, that had the information readily available. Ultimately, though, we came up with credible data.

I'm a history buff, and had thought I was on top of the question of presidents and slavery. I was quite amazed, and didn't hide my amazement from our action research team, when they discovered that two presidents who served after Lincoln — Andrew Johnson and Ulysses S. Grant — had been slave owners. While the students taped an extension on their chart, I explained that I was not totally surprised about Johnson because he had been a Southerner. But it was a shock that Grant had owned slaves. "He was the commander of the Union army in the Civil War," I explained. "When I first learned about the Civil War in elementary school, Grant and Lincoln were portrayed as saviors of the Union and freers of slaves."

When I told the entire class how Grant's slave-owning past had surprised me, Tanya, an African-American student, raised her hand and said, "That's nothing. Lincoln was a slave owner, too."

I asked for her source of information and she said she had heard that Lincoln didn't like blacks. I thanked her for raising the point, and told the class that while it was commonly accepted by historians that Lincoln was not a slave owner, his attitudes toward blacks and slavery were a source of much debate. I noted that just because a president didn't own slaves didn't mean that he supported freedom for slaves or equal treatment of people of different races.

I went into a bit of detail on Lincoln, in part to counter the all-too-common simplification that Lincoln unequivocally opposed slavery and supported freedom for blacks. I explained that while it's commonly believed that Lincoln freed enslaved Americans when he signed the Emancipation Proclamation, the document actually frees slaves only in states and regions under rebellion — it did not free slaves in any of the slaveholding states and regions that remained in the Union. In other words, Lincoln "freed" slaves everywhere he had no authority and withheld freedom everywhere he did. Earlier, in Lincoln's first inaugural address in March of 1861, he promised slaveholders that he would support a constitutional amendment forever protecting slavery in the states where it then existed — if only those states would remain in the Union.

Slave-Owning Presidents

By the time we finished our research, the students had found that 10 of the first 18 presidents were slave owners: George Washington, Thomas

Jefferson, James Madison, James Monroe, Andrew Jackson, John Tyler, James K. Polk, Zachary Taylor, Andrew Johnson, and Ulysses S. Grant.

Those that didn't. John Adams, John Quincy Adams, Martin Van Buren, William Henry Harrison, Millard Fillmore, Franklin Pierce, James Buchanan, and, despite Tanya's assertion, Abraham Lincoln.

The student researchers were excited to present their findings to their classmates, and decided to do so as part of a math class. I made blank charts for each student in the class, and they filled in information provided by the action research team: the names of presidents, the dates of their years in office, the total number of years in office, and whether they had owned slaves. Our chart started with George Washington, who assumed office in 1789, and ended in 1877 when the last president who had owned slaves, Ulysses Grant, left office.

We then used the data to discuss this topic of presidents and slave owning within the structure of ongoing math topics in my class: "What do the data tell us?" and "How can we construct new knowledge with the data?"

Students, for example, added up the total number of years in which the United States had a slave-owning president in office, and compared that total to the number of years in which there were non-slave-owning presidents in office. We figured out that in 69 percent of the years between 1789 and 1877, the United States had a president who had been a slave owner.

One student observed that only slave-owning presidents served more than one term. "Why didn't they let presidents who didn't own slaves serve two terms?" another student pondered.

Using the data, the students made bar graphs and circle graphs to display the information. When they wrote written reflections on the math lesson, they connected math to content. One boy wrote: "I learned to convert fractions to percent so I know that $10/18$ is the same as 55.5 percent. That's how many of the first 18 presidents owned slaves." Another girl observed, "I learned how to make pie charts and that so many more presidents owned slaves than the presidents who didn't own slaves."

During a subsequent social studies lesson, the three students who had done most of the research explained their frustrations in getting information. "They hardly ever want to mention it [slaves owned by presidents]," explained one student. "We had to search and search."

Specific objectives for this mini-unit, such as reviewing the use of per-cent, emerged as the lessons themselves unfolded. But its main purpose was to help students to critically examine the actions of early leaders of the United States and to become skeptical of textbooks and government web-sites as sources that present the entire picture. I figure that if kids start ques-tioning the "official story" early on, they will be more open to alternative viewpoints later. While discovering which presidents were slave owners is not an in-depth analysis, it pokes an important hole in the god-like mys-tique that surrounds the "founding fathers." If students learn how to be crit-ical of the icons of American past, hopefully it will give them permission and tools to be critical of the elites of America today.

Besides uncovering some hard-to-find and uncomfortable historical truths, I also wanted to encourage my students to think about why these facts were so hard to find, and to develop a healthy skepticism of official sources of information. I showed them two quotations about Thomas Jeffer-son. One was from a recently published fifth-grade history text book, *United States: Adventures in Time and Place* (Macmillan/McGraw Hill, 1998) which read: "Jefferson owned several slaves in his lifetime and lived in a slave-own-ing colony. Yet he often spoke out against slavery. 'Nothing is more certainly written in the book of fate than that these people are to be free'" (p. 314).

The other quotation was from James Loewen's *Lies my Teacher Told Me*. Loewen writes:

> Textbooks stress that Jefferson was a humane master, privately tor-mented by slavery and opposed to its expansion, not the type to destroy families by selling slaves. In truth, by 1820 Jefferson had become an ardent advocate of the expansion of slavery to the western territories. And he never let his ambivalence about slavery affect his private life. Jefferson was an average master who had his slaves whipped and sold into the Deep South as examples to induce other slaves to obey. By 1822, Jefferson owned 267 slaves. During his long life, of hundreds of different slaves he owned, he freed only three and five more at his death — all blood relatives of his (p. 140).

We talked about the different perspective each quote had toward Jefferson and toward what students should learn. My students' attention immediately turned to the set of spanking new history textbooks that had been delivered to our classroom that year as part of the districtwide social studies adoption. Some students assumed that our new textbook *United States* (Harcourt Brace, 2000) was equally as bad as the one I quoted from. One student suggested we just throw the books away. But I quickly pointed out they were expensive, and that we could learn from them even if they had problems and omissions.

I then explained what an omission was, and suggested that we become "textbook detectives" and investigate what our new social studies text said about Jefferson and slavery. I reviewed how to use an index and divided all page references for Jefferson among small groups of students. The groups read the pages, noted any references to Jefferson owning slaves, and then reported back to the class. Not one group found a single reference.

Not surprisingly, the students were angry when they realized how the text omitted such important information. "They should tell the truth!" one student fumed.

No Mention of Racism

I wanted students to see that the textbook's omissions were not an anomaly, but part of a pattern of ignoring racism in America — in the past and in the present.

In the next lesson, I started by writing the word "racism" on the board. I asked the kids to look up "racism" in the index of their social studies book. Nothing. "Racial discrimination." Nothing.

"Our school should get a different book," one student suggested.

"Good idea," I said, "but it's not so easy." I told my students that I had served on a committee that had looked at the major textbooks published for fifth graders and that none of them had dealt with racism or slavery and presidents.

Students had a variety of responses:

"Let's throw them out."

"Let's use the Internet."

"Write a letter to the people who did the books."

I focused in on the letter-writing suggestion and reminded them that before we did so, we had to be certain that our criticisms were correct. The students then agreed that in small groups they would use the textbook's index and read what was said about all the first 18 presidents, just as we had done previously with Jefferson.

None of the groups found any mention of a president owning a slave.

Letters as Critique and Action

In subsequent days, some students wrote letters to the textbook publisher. Michelle, a white girl, was particularly detailed. She wrote: "I am 11 years old and I like to read and write. When I am reading I notice every little word and in your social studies book I realize that the word "racism" is not in your book. You're acting like it is a bad word for those kids who read it." She went on to criticize the book for not mentioning that any presidents had slaves: "I see that you do not mention that some of the presidents had slaves. But some of them did. Like George Washington had 317 slaves. So did Thomas Jefferson. He had 267 slaves." She continued: "If you want to teach children the truth, then you should write the truth." (Michelle's letter and some of the student-made charts were also printed in our school newspaper.)

We mailed off the letters, and moved on to new lessons. Weeks passed with no response and eventually the students stopped asking if the publishers had written back. Then one day a fancy-looking envelope appeared in my mailbox addressed to Michelle Williams. She excitedly opened the letter and read it to the class.

Harcourt School Publishers vice president Donald Lankiewicz had responded to Michelle at length. He wrote that "while the word 'racism' does not appear, the subject of unfair treatment of people because of their race is addressed on page 467." He also argued: "There are many facts about the presidents that are not included in the text simply because we do not have room for them all."

Michelle wrote back to Lankiewicz, thanking him but expressing disappointment. "In a history book you shouldn't have to wait till page 467 to learn about unfair treatment," she wrote. As to his claim that there wasn't room for all the facts about the presidents, Michelle responded: "Adding more pages is good for the kids because they should know the right things from the wrong. It is not like you are limited to certain amount of pages.... All I ask you is that you write the word 'racism' in the book and add some more pages in the book so you can put most of the truth about the presidents."

Michelle never received a reply.

Improving the Lesson

Michelle and the other students left fifth grade soon after the letter exchange. In the flurry of end-of-year activities, I didn't take as much time to process the project as I might have. Nor did I adequately explore with students the fact that most non-slave-owning presidents exhibited pro-slavery attitudes and promoted pro-slavery policies.

But the larger issue, which critical teachers struggle to address, is why textbook publishers and schools in general do such a poor job of helping students make sense of the difficult issues of race. We do students a disservice when we sanitize history and sweep uncomfortable truths under the rug. We leave them less prepared to deal with the difficult issues they will face in their personal, political, and social lives. Granted, these are extremely complicated issues that don't have a single correct response. But it's important to begin with a respect for the truth and for the capacity of people of all ages to expand their understanding of the past and the present, and to open their hearts and minds to an ever-broadening concept of social justice.

I believe my students learned a lot from their research on presidents and slaves — and clearly know more than most Americans about which of the first 18 presidents owned slaves. I'm also hopeful they learned the importance of looking critically at all sources of information.

I know one student, Tanya, did. On the last day of school she came up to me and amid the congratulatory good-byes and said, "I still think Lincoln owned slaves."

"You are a smart girl but you are wrong about that one," I responded.

"We'll, see," she said, "You didn't know Grant had slaves when the school year started! Why should I always believe what my teacher says?"

Some of the students' names in this article have been changed.

Author's Note

About two years after I completed the research on slave-owning presidents with my students, a wonderful website called UnderstandingPrejudice.org was put up by folks at Wesleyan University. This site includes extensive information on presidents who owned slaves (see www.understandingprejudice.org/slavery). I learned from this website that three presidents not on my list also owned slaves: Martin Van Buren, William Henry Harrison, and James Buchanan. I was grateful for the additional information on this website, which opens up all sorts of new teaching possibilities.

Copies of the correspondence and PDFs of some of the handouts used in this lesson are available at www.rethinkingschools.org/rsr.

Unlearning the Myths That Bind Us

Linda Christensen

I was nourished on the milk of American culture: I cleaned the dwarves' house and waited for Prince Charming to bring me life; I played Minnie Mouse to Mickey's flower-bearing adoration, and, later, I swooned in Rhett Butler's arms — my waist as narrow and my bosom every bit as heaving as Scarlett's.

But my daddy didn't own a plantation; he owned a rough-and-tumble bar frequented by loggers and fishermen. My waist didn't dip into an hour-glass; in fact, according to the novels I read my thick ankles doomed me to be cast as the peasant woman reaping hay while the heroine swept by with her handsome man in hot pursuit.

Our students suckle the same pap. Our society's culture industry colonizes their minds and teaches them how to act, live, and dream. This indoctrination hits young children especially hard. The "secret education," as Chilean writer Ariel Dorfman dubs it, delivered by children's books and movies, instructs young people to accept the world as it is portrayed in these social blueprints. And often that world depicts the domination of one sex, one race, one class, or one country over a weaker counterpart. After studying cartoons and children's literature, my student Omar wrote: "When we read children's books, we aren't just reading cute little stories, we are discovering the tools with which a young society is manipulated."

Beverly Tatum, who wrote the book *Why Are All the Black Kids Sitting Together in the Cafeteria?* helps explain how children develop distorted views of people outside of their racial/cultural group:

> The impact of racism begins early. Even in our preschool years, we are exposed to misinformation about people different from ourselves. Many of us grow up in neighborhoods where we have limited opportunities to interact with people different from our own families.... Consequently, most of the early information we receive about "others" — people racially, religiously, or socioeconomically different

from ourselves — does not come as a result of firsthand experience. The secondhand information we receive has often been distorted, shaped by cultural stereotypes, and left incomplete....

Cartoon images, in particular the Disney movie *Peter Pan*, were cited by the children [in a research study] as their number one source of information. At the age of three, these children had a set of stereotypes in place.

Children's cartoons, movies, and literature are perhaps the most influential genre "read." Young people, unprotected by any intellectual armor, hear or watch these stories again and again, often from the warmth of their mother's or father's lap. The messages, or "secret education," linked with the security of their homes, underscore the power these texts deliver. As Tatum's research suggests, the stereotypes and worldview embedded in the stories become accepted knowledge.

I want my students to question this accepted knowledge and the secret education delivered by cartoons as well as by the traditional literary canon. Because children's movies and literature are short and visual, my students and I can critique them together. We can view many in a brief period of time, so students can begin to see patterns in media portrayals of particular groups and learn to decode the underlying assumptions these movies make. Brazilian educator Paulo Freire wrote that instead of wrestling with words and ideas, too often students "walk on the words." If I want my students to wrestle with the social text of novels, news, or history books, they need the tools to critique media that encourage or legitimate social inequality.

To help students uncover the values being planted by Disney, Mattel, and Nike, and to help them construct more just ones, I begin this "unlearning the myths" unit with two objectives. First I want students to critique portrayals of hierarchy and inequality in children's movies and cartoons. Then I want to enlist them to imagine a better world, characterized by relationships of respect and equality.

Exposing the Myths — How to Read Cartoons

Prior to watching any cartoons, I ask students to read the preface and first chapter of Dorfman's book *The Empire's Old Clothes: What the Lone Ranger, Babar, and Other Innocent Heroes Do to Our Minds.*

Students keep track of their responses in a dialogue journal. I pose the question: "Do you agree with Dorfman's position that children receive a 'secret education' in the media? Do you remember any incidents from your own childhood that support his allegations?"

This is difficult for some students. The dialogue journal spurs them to argue, to talk back, and create a conversation with the writer. Dorfman is controversial. He gets under their skin. He wrote:

> Industrially produced fiction has become one of the primary shapers of our emotions and our intellect....Although these stories are supposed to merely entertain us, they constantly give us a secret education. We are not only taught certain styles of violence, the latest fashions, and sex roles by TV, movies, magazines, and comic strips; we are also taught how to succeed, how to love, how to buy, how to conquer, how to forget the past and suppress the future. We are taught, more than anything else, how not to rebel.

Many students don't want to believe that they have been manipulated by children's media or advertising. No one wants to admit that they've been "handled" by the media. They assure me that they make their own choices and the media has no power over them — as they sit with Fubu, Nike, Timberlands or whatever the latest fashion rage might be. And Dorfman analyzes that pose:

> There has also been a tendency to avoid scrutinizing these mass media products too closely, to avoid asking the sort of hard questions that can yield disquieting answers. It is not strange that this should be so. The industry itself has declared time and again with great forcefulness that it is innocent, that no hidden motives or implications are lurking behind the cheerful faces it generates.

Justine, a senior in my Contemporary Literature and Society class, was bothered by Dorfman's quest "to dissect those dreams, the ones that had nourished my childhood and adolescence, that continued to infect so many of my adult habits." In her dialogue journal she responded:

> Personally, handling the dissection of dreams has been a major cause of depression for me. Not so much dissecting — but how I react to what is found as a result of the operation. It can be overwhelming and discouraging to find out my whole self image has been formed mostly

by others or underneath my worries about what I look like are years (17 of them) of being exposed to TV images of girls and their set roles given to them by TV and the media. It's painful to deal with. The idea of not being completely responsible for how I feel about things today is scary. So why dissect the dreams? Why not stay ignorant about them and happy? The reason for me is that those dreams are not unrelated to my everyday life. They influence how I behave, think, react to things....My dreams keep me from dealing with an unpleasant reality.

In this passage and others in her dialogue with Dorfman, Justine displayed discomfort with prying apart her identity and discovering where she received her ideas; yet she also grudgingly admitted how necessary this process was if she wanted to move beyond where she was at the time. Her discomfort might also have arisen from feeling incapable of changing herself or changing the standards by which she was judged in the larger society. But she knew such questioning was important.

In a later section of her journal, she wrote: "True death equals a generation living by rules and attitudes they never questioned and producing more children who do the same." Justine's reaction may be more articulate than some, but her sentiments were typical of many students. She was beginning to peel back the veneer covering some of the injustice in our society, and she was dismayed by what she discovered.

Charting Stereotypes

I start by showing students old cartoons because the stereotypes are so blatant. We look at the roles women, men, people of color, and poor people play in the cartoons. I ask students to watch for who plays the lead. Who plays the buffoon? Who plays the servant? I encourage them to look at the race, station in life, body type of each character. What motivates the character? What do they want out of life? What's their mission? If there are people of color in the cartoon, what do they look like? How are they portrayed? What would children learn about this particular group from this cartoon?

How does the film portray overweight people? What about women other than the main character? What jobs do you see them doing? What do they talk about? What are their main concerns? What would young children learn about women's roles in society if they watched this film and believed it? What roles do money, possessions, and power play in the film? Who has it? Who wants it? How important is it to the story? What would children learn about what's important in this society?

As they view each episode, they fill in a chart answering these questions. (For a ready-to-use copy of the chart visit www.rethinkingschools. org/rsr.) Students immediately start yelling out the stereotypes because they are so obvious.

Early in the unit, I show a Popeye cartoon, "Ali Baba and the 40 Thieves," that depicts all Arabs with the same face, same turban, same body — and they are all thieves swinging enormous swords. At one point in the cartoon, Popeye clips a dog collar on helpless Olive Oyl and drags her through the desert. Later, the 40 thieves come riding through town stealing everything — food, an old man's teeth, numbers off a clock — even the stripe off a barber pole.

The newer cartoons — like *Mulan*, *Aladdin*, and *Pocahontas* — are subtler and take more sophistication to see through. But if students warm up on the old ones, they can pierce the surface of the new ones as well.

On first viewing, students sometimes resist critical analysis. After watching a Daffy Duck cartoon, for example, Kamaui said, "This is just a dumb little cartoon with some ducks running around in clothes." Then students start to notice patterns — like the absence of female characters in many of the older cartoons. When women do appear, they look like Jessica Rabbit or Playboy centerfolds — even in many of the new and "improved" children's movies.

After filling in a few charts, collectively and on their own, students write about the generalizations children might take away from these tales. From experience, I've discovered that I need to keep my mouth shut for a while. If I'm the one pointing out the stereotypes, it's the kiss of death to the exercise. Besides, students are quick to find the usual stereotypes on their own: "Look, Ursula the sea witch is ugly and smart. Hey, she's kind of dark looking. The young, pretty ones only want to hook their man; the old, pretty ones are mean because they are losing their looks." Kenneth noticed that people of color and poor people are either absent or servants to the rich, white, pretty people. Tyler pointed out that the roles of men are limited as well. Men must be virile and wield power or be old and the object of "good-natured" humor. Students began seeing beyond the charts I'd rigged up for them. They looked at how overweight people were portrayed as buffoons in episode after episode. They noted the absence of mothers, the wickedness of stepparents.

Later in the unit Mira, a senior, attacked the racism in these Saturday morning rituals. She brought her familiarity with Native-American cultures into her analysis:

> Indians in "Looney Tunes" are also depicted as inferior human beings. These characters are stereotypical to the greatest degree, carrying tomahawks, painting their faces, and sending smoke signals as their only means of communication. They live in tipis and their language reminds the viewer of Neanderthals. We begin to imagine Indians as savages with bows and arrows and long black braids. There's no room in our minds for knowledge of the differences between tribes, like the Cherokee alphabet or Celilo salmon fishing.

A Black Cinderella?

After viewing a number of cartoons, Kenya scolded parents in an essay, "A Black Cinderella? Give Me a Break." She wrote: "Have you ever seen a black person, an Asian, a Hispanic in a cartoon? Did they have a leading role or were they a servant? What do you think this is doing to your child's mind?" She ended her piece: "Women who aren't white begin to feel left out and ugly because they never get to play the princess." Kenya's piece bristled with anger at a society that rarely acknowledges the wit or beauty of women of her race. And she wasn't alone in her feelings. Sabrina wrote, "I'm not taking my kids to see any Walt Disney movies until they have a black woman playing the leading role."

Both young women wanted the race of the actors changed, but they didn't challenge the class or underlying gender inequities that also characterize the lives of Cinderella, Ariel the Mermaid, and Snow White.

Kenya's and Sabrina's anger is justified. There should be more women of color who play the leads in these white-on-white wedding cake tales. Of course, there should also be more women of color on the Supreme Court, in Congress, and scrubbing up for surgeries. But I want students to understand that if the race of the character is the only thing changing, injustices may still remain.

So I have students read Mary Carter Smith's delightful retelling of Cinderella, "Cindy Ellie, A Modern Fairy Tale," which reads like laughter — bubbly, warm, spilling over with infectious good humor and playful language. In Smith's version, Cindy Ellie, who lived in East Baltimore, was "one purty young black sister, her skin like black velvet." Her father, "like so many good men, was weak for a pretty face and big legs and big hips." Her stepmother "had a heart as hard as a rock. The milk of human kindness had curdled in her breast. But she did have a pretty face, big legs, and great big hips....Well, that fool man fell right into that woman's trap."

Cindy Ellie's stepsisters were "two big-footed, ugly gals" who made Cindy Ellie wait on them hand and foot. When the "good white folks, the good Asian folks, and the good black folks all turned out and voted for a good black brother, running for mayor" there was cause for celebration, and a chance for Cindy Ellie to meet her Prince Charming, the mayor's son. With the help of her Godma's High John the Conqueror Root, Cindy Ellie looked like an "African Princess." "Her rags turned into a dazzling dress of pink African laces! Her hair was braided into a hundred shining braids, and on the end of each braid were beads of pure gold!...Golden bracelets covered her arms clean up to her elbows! On each ear hung five small diamond earrings. On her tiny feet were dainty golden sandals encrusted with dazzling jewels! Cindy Ellie was laid back!"

The students and I love the story. It is well told and incorporates rich details that do exactly what Sabrina, Kenya, and their classmates wanted: It celebrates the beauty, culture, and language of African Americans. It also puts forth the possibility of cross-race alliances for social change.

But, like the original tale, Cindy Ellie's main goal in life is not working to end the plight of the homeless or teaching kids to read. Her goal, like Cinderella's, is to get her man. Both young women are transformed and made beautiful through new clothes, new jewels, new hairstyles. Both have chauffeurs who deliver them to their men. Cindy Ellie and Cinderella are nicer and kinder than their stepsisters, but the Prince and Toussant, the mayor's son, don't know that. Both of the Cinderellas compete for their men against their sisters and the rest of the single women in their cities. They "win" because of their beauty and their fashionable attire. Both of these tales leave young women with two myths: Happiness means getting a man, and transformation from wretched conditions can be achieved through consumption — in their case, through new clothes and a new hairstyle.

I am uncomfortable with those messages. I don't want students to believe that change can be bought at the mall, nor do I want them thinking that the pinnacle of a woman's life is an "I do" that supposedly leads them to a "happily ever after." I don't want my female students to see their "sisters" as competition for that scarce and wonderful commodity — men. As Justine wrote earlier in her dialogue journal, it can be overwhelming and discouraging to find that our self-images have been formed by others, but if we don't dissect them, we will continue to be influenced by them.

Writing as a Vehicle for Change

Toward the end of the unit, students write essays critiquing cartoons. I hope that these will encourage students to look deeper into the issues — to challenge the servant/master relationships or the materialism that makes women appealing to their men. For some students the cartoon unit exposes the wizardry that enters our dreams and desires, but others shrug their shoulders at this. It's okay for some people to be rich and others poor; they just want to see more rich people of color or more rich women. Or better yet, be rich themselves. They accept the inequalities in power and exploitative economic relationships. Their acceptance teaches me how deep the roots of these myths are planted and how much some students, in the absence of visions for a different and better world, need to believe in the fairy tale magic that will transform their lives — whether it's a rich man or winning the lottery.

Many students write strong critiques following the viewing of the cartoons. But venting their frustration with cartoons — and even sharing it with the class — can seem an important but limited task. Yes, they can write articulate pieces. Yes, they hone their arguments and seek the just-right examples from their viewing. Through critiques and the discussions that follow, they are helping to transform each other — each comment or

observation helps expose the engine of our society, and they're both excited and dismayed by their discoveries.

But what am I teaching them if the lesson ends there? That it's enough
to be critical without taking action? That we can quietly rebel in the privacy of the classroom while we practice our writing skills, but we don't really
have to do anything about the problems we uncover, nor do we need to create anything to take the place of what we've expelled? Those are not the
lessons I intend to teach. I want to develop their critical consciousness, but
I also hope to move them to action.

For some the lesson doesn't end in the classroom. Many who watched
cartoons before we start our study say they can no longer enjoy them. Now
instead of seeing a bunch of ducks in clothes, they see the racism, sexism,
and violence that swim under the surface of the stories.

Pam and Nicole swore they would not let their children watch cartoons. David told the class of coming home one day and finding his
nephews absorbed in "Looney Tunes." "I turned that TV off and took them
down to the park to play. They aren't going to watch that mess while I'm
around." Radiance described how she went to buy Christmas presents for
her niece and nephew. "Before, I would have just walked into the toy store
and bought them what I knew they wanted — Nintendo or Barbie. But this
time, I went up the clerk and said, 'I want a toy that isn't sexist or racist.'"

Students have also said that what they now see in cartoons, they also
see in advertising, on prime-time TV, on the news, in school. Turning off
the cartoons doesn't stop the sexism and racism. They can't escape, and
now that they've started analyzing cartoons, they can't stop analyzing the
rest of the world. And sometimes they want to stop. Once a student asked
me, "Don't you ever get tired of analyzing everything?"

During a class discussion Sabrina said: "I realized these problems weren't
just in cartoons. They were in everything — every magazine I picked up,
every television show I watched, every billboard I passed by on the street."
My goal of honing their ability to read literature and the world through the
lens of justice had been accomplished at least in part. But as Justine wrote
earlier, at times my students would like to remain "ignorant and happy."
Without giving students an outlet for their despair, I was indeed creating

"factories of cynicism" (Bigelow, et al., 1994) in my classroom — and it wasn't pretty.

Taking Action

I look for opportunities for students to act on their knowledge. In Literature and U.S. History class, these occasions have presented themselves in the form of unfair tests and outrageous newspaper articles about our school, Jefferson High School in Portland, Oregon, that provoked spontaneous student activism (Bigelow, et al., 1994). But in my Contemporary Literature and Society class, I discovered that I had to create the possibility for action.

Instead of assigning the same classroom essays students had written in years before, I asked students to create projects that would move beyond the classroom walls. (For examples of student work visit www.rethinking schools.org/rsr.) Who could they teach about what they learned? I wanted their projects to be real. Who could their analysis touch enough to bring about real change? Students filled the board with potential readers of their work: Parents, peers, teachers, children's book authors, librarians, Disney, video store owners, advertisers.

My only rule was that they had to write a piece using evidence from cartoons or other media. Don't just rant in general, I told them. Use evidence to support your thesis. The examples might come from cartoons, advertisements, novels, your mother or father's advice. You might use lines from TV or movies. You don't have to stick to cartoons — use the world.

We discussed possible options:

◆ Focus on one cartoon — critique it, talk about it in depth. Write about *Mulan* or *Peter Pan*. Using the chart, analyze the representation of men, women, people of color, and poor people in that movie.

◆ Focus on the portrayal of one group. Write about how women, men, African Americans, Latinos, Arabs, overweight people or the poor are depicted and give examples from several cartoons or across time.

◆ Take an issue — like the representation of women — and relate it to your life and/or society at large.

One group of playful students wanted to create a pamphlet that could be distributed at PTA meetings throughout the city. That night they went home with assignments they'd given each other: Sarah would watch Saturday morning cartoons; Sandy, Brooke, and Carmel would watch after-school cartoons; and Kristin and Toby were assigned before-school cartoons. They ended up writing a report card for the various programs. They graded each show A through F and wrote a brief summary of their findings:

"Duck Tales": At first glance the precocious ducks are cute, but look closer and see that the whole show is based on money. All their adventures revolve around finding money. Uncle Scrooge and the gang teach children that money is the only important thing in life. Grade: C–

"Teenage Mutant Ninja Turtles": Pizza-eating Ninja Turtles. What's the point? There isn't any. The show is based on fighting the "bad guy," Shredder. Demonstrating no concern for the townspeople, they battle and fight, but never get hurt. This cartoon teaches a false sense of violence to kids: fight and you don't get hurt, or solve problems through fists and swords instead of words. Grade: D

"Popeye": This show oozes with horrible messages from passive Olive Oyl to the hero "man" Popeye. This cartoon portrays ethnic groups as stupid. It is political also — teaching children that Americans are the best and conquer all others. Grade: F

On the back of the pamphlet, they listed some tips for parents to guide them in wise cartoon selection.

Catkin wrote about the sexual stereotyping and adoration of beauty in children's movies. Her article described how she and other teenage women carry these messages with them still:

Women's roles in fairy tales distort reality — from Jessica Rabbit's six-mile strut in *Who Framed Roger Rabbit?* to Tinker Bell's obsessive vanity in *Peter Pan*. These seemingly innocent stories teach us to look for our faults. As Tinker Bell inspects her tiny body in a mirror only to find that her minute hips are simply too huge, she shows us how to turn the mirror into an enemy....And this scenario is repeated in girls' locker rooms all over the world.

Because we can never look like Cinderella, we begin to hate ourselves. The Barbie syndrome starts as we begin a lifelong search for the perfect body. Crash diets, fat phobias, and an obsession with the materialistic become commonplace. The belief that a product will make us rise above our competition, our friends, turns us into addicts. Our fix is that Calvin Klein push-up bra, Guess jeans, Chanel lipstick, and the latest in suede flats. We don't call it deception; we call it good taste. And soon it feels awkward going to the mailbox without makeup.

Catkin wanted to publish her piece in a magazine for young women so they would begin to question the origin of the standards by which they judge themselves.

Most students wrote articles for local and national newspapers or magazines. Some published in neighborhood papers, some in church newsletters. The writing in these articles was tighter and cleaner than for-the-teacher essays because it had the potential for a real audience beyond the classroom walls. The possibility of publishing their pieces changed the level of students' intensity for the project. Anne, who turned in hastily written drafts last year, said: "Five drafts and I'm not finished yet!"

But more importantly, students saw themselves as actors in the world. They were fueled by the opportunity to convince some parents of the long-lasting effects cartoons impose on their children, or to enlighten their peers about the roots of some of their insecurities. Instead of leaving students full of bile, standing around with their hands on their hips, shaking their heads about how bad the world is, I provided them the opportunity to make a difference.

References

Bigelow, Bill, et al. *Rethinking Our Classrooms, Volume 1: Teaching for Equity and Justice.* Milwaukee, WI: Rethinking Schools, 1994, p. 4.

Christensen, Linda. *Reading, Writing, and Rising Up: Teaching About Social Justice and the Power of the Written Word.* Milwaukee, WI: Rethinking Schools, 2000.

Dorfman, Ariel. *The Empire's Old Clothes: What the Lone Ranger, Babar, and Other Innocent Heroes Do to Our Minds.* New York: Pantheon, 1983, p. ix.

Smith, Mary Carter. "Cindy Ellie, A Modern Fairy Tale," in Goss, Linda (Ed.) *Talk That Talk: An Anthology of African-American Storytelling.* New York: Touchstone, 1989, pp. 396-402.

Shor, Ira and Freire, Paulo. *A Pedagogy for Liberation.* South Hadley, MA: Bergin & Garvey, 1987, p. 10.

Tatum, Beverly. *'Why Are All the Black Kids Sitting Together in the Cafeteria?' And Other Conversations About Race.* New York: Basic Books, 1997, pp. 4-5.

What Color Is Beautiful?

Alejandro Segura-Mora

M ost of my kindergarten students have already been picked up by their parents. Two children still sit on the mat in the cafeteria lobby, waiting. Occasionally one of them stands to look through the door's opaque windows to see if they can make out a parent coming. Ernesto, the darkest child in my class, unexpectedly shares in Spanish, "*Maestro*, my mom is giving me pills to turn me white."

"Is that right?" I respond, also in Spanish. "And why do you want to be white?"

"Because I don't like my color," he says.

"I think your color is very beautiful and you are beautiful as well," I say. I try to conceal how his comment saddens and alarms me, because I want to encourage his sharing. "I don't like to be dark," he explains.

His mother, who is slightly darker than he is, walks in the door. Ernesto rushes to take her hand and leaves for home.

Ernesto's comment takes me back to an incident in my childhood. My mom is holding me by the hand, my baby brother in her other arm, my other three brothers and my sister following along. We are going to church and I am happy. I skip all the way, certain that I have found a solution to end my brothers' insults. "You're a monkey," they tell me whenever they are mad at me. I am the only one in my family with curly hair. In addition to "monkey," my brothers baptize me with other derogatory names — such as *Simio* (Ape), *Chineca* (a twisted and distorted personification of being curly, and even more negative by the feminization with an "a" at the end), and *Urco*, the captain of all apes in the television program "The Planet of the Apes." As we enter the church, my mom walks us to the front of the altar to pray before the white saints, the crucified white Jesus, and his mother. Before that day, I hadn't bought into the God story. After all, why would God give a child curly hair? But that day there is hope. I close my eyes and pray with a conviction that would have brought rain to a desert.

"God, if you really exist, please make my hair straight," I pray. "I hate it curly and you know it's hard. So at the count of three, please take these curls and make them straight. One, two, three." With great suspense I open my eyes. I reach for my hair. Anticipating the feel of straight hair, I stroke my head, only to feel my curls. Tears sting my eyes. As I head for one of the benches, I whisper, "I knew God didn't exist."

For Ernesto, the pill was his God; for me, God was my pill. I wonder how Ernesto will deal with the failure of his pill.

A Teachable Moment

I can't help but wonder how other teachers might have dealt with Ernesto's comments. Would they have ignored him? Would they have dismissed him with a "Stop talking like that!" Would they have felt sorry for him because they agree with him?

As teachers, we are cultural workers, whether we are aware of it or not. If teachers don't question the culture and values being promoted in the classroom, they socialize their students to accept the uneven power relations of our society along lines of race, class, gender, and ability. Yet teachers can — and should — challenge white supremacist values and instead promote values of self-love.

Young students, because of their honesty and willingness to talk about issues, provide many opportunities for teachers to take seemingly minor incidents and turn them into powerful teaching moments. I am grateful for Ernesto's sincerity and trust in sharing with me. Without knowing it, Ernesto opened the door to a lively dialogue in our classroom about white supremacy.

To resurface the dialogue on beauty and skin color, I chose a children's book which deals with resistance to white supremacy (a genre defined, in part, by its scarcity). The book is *Nina Bonita*, written by Ana María Machado and illustrated by Rosana Fara (1996, available in English from Kane/Miller Book Publishers). The book tells the story of an albino bunny who loves the beauty of a girl's dark skin and wants to find out how he can get black fur.

I knew the title of the book would give away the author's bias, so I

covered the title. I wanted to find out, before reading the book, how children perceived the cover illustration of the dark-skinned girl. "If you think
this little girl is pretty, raise your hand," I said. Fourteen hands went up. "If
you think she is ugly, raise your hand," I then asked. Fifteen voted for ugly,
among them Ernesto.

I was not surprised that half my students thought the little girl was ugly.
Actually, I was expecting a higher number, given the tidal wave of white
dolls which make their way into our classroom on Fridays, our Sharing Day,
and previous comments by children in which they indicated that dark is
ugly.

When I asked my students why they thought the girl on the book cover
was ugly, one student responded: "Because she has black color and her hair
is really curly." Ernesto added: "Because she is black-skinned."

"But you are dark like her," Stephanie quickly rebutted Ernesto, while
several students nodded in agreement. "How come you don't like her?"

"Because I don't like black girls," Ernesto quickly responded. Several
students affirmed Ernesto's statement with "yes" and "that's right."

"All children are pretty," Stephanie replied in defense.

Carlos then added: "If you behave good, then your skin color can
change."

"Are you saying that if you are good, you can turn darker?" I asked, trying to make sure the other students had understood what he meant.

"White!" responded Carlos.

"No, you can't change your color," several students responded. "That
can't be done! "

"How do you know that your color can change?" I asked, hoping Carlos
would expand on his answer.

"My mom told me," he said.

"And would you like to change your skin color?" I asked.

"No," he said. He smiled shyly as he replied and I wondered if he may
have wished he was not dark-skinned but didn't want to say so.

Carlos's mother's statements about changing skin color reminded me of
instances in my family and community when a new baby is born. "Oh, look
at him, how pretty and blond looking he is," they say if the baby has Euro-

pean features and coloring. And if the babies come out dark, like Ernesto? Then the comments are, "¡Ay! Pobrecito, salió tan prietito" — which translated means, "Poor baby, he came out so dark." I hear similar comments from co-workers in our school's staff lounge. A typical statement: "Did you see Raul in my class? He has the most beautiful green eyes."

It is no surprise that so many students must fight an uphill battle against white supremacist values; still other students choose not to battle at all.

Challenging the Students

In an attempt to have students explain why they think the black girl in Nina Bonita is ugly, I ask them, "If you think she is ugly for having dark skin, why do you think her dark skin makes her ugly?"

"I don't like the color black," volunteers Yvette, "because it looks dark and you can't see in the dark."

"Because when I turn off the light," explains Marco, "everything is dark and I am afraid."

Although most of my kindergarten students could not articulate the social worthlessness of being dark-skinned in this society, I was amazed by their willingness to struggle with an issue that so many adults, teachers included, ignore, avoid, and pretend does not exist. At the same time, it was clear that many of my students had already internalized white supremacist values.

At the end of our discussion, I took another vote to see how students were reacting to Nina Bonita; I also wanted to ask individual students why they had voted the way they had. This second time, 18 students said the black girl was pretty and only 11 said she was ugly. Ernesto still voted for "ugly."

"Why do you think she is ugly?" I asked, but this time the students didn't volunteer responses. Perhaps they were sensing that I did not value negative answers as much as I did comments by students who fell in love with Nina Bonita. In their defense of dark skin, some students offered explanations such as, "Her color is dark and pretty," "All girls are pretty," and, "I like the color black."

Our discussion of Nina Bonita may have led four students to modify their values of beauty and ugliness in relation to skin color. Or maybe these four students just wanted to please their teacher. What is certain, however, is that the book and our discussion caused some students to look at the issue in a new way.

Equally important, *Nina Bonita* became a powerful tool to initiate discussion on an issue which will affect my students, and myself, for a lifetime. Throughout the school year, the class continued our dialogue on the notions of beauty and ugliness.

(One other book that I have found useful for sparking discussion is *The Ugly Duckling*. This fairy tale, which is one of the most popular among early-elementary teachers and children, is often used uncritically. It tells the story of a little duckling who is "ugly" because his plumage is dark. Happiness comes only when the duckling turns into a beautiful, spotless white swan. I chose to use this book in particular because the plot is a representation of the author's value of beauty as being essentially white. I want my students to understand that they can disagree with and challenge authors of books, and not receive their messages as God-given.)

When I have such discussions with my students, I often feel like instantly including my opinion. But I try to allow my students to debate the issue first. After they have spoken, I ask them about their views and push them to clarify their statements. One reason I like working with children is that teaching is always a type of experiment, because the students constantly surprise me with their candid responses. These responses then modify how I will continue the discussion.

I struggle, however, with knowing that as a teacher I am in a position of power in relation to my young students. It is easy to make students stop using the dominant ideology and adopt the ideology of another teacher, in this case my ideology. In this society, in which we have been accustomed to deal with issues in either/or terms, children (like many adults) tend to adopt one ideology in place of another, but not necessarily in a way in which they actually think through the issues involved. I struggle with how to get my students to begin to look critically at the many unequal power relations in our society, relations which, even at the age of five, have already shaped even whether they love or hate their skin color and consequently themselves.

At the end of our reading and discussion of the book, I shared my feelings with my students. "I agree with the author calling this girl *Nina Bonita* because she is absolutely beautiful," I said. "Her skin color is beautiful."

While I caressed my face and kissed my cinnamon-colored hands several times happily and passionately, so that they could see my love for my skin color, I told them, "My skin color is beautiful, too." I pointed to one of my light-complexioned students and said, "Gerardo also has beautiful skin color, and so does Ernesto. But Gerardo cannot be out in the sun for a long time because his skin will begin to burn. I can stay out in the sun longer because my darker skin color gives me more protection against sunburn. But Ernesto can stay out in the sun longer than both of us because his beautiful dark skin gives him even more protection."

Despite our several class discussions on beauty, ugliness, and skin color, Ernesto did not appear to change his mind. But hopefully, his mind will not forget our discussions. Ernesto probably still takes his magic pills — which, his mother later explained, are Flintstones Vitamins. But I hope that every time he pops one into his mouth, he remembers how his classmates challenged the view that to be beautiful, one has to be white. I want Ernesto to always remember, as will I, Lorena's comment: "Dark-skinned children are beautiful and I have dark skin, too."

The names of the children in this article have been changed.

Out Front

Annie Johnston

My prep period was half over. I still had to prepare for a sub the next day and copy the materials for my next class when a student appeared at my door. Nervously clutching a bathroom pass as her eyes darted from the room number to me, she asked, "Are you the one who does that support group for…." Her voice trailed off.

"The lesbian, gay, bisexual, and questioning youth support group?" I responded. "Yes. They meet Thursdays at lunch. They are working on a conference of gay/straight alliances around the Bay Area. It's not a large group…." As my explanation continued I could see I had lost her.

"That's not what I want," she said. "I need to talk to someone, right away."

Oh dear, I thought, crisis management. This is not what I can do today. I had to leave early to get my daughter to an appointment. But instead I said, "What do you need to talk about?"

Slowly and hesitantly it came out. A good friend was attracted to her. She might actually be interested. That scared her to her very core. She sought me out because my room number was announced weekly as the location of the support group meetings. I took her name, found out what period she could stand to miss, and spent the rest of my prep period finding someone in the health center who would be positive about the possibility that this child might have feelings for someone of the same sex. I was lucky. More often, I end up playing amateur psychologist.

I teach history at Berkeley High School, considered one of the better schools for queer-identified youth (an all-inclusive term, preferred by the

---

*For many years, "queer" was a pejorative only acceptable when used among gay people. But as the definition of this movement has expanded to include lesbian, bisexual, transgender, and questioning people, many youth openly began using "queer" as an all-inclusive term. This was probably popularized by the short but exciting existence of the group "Queer Nation," which did a lot of in-your-face guerrilla theater against heterosexism. "Gay," on the other hand, was an acceptable term in general usage denoting all

students, for queer and questioning youth).* Yet even at Berkeley, there are limits to the school's openness to queer youth, who tend to graduate early or leave for a semester or two of "Independent Studies." The Independent Studies program is an alternative track in which students only meet with each teacher for one-half hour per week and do all their work on their own.

I have been teaching at Berkeley for more than eight years and have been coming out to my classes since my first year. There are a few other staff in this school of 3,000 students who do not hide our sexuality. We know that we have to be seen — that it's important not just for the gay youth but for all the students to have gay role models. We also know that at Berkeley, because of district and city policies forbidding discrimination on the basis of sexual orientation, we won't be fired.

The situation is better at Berkeley than at most schools across the country. But even at Berkeley, homophobia is a constant reality. Girls who are close friends and lean over each other's desk are called "lezzies." Boys who seem in any way weak or "womanly" are called "faggots." Despite advances in the struggle against homophobia in our schools, there is still a long, long way to go.

One teacher described a situation in which a young man, who had been consistently called "faggot" by his peers, took an all-too-typical approach to stop the taunting. He came into her class one day and went up to a shy, relatively unpopular girl and, in front of his buddies, proceeded to make sexually humiliating remarks. He was conforming to teenage male culture, in which "Hey, baby, why don't you suck my...." means, "See, I'm a real man." The club of homophobic ridicule is held over the heads of all young people — it is one of the main means by which gender roles are enforced.

Backlash Era

In this backlash era, out teacher role models are an endangered species. Even in the progressive Bay Area, there have been major flaps over a

---

homosexual people and had a respectful connotation. Among youth now, however, "gay" is a slang adjective with extremely negative overtones. I use "queer" when talking about youth, partly because it covers so many bases, and so many youth aren't sure what base they'll end up playing. I use "gay" when talking about older people because we came of age when "gay" (or lesbian-gay-bisexual-transgender) was the proper term.

teacher allowing a brief discussion of the coming-out episode of the TV show "Ellen" in 1997, and a teacher simply letting it be known to her classes that she is lesbian.

At the same time, gay/straight alliances are growing at a phenomenal rate. When students in Salt Lake City formed a gay/straight alliance in 1995, the district banned all clubs rather than allow the alliance to meet. But protesting students walked out *en masse* and marched to the state capital, forcing the state legislature to intervene and countermand the district. In addition, there have been significant legal victories in recent years — in particular the case brought by Jamie Nabozny, which held school administrators in Ashland, Wisconsin liable when a gay student was harmed by harassment that the administrators had ignored despite the existence of a district anti-harassment policy. Many districts have also been more open to training staff on how to create a safe environment for lesbian and gay youth.

At my school, the lesbian, gay, bisexual, and questioning youth support group is an important place for students to find each other and establish a supportive community. It is difficult, however, for those students to be activists around gay issues at school. They face constant harassment and ridicule. It is equally difficult for students who are unsure of their sexual identity to take the radical step of coming to such a gay-identified group.

Take the situation facing Jake, who was ridiculed by other students for the entire semester in my World History class. He came midyear, he said, because he had been so ostracized in his last school. He had a manner about him that just spoke of weirdness and difference. By the end of four months, students would write things on the board about him, no one would work with him, and he would take it all in as if he deserved it. After he brought in a crucifix he'd made in shop class and announced to me that the bloody body hanging from it was himself, I redoubled my efforts to get him seen by a counselor, but to no avail. It was May by that time, the university interns who helped out at the health center were gone for the year, and there was really no one who could help.

Jake spent time hospitalized over the summer for severe depression and on suicide watch, I think. He spent more time hospitalized in the fall. After he left the hospital, he came by to tell me he had known he was gay since he was seven years old. He'd been in denial, hoping and praying that something would change him.

I'm not sure where Jake got the strength, but he finally decided to stand up for himself, to shove the hatred and ridicule back at his tormentors. He also began reading books about gay male sexuality, and came to a staff development inservice I had organized to speak to teachers about the damage a homophobic environment does to youth.

Jake started to like himself, and it changed his life. He came back to Berkeley High and developed a number of friends. And while he still got gay-bashed, the last time he got kicked and punched he lodged an official complaint rather than just turning the other cheek.

Jake could have been a statistic. According to a study done by Paul Gibson for the U.S. Department of Health and Human Services, gay youth are two to three times more likely to commit suicide and comprise up to 30% of all completed suicides.

Help!

As an openly gay teacher, I do what I can to help the Jakes of our school. I talk to the social living classes, work with others to organize staff inservices, get students to speak on panels about their experiences, and advocate for the youth who end up on my doorstep. I struggle with how to make support services available to all students, not just those who come to the lesbian, gay, bisexual, and questioning youth group. This is particularly crucial for students of color, for whom the issue of identity is much more complex.

I know I should do more, but I can't. "Out lesbian teacher" is not my only identity. I can take the lead on these issues for only so long without getting burned out. I need allies, and so do the youth. I need young gay teachers who are supported and encouraged to act as out role models in the schools, instead of being scared that they will be persecuted and driven from their jobs. I need straight teachers to sponsor forums on the issue and push for an "anti-slur" policy.

You don't always get what you need, but you don't get much of anything unless you ask. So here are a few things I would ask of other teachers:

◆ Set a clear anti-homophobic standard for what is acceptable language and behavior in your classrooms and your schools.

* Incorporate gay issues into the curriculum — not just in social living classes when talking about sex, but in history, English, science, and Spanish.
* Support gay teachers' ability to be out role models for our youth.

Anti-Slur Policy

Establishing policies on language and behavior is sometimes the best place to start. Even at Berkeley, it has been difficult to develop a culture in which anti-gay language in unacceptable. When I asked a group of queer-identified youth what teachers had done to make a positive difference in combating homophobia, they could not think of a single thing. One year, one teacher tried to make an issue of anti-gay language, but she was quickly overwhelmed by students' negative responses. For the remainder of the semester, not a single student in her class suffered any consequences for using anti-gay language.

Once, after a 45-minute argument with students in my class over why anti-gay language is harmful, Ryanna, still unconvinced, said: "I'll do it, Ms. Johnston, because I respect you. But I just want you to know that none of my other teachers ever has demanded this of me. It is extremely difficult to remember to watch my language here when this is the language I use at home all the time, and when every other teacher in the school considers it acceptable."

Despite her reluctance, however, Ryanna managed to watch her language. Moreover, during the initial class discussion, many other students expressed their disapproval of anti-gay language, and reevaluated words they had been using.

Such conversations and policies have a ripple effect. One closeted bisexual student told me that he later felt able to raise gay issues in a current events discussion, knowing a large number of the students in the room would take them seriously. In this case, events that affected gay people became a normal, acceptable thing to talk about.

These conversations require a large chunk of class time. Further, policies must be backed up by immediate consequences when students forget or violate the rules. For instance, many students don't understand why calling a test they hated "gay" is insulting to gay people. They don't connect the emergence of "gay" as a slang word, meaning "really yucky," to homophobia. It takes teaching to make that connection. Usually a talking-to in the hallway is adequate, although not always. Once in a while, a student will be unwilling to suppress his or her homophobia and will use homophobic remarks to seriously taunt another student. In such cases, teachers need to be aware that gay-baiting is a form of sexual harassment and that state education codes require schools to create a safe place for all students.

Curriculum Issues

An anti-slur policy reduces the amount of negative vibes, but is not sufficient to create a classroom that welcomes the existence of queer people. To take this further step, teachers must include queers and queer issues in their curriculum. It's likely that a tenth of the population is gay in this country, and gay people play a major role in our society. Students must see that fact reflected in what we teach. "Gay" has to be integrated into our picture of current events, historical reality, literary themes, and scientific exploration. We need curriculum in which "gay" is not relegated to the "Sexuality and Sexually Transmitted Diseases" discussion in health and social living classes.

Every subject area has openings for such curriculum, but it takes a conscious effort to develop or access and incorporate the materials. In U.S. history, for instance, when we teach the Civil Rights Movement, we can examine the role of Bayard Rustin, an out civil rights activist who helped organize the 1963 March on Washington. We can include the gay liberation movement as a civil rights movement. We can have students study the Black Panther Party's position on homosexuality. Here is what Huey Newton approved as the official Black Panther position on the subject:

> Homosexuals are not given freedom and liberty by anyone in this society. Maybe they might be the most oppressed people in the society....A person should have the freedom to use his body whatever way he wants to. The Women's Liberation Front and Gay Liberation Front are our friends, they are our potential allies and we need as

many allies as possible....We should be careful about using terms which might turn our friends off. The terms "faggot" and "punk" should be deleted from our vocabulary, and especially we should not attach names normally designed for homosexual men to men who are enemies of the people, such as Nixon or Mitchell. Homosexuals are not enemies of the people.

There are countless pieces of literature with lesbian and/or gay themes, ranging from *Coffee Will Make You Black* by April Sinclair, to *Giovanni's Room* by James Baldwin, to *Rubyfruit Jungle* by Rita Mae Brown. A multitude of famous literary icons have been lesbian or gay, such as Sappho, James Baldwin, Adrienne Rich, and E. M. Forster. Biology classes that discuss human reproduction can include the role of artificial insemination in allowing a growing number of lesbians and gay men to become parents. The ongoing "biology versus environment" debate — i.e., whether sexual preference is determined largely through genetics or environmental factors — can be one of the topics students can choose to research and debate. Physical education teachers can talk openly and respectfully about gay athletes such as diver Greg Louganis and tennis star Martina Navratilova.

If we acknowledge gay people's contributions in every area of our society, young people's perceptions of what it means to be gay can go beyond the often-threatening issue of sexuality.

From elementary school on, teachers need to talk about gay people so children learn they are a normal part of our society. Many students have lesbian and gay family members whom they love. They must not feel they have to hide or be embarrassed by these relationships.

My eight-year-old daughter, for instance, has decided she will not compromise on telling the world she has two moms, no matter what the consequences. Last year, she had a confrontation with a bunch of kindergarten boys who accused her and her friend of being gay because she was leaning on her friend's shoulder for support due to a twisted ankle. She told them there was nothing wrong with being gay. Then she announced that, besides, both her moms were gay.

The boys really went to town on that. The ridicule they subjected her to reduced her to tears. After 10 minutes of crying in the bathroom she returned to class and was given detention — her first — for tardiness. She called it the worst day of her life and said, "And Mom, how am I going to make it through high school?"

In every class, every semester, after I come out I find out about the aunts, cousins, brothers, and friends that young people are normally forced to be silent about. Children desperately need teachers to counter these taboos, to talk about gay people naturally, unabashedly, and positively.

Role Models

A queer-friendly school is one in which there are positive lesbian and gay role models, not just for queer students but for all students. Whether students are gay or bi or straight, they need to experience gay teachers as people who enrich their lives and care about them. An environment in which lesbian, gay, and bisexual teachers can be out to their students is critical to breaking down the culture of homophobia.

But it is extremely difficult to be out in a school setting. You feel isolated and pegged. In many districts, you can be fired for being out in the classroom. At the least, one risks censure by the administration and homophobic reactions from parents. Every gay teacher fears being targeted and persecuted if word gets out.

Consider my experience with Calley, who was a bright, energetic 14-year-old when first she came to my classroom. She had spent junior high fighting with the Little League coach to be able to play on the all-boys baseball team. She spent her freshman year trying out boyfriends and sporting large hickeys. By her sophomore year, she'd had enough of all that. She began attending the lesbian/gay support group meetings in my classroom and signed up to be a proctor for me. Her mother searched her backpack and read her journal, in which she had a number of poems that made her feelings about sexuality quite explicit. Calley's mother immediately wanted to drag Calley to a therapist. And her mother was looking for someone to blame. I was a handy target.

In a conservative community hell-bent on targeting gays, I'd have been mincemeat. But at Berkeley, where there is no such organized opposition to the rights of gays, and where many straight colleagues and administrators are supportive of gays, Calley's mother could do little about me.

Calley ran away from home that summer, returning to an uneasy truce in the fall. She is out and has a strong circle of friends, but clearly it will be many years before she feels again the support of a loving family.

Gay teachers need to take more risks to provide strong out models of what it means to be gay. We cannot do that, however, without a supportive environment. Straight teachers can help to create such support.

If straight faculty members at my high school would raise a concern about the homophobia they so constantly see in their classes, it would be easier to develop an anti-slur policy. If there were any other teachers developing curriculum that included gay issues (besides when discussing HIV), I would feel supported. These actions do not require a particular sexual orientation. They only require concern and a commitment to act against homophobia.

PART 3

Education Policy and Politics

Schools More Separate: A Decade of Resegregation

Gary Orfield

Half a century ago the U.S. Supreme Court concluded that school segregation was unconstitutional and "inherently unequal." After this landmark ruling, particularly during the Civil Rights Movement era, schools in the United States became notably less segregated, especially in the South.

But in the 1990s a new trend emerged. During that decade, three major Supreme Court decisions authorized a return to segregated neighborhood schools and limited the reach and duration of previous desegregation orders. By 2001 the desegregation of black students had receded to levels not seen in three decades. As the nation's public schools became steadily more nonwhite, schools in large cities — and increasingly, in suburban areas as well — reflected serious patterns of segregation, with blacks and Latinos more and more likely to attend segregated schools.

Background

A battle that began early in the 20th century to try to bring equality to the segregated black schools of the South had become, by the 1960s, an all-out attack on the entire structure of racially separate schools in the 17 states which mandated segregation by law. This struggle was never just for desegregated schools, nor was it motivated by a desire on the part of black students to simply sit next to white students. It was an integral part of a much broader movement for racial and economic justice supported by a unique alliance of major civil rights organizations, churches, students, and leaders of both national political parties.

From 1954 until 1964, efforts to enforce mandated desegregation faced almost uniform local and state resistance in the South. A handful of civil rights lawyers, most of them from the NAACP Legal Defense Fund, sued local school boards, trying to force the initiation of desegregation. Most of these lawsuits, however, were heard in courts presided over by conservative federal judges. By 1964, as Congress considered whether to prohibit discrimination in all programs receiving federal aid, 98% of Southern blacks were still in totally segregated schools.

The only period in which there was active positive support for desegregation by both the courts and the executive branch of the government was the four years following the enactment of the 1964 Civil Rights Act. During this period federal education officials, the Department of Justice, and the high courts all maintained strong and reasonably consistent pressure for achieving actual desegregation. During this period desegregation policy was transformed from a very gradual anti-discrimination policy to one of rapid and full integration.

It was in this period that the South moved from almost total racial separation to become the nation's most integrated region.* The region went from virtually total apartheid to being the most integrated region in the U.S. between 1964 and 1970. During this time, the South had the highest level of integration and the most substantial contact between black and white students. Today it remains the only region in which whites typically attend schools with significant numbers of blacks.

But the 1968 election that brought Richard Nixon to the White House was a turning point, leading first to a shutdown of the enforcement machinery of the federal education office, and then to a change of position: The Justice Department began urging the Supreme Court to slow down or reverse desegregation requirements. Nixon's appointment of four justices to the U.S. Supreme Court set the stage for key 5-4 decisions against desegregation across city-suburban lines and against equalizing finances among school districts. By 1974 it was clear that there was no feasible way to provide desegregated education for millions of black and Latino children attending heavily minority central-city schools.

When education officials moved to revive school desegregation enforcement under the Carter administration, Congress took the authority away

---

*The South is defined as: Alabama, Arkansas, Florida, Georgia, Louisiana, Mississippi, North Carolina, South Carolina, Tennessee, Texas, and Virginia.

from them (although the Justice Department under Carter did initiate a number of important lawsuits seeking to find ways to promote city-suburban desegregation in special circumstances and to coordinate the desegregation of housing with school integration policy).

Subsequently, the Reagan administration brought about a rapid repeal of the federal desegregation assistance program and a shift in the Justice Department to a position of strong opposition to desegregation litigation, opposing even the continuation of existing desegregation plans. This administration developed theories that desegregation had failed and that existing desegregation orders should be canceled after a few years. The Justice Department began to advocate such a policy in the federal courts in the mid-1980s.

The long battle to change the Supreme Court by the Nixon, Reagan, and George H. Bush administrations succeeded in creating a court with a fundamentally different approach to civil rights by the late 1980s. The Rehnquist Court, led by a consistent dissenter against school desegregation law, adopted the assumptions that the history of discrimination had been cured, that enough had been done so the orders should be ended, and that there was a serious danger of discrimination against whites if civil rights requirements were to continue. In three decisions in the 1990s, the Court defined desegregation as a temporary remedy and found that school boards released from their orders (and thus deemed "unitary") could reinstate segregated schools.

The Rehnquist Court concluded that positive policies taking race into account for the purpose of creating integration were suspect and had to demonstrate both a compelling reason and proof that the goal could not be realized without considering race. These policies led some lower courts to forbid even voluntary action for desegregation, such as magnet schools with desegregation policies for admissions. Such orders have been handed down, for example, in Virginia, Maryland, and Boston.

There is considerable confusion about the current status of desegregation law, but the basic trend is toward dissolution of desegregation orders and a return to patterns of more serious segregation. There has been no major push to integrate schools since the early 1970s. The courts, Congress, and the executive branch all reduced enforcement a generation ago. Significant federal aid aimed at helping interracial schools succeed ended in 1981. Many states have quietly abandoned the offices, agencies, and policies they set up to produce and support interracial education.

Benefits of Desegregation, Costs of Segregation

Desegregation was not ordered as an educational treatment but instead to end deeply rooted patterns of illegal and unequal separation of students. Nevertheless there is evidence that desegregation both improves test scores and changes the lives of students. More importantly, there is also evidence that students from desegregated educational experiences benefit in terms of college-going, employment, and living in integrated settings as adults. There are also well-documented and relatively simple instructional techniques that increase both the academic and human-relations benefits of interracial schooling.

A recent study of elite law schools, for example, shows that almost all of the black and Latino students who made it into those schools came from integrated educational backgrounds. And minority students with the same test scores tend to be much more successful in college if they attended interracial high schools.

In addition, recent surveys show that both white and minority students in integrated school districts tend to report, by large majorities, that they have learned to study and work together and that they are highly confident about their ability to work in such settings as adults. Students report that they have learned a lot about the background of other groups and feel confident about the ability to discuss even controversial racial issues across racial lines. In other words, students report great confidence about skills many adults are far from confident about.

Studies exploring the life experiences of black students attending suburban white high schools show that such students experience far higher graduation and college admission rates than those left in central city schools, frequently attain an ability to be fluently bicultural, and, as adults, are often able to work with and offer guidance on issues that require these skills.

Interestingly, the period of growing desegregation coincided with the period of the most dramatic narrowing of the test score gap ever recorded for blacks and whites. This cannot be attributed simply to desegregation but may well be a product of the broad reforms that were associated with the Civil Rights Movement, according to a 1998 study by RAND Corporation researcher David Grissmer and an earlier study by Daniel Koretz.

In the 1990s, on the other hand, as patterns of racial segregation reappeared and accelerated, racial gaps in achievement grew, and the high-school graduation rate of black students decreased.

Although there is a great deal of debate about the scale of the benefits produced by desegregation, there is no doubt that segregated schools are unequal in easily measurable ways. To a considerable degree this is because the segregated minority schools are overwhelmingly likely to have to contend with the educational impacts of concentrated poverty (defined as having 50% or more of the student population eligible for free or reduced-price lunch), while segregated white schools are almost always middle class. Highly segregated black and/or Latino schools are many times more likely than segregated white schools to experience a concentration of poverty. This is the legacy of unequal education and income, and the continuing patterns of housing discrimination.

Anyone who wants to explore the continuing inequalities need only examine the test scores, dropout rates, and other statistics for various schools in a metropolitan community and relate them to statistics for school poverty (percent of students receiving free or reduced-price lunch) and race (percent black and/or Latino) to see a distressingly clear pattern. There is a very strong correlation between the percentage of low-income students in a school and its average test score. Therefore, minority students in segregated schools, no matter how able they may be as individuals, usually face a much lower level of competition and average preparation than other students. Such schools tend to have teachers who are themselves much more likely to be teaching a subject they did not study and with which they have had little experience. There are not enough students in these schools ready for advanced and AP courses, and those opportunities may be eliminated even for students who are ready because there are not sufficient students to fill a class. Many colleges give special consideration to students who have taken AP classes, ignoring the fact that such classes are far less available in segregated minority high schools.

These problems are most serious when racial segregation is reinforced by class segregation, but they are also serious for the black middle class. For one thing, black middle-class families tend to live in communities with far more poor people than white middle-class families do, and often share schools with lower-class black neighborhoods.

The basic message is that, a half century after the Supreme Court struck down "separate but equal" schools, segregation still tends to produce deeply unequal education experiences for students of color, and that even where integrated schools have better opportunities, this does not ensure equal access to those opportunities. Desegregation at the school level appears to be a necessary, but far from sufficient condition for equitable practices.

Can Separate Be Equal?

Critics of desegregation often argue that it would be better to spend the money on improving schools where they are. The suggestion is that while a great deal of money is being spent on desegregation, we are ignoring alternative solutions that have been shown to produce academic gains in segregated neighborhood schools.

In reality, such solutions do not exist.

Before the Supreme Court ordered desegregation in 1954, the nation had been operating for 58 years under a constitutional mandate to equalize the segregated schools. This approach had been a massive failure. School boards consistently provided segregated and strikingly unequal schools. Minority communities' efforts to improve their schools were regularly defeated because they did not have enough political power to force changes in local politics, and neither the courts nor Congress nor any state government showed any interest in strongly enforcing the equality requirement.

Even after the Supreme Court acted, dramatic inequalities continued to exist between minority and white schools in many districts, and were often part of the proof presented to courts as a basis for desegregation orders.

Civil rights groups engaged in decades of unsuccessful battles to equalize segregated schools before desegregation was ordered. This long history in thousands of communities produced great skepticism about the willingness of the majority to make minority schools equal. From the 1980s through the early 2000s, the basic educational goal of both national parties was to improve schools by imposing "tough standards." No priority was given by education officials of any administration in this period to desegregation. In 1989, President George H. Bush and the nation's governors, led by then Arkansas Gov. Bill Clinton, embraced the goal of racial equity in education by 2000, which Congress embodied in the Goals 2000 legislation. Almost all the states adopted sweeping state reforms based on more course requirements and mandatory testing. Those reforms ignored the issue of race and class segregation. The idea was to equalize outcomes within the existing structure of segregated schools.

During this period there was a substantial increase in compensatory resources directed at improving impoverished schools and bringing strong pressure to bear on their teachers and administrators to raise achievement. But despite these initiatives, racial differences in achievement and graduation began to expand in the 1990s, after having closed substantially from the 1960s into the mid-1980s. There is no evidence that we have learned how to make segregated, high-poverty schools equal on a systemic scale.

Changes in Schools and Students

The nation's schools have changed in amazing ways since the civil rights era. By 1999 the number of black and Latino students in the nation's public schools was up 5.8 million, while the number of white students had declined by 5.6 million. By 2001, minority student enrollment was approaching 40% of all U.S. public school students, nearly twice the percentage of minority students during the 1960s.

The schools reflect the transformation of the U.S. population in an era of low birth rates and massive immigration. Latino students, a group that was just 2 million in 1968, had grown to 6.9 million by 1998, an extraordinary increase of 245% in just 30 years. In 1968 there were more than three times as many blacks as Latinos in our schools, but by 1998 there were seven Latino students for every eight blacks, and Latinos were projected to soon outnumber black students.

This is an extraordinary switch. Our schools will be the first major institutions to experience nonwhite majorities.

Although white residents of many central cities have experienced living in predominantly nonwhite communities for years, we will increasingly see entire metropolitan areas and states where there will be no majority group, or where the majority group will be Latino or African-American. This will be a new experience in American educational history. We will be facing either pluralism in schools on an unprecedented level, with millions of whites needing to adjust to minority status, or the possibility of very serious racial and ethnic polarization, reinforced by educational inequalities, with the possible exclusion of the majority of students from access to educational mobility. We will, in the process, be affecting the kind of relationships and experiences that prepare people to function in multiracial civic life and workplaces.

The United States is in the midst of its largest immigration ever in terms of numbers (not percentages) of newcomers, and the people coming since 1965 have been overwhelmingly Hispanic and Asian. Obviously statistics showing only levels of black segregation from whites would seriously oversimplify the complexities of the situation. We are well into a period in which we need new ways of describing and understanding the population.*

Ground Gained, Ground Lost

While desegregation has encountered setbacks, it's important to note we are not back where we began. In the South, a black student is 32,700 times more likely to be in a white-majority school than a black student in 1954, and 14 times more likely than a black student when the Civil Rights Act was passed in 1964.

But ground has been lost. During the 1990s the proportion of black students in majority-white schools decreased by 13%, to a level lower than any

---

*Until recently Hawaii was the only U.S. state with a clear majority of nonwhite students. The data for 1998-99 showed that there were six states, plus the District of Columbia, in which whites were the minority. They included the nation's two largest states, California and Texas, which serve nearly 10 million students.

year since 1968. More than 70% of the nation's black students were in predominantly minority schools, up significantly from the low point in 1980. By 2001 one-sixth of the nation's black students and one-ninth of all Latinos were being taught in what we refer to as "apartheid schools," which are virtually all nonwhite and where enormous poverty, limited resources, and social and health problems of many types are concentrated.*

Meanwhile, the data show that white students are by far the most segregated in schools dominated by their own group. Whites on average attend schools where less than a fifth of the students are from all of the other groups combined. In spite of rapid increases in minority enrollment overall, white students in most states had relatively few minority classmates. Even in the District of Columbia, where less than one student in 20 was white, the typical white student was in a class with a slight majority of whites.

This white segregation is a result of continuing residential segregation, the Supreme Court's decision to exclude suburbs from a role in urban desegregation remedies, and the historic fact that northern metropolitan areas are typically organized into many more small districts than those in the South. New suburbs continue to be marketed overwhelmingly to whites, even in metropolitan communities with large nonwhite middle-class populations. Many of the most rapidly resegregating school systems since the mid-1980s are suburban. Clearly, segregation and desegregation are no longer merely urban concerns but wider metropolitan issues.

Summary

The United States has the most diverse group of students in its history, and all the basic trends indicate the diversity will become even greater. Among our school-age population we have only a generation before the entire country becomes majority nonwhite or non-European in origin.

---

*In 1968, more than half (54.8%) of Latinos were in predominantly nonwhite schools, but almost half attended majority-white schools. By 1998, more than three-fourths (75.6%) of Latinos were in predominantly minority schools, and less than a fourth were in majority-white schools. By this measure Latinos have been substantially more segregated than black students since 1980, although black resegregation gradually narrowed the gap in the 1990s.

Diversity is growing rapidly in the nation's suburban rings, which have become the center of American life and politics.

Yet our schools remain largely segregated and are becoming more so. Segregated schools are still highly unequal. Segregation by race relates to segregation by poverty and to many forms of educational inequality for African-American and Latino students; few whites experience impoverished schools. Efforts to overcome the effects of segregation through special programs have had some success, but there is no evidence that they have equalized systems of segregated schools.

Race matters strongly and segregation is a failed educational policy. Any policy framework must explicitly recognize the importance of integrated education not only as a basic education goal but also as a compelling social interest. A great deal of long-lasting progress was achieved when this issue was last seriously addressed, a third of a century ago. If we are not to lose those gains and if we are to be ready for a profoundly multiracial society with no racial majority, we must begin to face the trends documented here and devise solutions that will work.

This is condensed from reports by the Civil Rights Project of Harvard University. For a link to the complete texts of the reports see www.rethinkingschools.org/rsr.

Neighborhood Schools: Déjà Vu

Robert Lowe

When I was a child, I attended Lincoln School. It was one of those sturdy, red brick, vaguely colonial affairs that stood almost unobtrusively amid the large homes of affluent suburbia. Lincoln was neither especially intimidating nor inviting, but it was a neighborhood school. It lacked a cafeteria not because of limited funds but because all the children walked home for lunch every day. During the cold months, kids plied its skating rink before school, during "gym," following dismissal, and after dinner. During warm weather, children scrambled over the playing fields until dark. Perfect attendance was virtually automatic at parent-teacher conferences and science fairs, and the gymnasium was filled for meetings of the Cub Scout pack and cultural events.

Perhaps nostalgia for such experiences partly fuels the periodic push to re-create neighborhood schools in cities throughout the country. Media and policymaker wisdom contrasts the "natural" geography of education, which integrates school and community in neighborhood institutions, with the "unnatural," community-fragmenting consequences of busing. By removing costly transportation requirements mandated by what is viewed as an intrusive government, it is assumed that neighborhood schools will flourish as centers of educational excellence.

Yet a policy of returning education to local schools suggests historical amnesia about both neighborhood schools and busing, and threatens to increase racial inequality in education.

Historian Carl Kaestle traces "the staunchly defended American tradition of neighborhood schools" to the 18th century.[1] In rural America, these schools for white children belonged to and reflected the culture of the surrounding community. They also typically were ill-funded affairs that housed a multitude of students in miserable one-room buildings where untrained teachers presided. A tradition of scrappy, parochial-minded schools in the countryside survived into the 20th century, when greater professional training of teachers and the consolidation of schools provided expanded educational opportunities to students. Consolidation, however, spelled the end of neighborhood schools for many. Though rural communities initially resisted this change, busing became an uncontroversial way of transporting white children to improved institutions. In contrast, a failure to provide busing to African-American children in the South often meant that education beyond the earliest grades was denied them.

The greater population density of cities ensured the long-term survival of urban neighborhood schools, but their uneven quality reflected the unequal distribution of power between neighborhoods differentiated by class and race. In the 1960s and 1970s, the fiercest resistance to busing for school integration often came from ethnic, white working-class areas like South Boston and the northwest side of Chicago, where loyalty to neighborhood schools certainly was not based on their putative excellence.

High quality simply never was the hallmark of neighborhood schools in general, but segregation was. What my suburban school had in common with neighborhood schools in cities and rural areas was its racial exclusivity. Similarly, the nationwide effort to restore neighborhood schools has little basis for promising excellent schools, but it can and will deliver racially separate ones. This is the unstated attraction for many of the white policymakers who propose an agenda that will close the era of *Brown v. Board of Education*. If glorifying neighborhood schools partly sanitizes this sea change in educational policy, so too does the way busing is represented.

'Forced Busing'

Plans to abandon public transportation to promote desegregation almost universally are framed as ending "forced busing." This phrase is one of those curious word combinations — like "critical thinking" or "authentic assessment" or "school choice" — that carries a built-in opinion about the value of what is being described. "Forced busing" obviously is something bad, and the term's widespread use suggests satisfaction with the movement to end it. In addition, the phrase assumes an illegitimate use of government power — one that denies the freedom to attend neighborhood schools and coerces attendance elsewhere.

Yet exactly who has been coerced is a question that often gets finessed. During the 1972 presidential campaign, the white voters attracted to George Wallace certainly knew the answer when he colorfully and consistently denounced busing as "social scheming" by "anthropologists, zoologists, and sociologists."[2] The fundamental problem with mandatory busing was that it interfered with what many whites perceived as their right to separate schools — either by requiring them to bus out of their neighborhood schools or by permitting blacks to bus in. Busing was not required by the U.S. Supreme Court until 16 years of experience beyond *Brown v. Board of Education* made it clear that white resistance to desegregation in many cities would perpetually confine African Americans to separate schools.

The notion that neighborhood schools are somehow innocent of government power is also patently false. In Northern cities, school district authorities' willful gerrymandering of attendance areas produced segregation where the location of schools naturally would have yielded integration. Moreover, there was nothing "natural" about suburban schools like mine. They were shaped by federal decisions to build highways rather than urban infrastructure and to support racially homogenous enclaves through the mortgage policy of the Federal Housing Authority.

The Courts

Historical amnesia is not the only reason opposition to busing was once broadly identified with racism but is now widely perceived as promoting the common good. Another reason is that the courts now legitimate such a perspective. An activist federal judiciary that once struck down legally enforced segregation and ultimately struck down ineffectual desegregation plans now significantly bears the influence of conservative Reagan and Bush appointees. These transformed federal courts have been declaring "unitary" (no longer marked by separate and unequal divisions that require corrective action) those school districts that had been under desegregation orders. Neither existing segregation nor grave racial disparities in student performance have deterred the courts from releasing urban districts from their oversight. Relatedly, there are many cities where whites hold political power but the school systems enroll mostly students of color. The legal climate is ideal for them to restore neighborhood public schools in the hope of attracting whites with the implicit promise of racial exclusivity. Furthermore, what Gary Orfield and Susan Eaton refer to as "dismantling desegregation" simply is not evoking much protest or even contention.[3]

This is a far cry from the mid-1950s when African Americans in Yazoo City, Mississippi, and other Southern towns risked their jobs — and lost them — for petitioning for desegregated schools. It is distant as well from the mid-1960s when massive demonstrations and boycotts hit Chicago, Milwaukee, New York City, and other cities to protest the failure of school districts to desegregate.

The basic explanation for the lack of organized opposition to resegregation, of course, is that desegregation hardly has been an unqualified success for African Americans. Put simply, it has been implemented on terms favorable to whites, and even privileged treatment has not been sufficient to keep many whites from choosing private schools or from moving to the suburbs. For some African-American students, their disproportionate burden of busing has been compensated by access to resources and opportunities unavailable in neighborhood schools. For others, however, it has meant either busing to poor quality and nearly segregated schools far from home or traveling to schools internally segregated by tracking that provide challenging curricula almost exclusively to white students.

Dual Approach

Certainly the failure to achieve or preserve racially balanced schools in many districts, and the failure to treat African-American students equally in others, casts doubt on unequivocally continuing a policy of busing for the purpose of promoting desegregated schools. Depending on the context, in fact, African Americans over the past 200 years have sought equal education by alternately pursuing desegregation and separate-but-equal schools. Beginning in the late 1960s, for example, many African Americans sought community control of their schools out of frustration with the slow pace of desegregation and out of anger at the hostile treatment of many black students in predominantly white schools. Three decades earlier, W. E. B. Du Bois backed away from his previous insistence on desegregation in an often-quoted passage that tactically supported separate schools:

> The Negro needs neither separate nor mixed schools. What he needs
> is Education. What he must remember is that there is no magic either
> in mixed schools or segregated schools. A mixed school with poor
> unsympathetic teachers, with hostile public opinion, and no teaching
> of the truth concerning black folk is bad. A segregated school with
> ignorant placeholders, inadequate equipment, poor salaries is equally
> bad. Other things being equal the mixed school is the broader more
> natural basis for the education of all youth. It gives wider contacts; it
> inspires greater self-confidence; and suppresses the inferiority complex.
> But other things seldom are equal, and in that case, Sympathy, Knowl-
> edge, and the Truth outweigh all that the mixed school can offer.[4]

The parents of color whose children attend urban schools today should
collectively have the authority to decide whether either or both strategies
for equal education should be pursued. The policy of merely re-creating
neighborhood schools, however, is fundamentally a white initiative. Unless
a return to neighborhood schools includes control by the neighborhood
and guarantees adequate resources, it threatens to create institutions that
are worse than those of the pre-*Brown* South. It would reproduce the separate but unequally funded schools of the Jim Crow era without providing
their community-connected, all-black staffs, who often committed themselves to developing students' "highest potential."[5]

---

[1] Kaestle, Carl F. *Pillars of the Republic: Common Schools and American Society, 1780-
1860.* New York: Hill and Wang, 1983, p. 27.

[2] Greenshaw, Wayne. *Watch Out for George Wallace.* Englewood Cliff, NJ: Prentice-
Hall, 1976, p. 40.

[3] Orfield, Gary and Eaton, Susan E. *Dismantling Desegregation: The Quiet Reversal of
Brown v. Board of Education.* New York: The New Press, 1996.

[4] Du Bois, W. E. B. "Does the Negro Need Separate Schools?" *Journal of Negro Education*
4. July 1935, p. 335.

[5] Walker, Vanessa Siddle. *Their Highest Potential: An African American School Community in the Segregated South.* Chapel Hill: University of North Carolina Press, 1996.

'Choice' and Other White Lies

Makani Themba-Nixon

In 1966, at six years old, I was one of six black children in a busing "experiment" to "integrate" an all-white elementary school in the New York City borough of Queens. Far above the Mason-Dixon Line, my parents thought I would be safe from the savage anti-integration sentiment they saw displayed in Little Rock, Arkansas or Jackson, Mississippi.

Boy, were they wrong.

Every day, the six of us would anxiously touch hands as we took the early morning ride from Hollis, in southern Queens, to the northern community of Little Neck. Hollis was a newly black and middle-class community back then — made newly black by the hurried panic of whites moving to places like Little Neck, where they thought they'd be "safe."

Our coming made them feel unsafe. And we were not prepared for the their violence and hatred.

Teachers, students, and parents taunted us constantly. Other students were given special dispensation not to hold our hands or in any way have contact with us. After a day of abuse in school, we would leave school as we entered — dodging rocks and epithets. The rocks never hit anyone. The epithets did. They hit and burrowed deep into our souls.

This is how the "choice" movement began — with the rock throwers and the naysayers. It was, and is, a movement rooted in fear. It was, and is, a movement that flees from public education rather than fight for public schools that serve all children, regardless of color or income.

It is no coincidence that this country's first school voucher movement gave public dollars to white students in Virginia to attend private, segregated schools, following the 1954 *Brown v. Board of Education* decision by the U.S. Supreme Court legally banning racially separate and unequal education.

At the time, conservatives were in the forefront of opposition to the Supreme Court decision. Today, conservatives are once again taking a strong interest in school vouchers — only this time in the guise of concern for black folk.

Aided by millions in funding from conservative think tanks and public relations firms, today's voucher movement has a much slicker image. And it is attracting diverse faces.

A high-profile, big-ticket ad campaign is pushing the idea of school vouchers in the African-American community, although the campaign uses the more appealing term "choice." The ads — and their backers — are part of the complex relationship of school reform to race.

For example, the television and radio ads sponsored by the Black Alliance for Educational Options (BAEO) have been numerous, plaintive, and compelling. Black folk. Regular. Sincere. Speaking directly about their aspirations for their children's education and lives.

Given prevailing stereotypes of black apathy and neglect, the ads would be right on target if it weren't for the group's solution: school vouchers.

While the ads target the black community, the white conservatives bankrolling and controlling the school voucher movement have a far broader agenda. (Contributors to the BAEO have included prominent conservative organizations such as the Lynde and Harry Bradley Foundation, the Walton Family Foundation, and Milton and Rose D. Friedman Foundation.) Instead of providing the money needed to improve public schools, they want to use public tax dollars on vouchers for private schools. Since most voucher plans do not approach the cost of tuition at the best private schools, it's clear that in the long run, vouchers are a way to help the (mostly white) well-to-do flee public schools. The overwhelming majority of students of color, meanwhile, will remain in even more poorly funded public schools.

The difference between the "choice" movement and authentic school reform is the difference between abandonment and accountability. Vouchers enable parents to withdraw public education dollars and spend them at private schools. It is the ultimate breach in the social contract. Taxpayers are no longer a community unit committed to maintaining public education for all. They are individual consumers out for the best deal.

At the heart of the *Brown* decision was its understanding of the relationship of race to resources and educational quality. Yet conservative groups downplay the importance of funding. A case in point: One BAEO press release touted research claiming that it's "choice" — not books, good teachers, and a rigorous curriculum — that advances black education.

According to the BAEO, the only choice that matters is choosing a better school over a struggling school. But this sidesteps the underlying problem: that the bad schools are concentrated in black and brown communities. We need to fight to improve the entire system, not for a better place within it for select individuals.

The conservatives are not interested in real reform because it costs too much money. Clearly, money matters. Who gets it and for what purpose is at the heart of the education debate. These are decisions that have been fraught with racism, controversy, and even intrigue for centuries. School vouchers are no different.

This is not to deny that many schools are in trouble. But the answer lies in wholesale reform, not in a few of us taking the money and running.

Black-White Inequality

Inequitable funding and the resulting low-quality schools stem from yet another broken promise of Reconstruction.

After the Civil War, blacks fought for access to the nation's "great equalizer," public education, as part of the tremendous debt owed us. (The debt concerning education is a literal one. Under slavery, in a practice that continued with "indentured" children in post-slavery years, it was common for black children to be "loaned out" as apprentices in exchange for cash to support the private school tuition of their "owner's" children. In other words, for at least three centuries white children of the gentry were educated as a direct result of wages provided by black children who were deprived of education.[1]

The right of blacks to quality education was an important part of the struggle during Reconstruction. In fact, African Americans led the fight for free public schools for all, and working in alliance with whites brought such a victory to the South for the first time.

The 1954 *Brown* decision came after almost a century of sustained organizing and agitation. Many thought that *Brown* would force an equitable division of resources and end the separate and unequal schooling that was the hallmark of U.S. education. But whites rebelled. When all else failed, they moved out of cities with any significant black population, thereby accelerating the march toward sprawl and suburbanization. They even started their own private schools to avoid contact with blacks.

This is the true beginning of the "choice" movement. It's a fascinating transition that "choice," so often used to support segregation and white flight, is now allegedly designed to help black children.

It's not the first time that conservatives have changed their tune in order to advance their interests. Just a century ago, these same interests were working to ban private schooling and make public schools mandatory. They introduced state laws designed to outlaw Catholic schools (for the Irish), Hebrew schools, and German schools organized by the many immigrant families trying to hold on to their heritage on these shores. The Ku Klux Klan was a major advocate of these mandatory public school attendance laws. They were concerned that children in private schools would be taught "foreign values" that would pose a threat to the "American way of life."

Fright and Flight

With the advent of school integration, it is now public schools that are the "threat." Fear of attending school with people of color and concerns over issues such as sex education and multicultural curricula are driving ever more white families to private schools or home schooling. It's impossible to understand the voucher movement without looking at this broader context.

The conservatives pushing school vouchers are not committed to fighting for better schools for all. They are seeking to pull much-needed resources out of public schools and to funnel the money into private schools. Fundamentally, they are looking for new ways for whites to maintain segregation and privilege. (Nationwide, 78% of private school students are white; 9% are African American and 8% are Latino.)

In order to keep white families in public schools following desegregation mandates, magnet schools and in-school academies became especially popular. Tracking has also been used to maintain separate and unequal schooling, even in nominally integrated schools. A study by the Applied Research Center, *No Exit? Testing, Tracking, and Students of Color in U.S. Public Schools,* found that tracking is most common in schools with significant numbers of African-American and/or Latino students. Further, white students — regardless of test scores, grades, or behavior — are much more likely to be placed in "higher tracks" or academic programs.[2]

College Admissions

Perhaps the best example of the conservative movement's unabashed commitment to white privilege is found in its efforts at the post-secondary level.

As high-paying factory jobs of the industrial economy disappear, a college education is now critical to ensure a life without poverty. As a result, college admissions, especially at the graduate level, have become highly competitive. In recent years, there has been a proliferation of lawsuits and policies at both the state and federal level designed to limit access to college (especially graduate school) for students of color, and to expand access for whites. Special outreach measures like affirmative action have been under growing attack. One of the clearest examples is California, where a 1996 ballot measure curtailed the ability of colleges and universities to consider racial diversity as part of their hiring and admissions criteria.

At the same time, whites are suing for race-conscious admissions to gain unprecedented access to historically black colleges and universities so that they have expanded options for college education. For example, Alabama State University has been subject to a 1995 federal court ruling by District Judge Harold L. Murphy, requiring that it set aside nearly 40% of its academic grants budget for scholarships to whites. The state has augmented the university's $229,000 contribution with public funds, bringing the "whites only" scholarship fund to $1 million a year. Until recently, a white student applying for such a scholarship needed only a "C" average. African Americans vying for admission to the university, meanwhile, had to earn almost a full grade point higher to even merit consideration. (According to press reports, the university has since raised the grade point average required for white scholarships, partly in response to a lawsuit by an African-American student.)

Aside from the irony of such a policy that cuts off African Americans from institutions established to help address the deep inequalities of slavery and its aftermath, there are no accompanying requirements for historically white colleges and universities. On the contrary, affirmative action efforts to integrate such historically white universities are under attack.

Back to the Future

After centuries of fighting for equal education, more and more African Americans are understandably weary. For those who can afford to augment vouchers and get their kids into a great private school, vouchers might sound like a good idea. But for the rest of us, vouchers undermine the ability of African-American kids to get an education at all, because they further defund the public schools where the overwhelming majority of our kids will remain.

Vouchers also divert resources and responsibility from the public sector and move them all to the market. It's all about getting the money, yet without any accountability.

In the days of the historic *Brown* case, many black people put their lives on the line in the fight for quality public schools for all. This was the real choice movement. It wasn't about slick ad campaigns. It was a movement that took place in the basements of churches and at the kitchen tables of mamas and grandmas who cared deeply for all their community's children.

The new choice movement, with its clandestine commitment to advancing white privilege and its crass consumer approach to education, is a betrayal of this legacy.

This article is adapted from a piece that originally appeared on the website SeeingBlack.com.

---

[1] See Peggy Cooper Davis, *Neglected Stories: The Constitution and Family Values* (Hill and Wang, 1997); or Herbert Aptheker, *American Negro Slave Revolts* (International Publishers, 1983).

[2] For a link to the Applied Research Center report, visit www.rethinkingschools.org/rsr.

For-Profits Target Education

Barbara Miner

In September 1990, the TV show "Good Morning America" was broadcast from South Pointe Elementary School in Dade County, Florida. It was the first day of school in what was to be a new and glorious era in education: for-profit, private companies running public schools.

South Pointe was run by Education Alternatives, Inc. (EAI), the first for-profit private firm under contract to run a public school. At the time South Pointe was the darling of the privatization movement. John Golle, head of EAI, was boasting that his company could run public schools for the same amount of money, improve achievement, and still make a profit. "There's so much fat in the schools that even a blind man without his cane would find the way," he told *Forbes* magazine in 1992.

EAI's rhetoric, however, never matched its educational and financial reality. The company soon found it couldn't, in fact, run public schools for less than the districts it contracted with, and its promises of academic improvement proved elusive. By the spring of 2000, EAI was in the midst of a corporate and educational meltdown. The company, which had changed its name to Tesseract Group Inc., was millions of dollars in debt, got kicked off the NASDAQ stock exchange when its stock price tumbled to pennies a share, and couldn't even afford the postage to mail report cards home to parents at one of its remaining charter schools in Arizona. Not long after, the company was in bankruptcy.

The tale of EAI is more than historical anecdote. It provides important insight into the problems facing one of the hottest and most controversial trends in education: the move by for-profit companies to run public schools.

What Is Privatization?

Privatization, while couched in rhetoric extolling the ability of the marketplace to unleash creativity and innovation, at heart is a way for profit-seeking companies to get their hands on a bigger share of the $350 billion-a-year K-12 education "industry." Wall Street has shown interest in this idea, but with a single focus: Can for-profit education management companies make a profit?

By 2002 the verdict was decidedly still out on that question. While some privately held companies had reported modest profits, there was not a single for-profit, publicly held educational management company that had shown an ongoing ability to make money. Edison Schools, the biggest and most important for-profit firm, had lost more than $233.5 million in the preceding decade.

But the controversy goes beyond whether private companies can eke out profits from already underfunded school districts. Privatization inherently leads to private control; it undercuts the democratic oversight and decision-making of a public institution. And privatization turns those institutions over to forces focused first and foremost on making money, not on the best interests of children and society at large. Issues of educational quality inevitably take a back seat to whether investors are reaping profits from their investments.

Private-sector involvement in public education is not a new phenomenon. For decades, public schools have purchased any number of products and services from private companies, such as textbook publishers and bus companies. But since 1990 privatization has taken on new meaning, as for-profit companies have tried to get involved in education at a qualitatively different level. Their goal: to run entire schools and districts, from the hiring of teachers to the development of curriculum to the teaching of students. In the process, they have planned to "compete" with publicly run schools and revise the very definition of public education, transforming it from a public service into a source of private profit.

The Wall Street term for such companies is Educational Management Organizations (EMOs.) And if you like HMOs (Health Management Organizations), as many on Wall Street do, you'll love EMOs. Investors, in fact, have often been fond of comparing public education to the health care industry before the nationwide ascendancy of HMOs. "Education today, like health care 30 years ago, is a vast, highly localized industry ripe for change," Mary Tanner, managing director of Lehman Brothers, said at a 1996 Education Industry Conference in New York City. "The emergence of HMOs and hospital management companies created enormous opportunities for investors. We believe the same pattern will occur in education."

In 2002, key players in privatization included:

- **Edison Schools Inc.**, formed in 1992 and based in New York City. Edison is by far the biggest and most important company in the field. In 2002 it ran 136 schools serving 75,000 students in 22 states and the District of Columbia. Edison has managed to survive while other companies have fallen by the wayside. In July 2001, for example, in an example of the industry consolidation, Edison acquired the privately held company LearnNow. Edison is the only publicly held company among the major for-profit education management companies. Key investors have included Microsoft co-founder Paul Allen ($71 million through his Vulcan Ventures in 1999), J.P. Morgan Chase & Co., and Investor AB, a Swedish holding company.

- **Chancellor Beacon Academies**, formed by the merger in January 2002 of Beacon Education Management of Westborough, Massachusetts and Miami-based Chancellor Academies, Inc. By 2002, the new company was the second largest for-profit school management company in the United States, serving about 19,000 students on 46 campuses in eight states and the District of Columbia.

- **Mosaica Education Inc.**, of San Rafael, California. By 2002 Mosaica was running 22 schools in 11 states. In June 2001 it took over the struggling Advantage Schools Inc.

- **National Heritage Academies**, of Grand Rapids, Michigan. National Heritage ran 28 schools in 2002, mostly in Michigan and North Carolina. It emphasized moral values and character education in a setting that opponents claimed was thinly veiled religious education.

Many investors have spoken bullishly of Edison and the other for-profit school management companies. Michigan industrialist J. C. Huizenga, who invested more than $50 million in National Heritage Academies, characterized for-profit education this way to *Business Week* magazine in 2001: "This is a breakthrough business opportunity."

Others have been more cautious. Allen Greenberg, editor of the *Phila-*

delphia Business Journal, wrote in 2001: "I took a look at some of Edison's recent filings with the Securities and Exchange Commission. It's not a pretty picture." His bottom-line analysis: Edison's financials "should give even the most ardent supporters of privatization cause to go slow."

Even Edison was forced to bluntly acknowledge its unprofitability. In filings with the Securities and Exchange Commission (SEC), Edison repeatedly noted: "We have not yet demonstrated that public schools can be profitably managed by private companies and we are not certain when we will become profitable, if at all."

Tough Sledding For Edison

From 2000 to 2002, Edison suffered setbacks in several high-profile school districts.

- In New York City, it lost a community/parental vote on whether the company should manage five New York schools. The vote was doubly embarrassing because it came in the city where Edison was headquartered, and because it was the parents who rejected Edison. (This was the only instance, as of 2002, where Edison's future was decided by the votes of parents, not politicians.)

- In Wichita, Kansas, the school board voted unanimously to take back two of Edison's four schools in the district: Edison-Ingalls and Edison-Isely, both elementary schools. At Ingalls, enrollment dropped from a high of 722 in 1997 to 426 in 2002, while more than half of the teaching staff left after the end of the 2000-2001 school year. At Isely, enrollment dropped from about 280 to 200. Edison claimed the teachers left Ingalls because they did not like the company's longer school year. But a number of teachers told *The Wichita Eagle* newspaper that they were driven out by intolerable working conditions. "The work environment was horrifically hostile," said teacher Jeanette Falley. In addition, the school's principal and assistant principal were removed after school personnel were caught improperly helping students on standardized tests.

- In Dallas, the school board forced Edison to renegotiate its five-year contract when it was found that Edison would have otherwise received

$20 million more than the actual cost of running its seven schools.

◆ In San Francisco, parents and school board members revoked Edison's charter when test scores showed that the school's performance was the absolute worst of all the city's schools. Under political pressure, the state stepped in and granted Edison an independent charter so the school could keep going.

The San Francisco battle also highlighted issues of whether Edison has genuine parental support, after it hired a professional organizing and marketing company, Digital Campaigns, to whip up support among parents. Digital Campaigns boasted on its website that Edison was able to attract only five parent signatures on a petition until the company stepped in to help. Caroline Grannan, a San Francisco public school parent and co-founder of Parents Advocating School Accountability, noted: "It's impossible to know how many 'happy parents' would be speaking up without the professional organizing operation."

It is in the Philadelphia school district, which was taken over by the state of Pennsylvania in 2002, that Edison perhaps has the most on the line. Edison was given 20 of the district's schools to run that year, more than twice as many as it runs in any other city. (Edison initially asked for control of the district's central administration and as many as 100 schools, but that plan was sharply curtailed amid public clamor.) Other schools within the city were given over to other private companies — Chancellor Beacon, for example, received five — as well as to Temple University and the University of Pennsylvania.

Edison's Academic Woes

One of the biggest controversies in all of the districts where Edison operates is whether Edison schools actually perform better than public schools. Edison says yes, but the company's performance indicates otherwise. Some examples:

◆ Dallas Superintendent Mike Moses told *The American School Board Journal* in 2001 that "we looked at their seven schools against seven comparable schools, and truthfully, Edison's performance was not superior."

◆ Gerald Bracey, author of the book *The War Against America's Public*

Schools (Allyn and Bacon, 2001), issued a report in 2002 on Edison's claims of improved academic achievement, and said that Edison makes "hyperbolic conclusions, using data that can only be described as questionable."

◆ A study of 10 Edison schools conducted for the National Education Association by researcher Gary Miron of the Evaluation Center at Western Michigan University, found that Edison schools were performing at the same level as comparable public schools, or slightly worse overall. "Our findings suggest that Edison students do not perform as well as Edison claims in its annual reports," the report said. An earlier report by the American Federation of Teachers reached similar conclusions.

◆ U.S. Rep. Chaka Fattah (D-Pennsylvania) reviewed Edison's claims of improved achievement in 2001 and found that "the overwhelming majority of Edison schools perform poorly, in many cases faring worse than some Philadelphia schools."

Edison disputes such reports as political sniping. The RAND Corp., a respected independent research group, was hired by Edison to analyze the company's academic achievement. The report was to be completed in late 2003 or 2004.

Given these concerns, why would a school district contract with a for-profit company?

At least in part, the answer lies in the intensive lobbying and political connections of privatization advocates. While there may be doubts about the educational value of privatization, the movement has the support of well-heeled investors with strong ties to political power brokers.

Another part of the answer lies in the belief that there are quick fixes that will improve schools, especially in underfunded urban districts. School districts are sometimes open to privatization because officials are tired of fighting taxpayers and state legislators for the increased money they know is essential to get the job done, and are equally tired of being blamed for failures they believe are beyond their control.

Finally, the power of the school privatization movement cannot be separated from the growing clout of market ideology, not only in the United

States but around the world. As "globalization" becomes not just a market strategy but an increasingly dominant world view, the very concept of institutions designed to serve the public good, rather than generate money for stockholders, is often seen as hopelessly idealistic and anachronistic.

Ultimately, for-profit firms will not live or die on their educational record but on their ability to generate profits. And so far, that record is dismal. In the long run, the problem facing Edison is the same problem that faced the now-bankrupt Tesseract, formerly known as EAI: Despite public perception, there is little "fat" in urban public school budgets. Nor are there any "silver bullets" that will magically improve schools.

Because education is a labor-intensive industry, there are only two ways to make money: cut wages or cut services. (A variation on "cutting wages" is to hire younger, lower-paid staff. A variation on "cutting services" is to control student admissions, so students who are more difficult to educate go elsewhere.) Like Tesseract, Edison has been plagued by charges that it saves money by hiring less experienced teachers and that it doesn't adequately serve special education students.

Edison also has come under fire for cutting staff to the point where basic school operations and discipline are compromised. The company announced in 2002, for example, that its plan for Philadelphia included cutting the costs of support staff. (This fit the pattern established earlier by EAI: When EAI went into its first multi-school contract in Baltimore in 1992, one of the first things it did was replace $10-an-hour, unionized paraprofessional workers with $7-an-hour "interns" who did not have benefits.) Later, Edison was forced to reinstate some non-teacher support staff, at company expense, after a series of lunchroom fights, incidents of vandalism, and other problems at middle schools.

The Real Winners

Edison's over-optimistic profit projections have led many investors to shy away from the company. After trading at more than $30 a share in early 2001, the stock price had plummeted to $1.56 by early 2003, after trading at one point for as little as 14 cents per share.

That doesn't mean, however, that some people haven't made a lot of money off of Edison. Company founder Chris Whittle, for example, has parlayed his stock holdings into considerable wealth. In one day alone in 2001, some 650,000 shares held indirectly by Whittle were sold for more than $15 million. According to a proxy statement filed later that year, Whittle still owned 3.7 million shares of Edison stock, and he and his associates had options on an additional 4.4 million shares.

A few other examples:

- Benno Schmidt Jr., Edison board chair, made more than $400,000 in Edison stock sales in 2001, on top of his six-figure salary.
- Christopher Cerf, chief operating officer for Edison, made $880,000 in Edison stock sales in 2001.
- Jeffrey Leeds, an Edison director, made more than $2 million off Edison stock sales in 2001.
- In 2002 Deborah McGriff, a former superintendent of the Detroit schools and a vice president of Edison (and wife of voucher and privatization proponent Howard Fuller) sold 15,325 shares of the roughly 200,000 stock options she held when the company first went public — for a gain of $348,184.

Edison was not the only company that provided major windfalls for its executives. EAI founder and CEO Golle, ever the shrewd businessman, knew when to make his move. In the fall of 1993, over a two-month period when EAI stock was riding high, Golle made a net profit of approximately $1.75 million on sales of 50,000 shares of EAI stock.

The for-profit education privatization movement is not likely to go away just because the companies are not yet making profits. A lot of people with a lot of money are in this for the long run. Nonetheless, advocates of improved schools shouldn't be fooled that privatization is somehow about education reform. In the end, power and money — who gets more and who gets less — remain at the heart of the privatization struggle. Educational improvement is a sideshow.

Learning to Read 'Scientifically'

Gerald Coles

The first week after becoming president in 2001, George W. Bush sent Congress an educational reform "blueprint" that included a reading initiative mirroring policies that had supposedly produced an educational "miracle" in Texas when Bush was governor.

Bush promised to eliminate the nation's "reading deficit" by "ensuring that every child can read by the third grade." To do so, he proposed applying "the findings of years of scientific research on reading" to "all schools in America." Bush stressed that these research findings were "now available," especially in a report of the National Reading Panel (NRP) which reviewed "100,000 studies on how students learn to read" and provided a guide for "scientifically based reading instruction." Bush said his legislation would provide funds for reading instruction — but only if the instruction were "scientifically based."

Never, it seems, has this nation had a more scientifically minded president. Shortly after releasing his reading proposal, Bush rejected a policy for reducing carbon dioxide emissions in power plants because, he said, the science is "still incomplete." He also terminated plans to reduce the amount of arsenic in drinking water because, he said, he wanted to determine if the proposed reductions were "supported by the best available science." He went on to withdraw the United States from an international agreement to reduce global warming because, he said, the "state of scientific knowledge of the causes of, and solutions to global climate change" was "incomplete."

Although many have questioned Bush's intellectual ability to do the job, these decisions demonstrate that we have a president who evidently has studied an array of scientific literature and has been able to formulate various policy judgments based on the empirical evidence. One might conclude that the reading research must indeed be sound for Bush to have given it his one empirical imprimatur.

Too bad that's not the case.

Bush and 'The Basics'

The type of "reading education" Bush has in mind can be gleaned from remarks made in 1996 when he advised Texas teachers to get "back to the basics" — that is, return to traditional education that focuses on basic skills, basic facts, and a traditional curriculum, and reject all classroom reforms that include children's perspectives and thereby reduce the authority of the teacher.

"The building blocks of knowledge," Bush explained, "were the same yesterday and will be the same tomorrow. We do not need trendy new theories or fancy experiments or feel-good curriculums. The basics work. If drill gets the job done, then rote is right."

Although advocates of what is now being called "scientifically based" reading instruction might take issue with the "rote" comment, Bush accurately described the essentials of this teaching philosophy. "Trendy" is code for whole language, cooperative learning, meaning-emphasis learning (reading instruction that stresses comprehension and teaches skills as part of students' reading for meaning), and critical literacy (reading instruction that examines and questions values, assumptions, and ideologies in written material) — that is, anything that is an alternative to the "basics."

"Basics," meanwhile, is code for beginning reading instruction that emphasizes exclusively the explicit, direct, and systematic instruction of skills and minimizes the need for meaning and comprehension until the skills are learned. Under such an approach, teachers follow pre-established reading programs that move children through a step-wise process from small parts of language to larger ones. While advocates of this instruction method insist it is "balanced" — that is, instruction balances reading for meaning with learning skills for reading — a close look reveals that the comprehension end of the seesaw remains close to the ground for a long time.

The Scientific Aristocracy

Demands for so-called "scientifically based" reading education preceded Bush's initiative. Beginning in the mid-1990s, reading research funded by the National Institute of Child Health and Human Development (NICHD), a branch of the National Institutes of Health, was being touted as a scientific gold standard which justified scripted skills-emphasis instruction (that is, instruction using a reading program that has prescribed, sequential lessons that teachers and students must follow). The "Chief" (actual title) of the NICHD reading research division, Reid Lyon, was a persistent spokesman for scripted instruction in policy hearings across the country. Lyon and NICHD-supported researchers usually had an easy time of it, because alternative views at these hearings were few, if any. In the Bush reading legislation, the reading division of NICHD was included in the processes for disseminating information about the reading legislation, for setting standards for "scientific" research, and for reviewing and judging applications.

In 2000, NICHD arranged for Congress to "request" that it form the National Reading Panel to report on the best scientific information on reading. Given NICHD's dominant role in selecting the panel and administrating its work, its conclusions were predictable. Typical of the media reports announcing the panel's findings was one in *Education Week*, whose headline read, "Reading Panel Urges Phonics For All in K-6." Although the report urged more than phonics, the headline was generally correct because the panel stressed the need for an early mastery of sound-symbol connections and similar skills through explicit, systematic, direct instruction. Implicit in the panel's report and explicit in most media reports was the rejection of a whole language approach to literacy.

In *Misreading Reading: The Bad Science That Hurts Children* (Heinemann, 2000), I reviewed the NICHD reading research and related studies, and documented the shoddy research in this work and its failure to support skills-emphasis instruction.

But before providing a few illustrations of the report's deficiencies, I want to return to Bush's description of the report.

The '100,000' Studies

Bush's legislative proposal stated that the panel reviewed 100,000 studies on reading, a number that was often repeated in the media. Unmentioned is the fact that the number does not remotely describe the actual number of studies used in the panel's analysis.

The panel did begin by looking at the research studies on reading and found that approximately 100,000 had been published since 1966. However, the panel used several criteria for extensive pruning of this number. For example, the studies had to deal with reading development from preschool through high school, and therefore excluded studies on many reading topics such as literacy skills in occupations or brain functioning and literacy activity. The studies also had to meet the Panel's definition of "scientific research," which was limited almost entirely — and narrowly — to quantitative, experimental studies.

Perhaps most important, the panel used only studies relating to the instructional topics which the panel majority had decided were key areas of good reading instruction. As panel member Joanne Yatvin, an Oregon principal, wrote in her "Minority View" dissenting from the report's conclusions: "From the beginning, the Panel chose to conceptualize and review the field narrowly, in accordance with the philosophical orientation and research interests of the majority of its members."

This questionable procedure eliminated a variety of important instructional issues contained in the research literature, such as the relationship of writing and reading, meaning-emphasis instruction, the interconnection of emotions and literacy learning, and approaches for responding to children's individual literacy needs. This panel of experts had no qualms about exercising *a priori* its judgment on what is central to successful reading instruction, and ignoring contrary views of other leading reading researchers on what comprises the best way to learn to read. The panel knew best.

After this pruning of the "100,000" studies, what remained were 52 studies on phonemic awareness, 38 studies for phonics, 14 for fluency, and 203 for 16 categories of comprehension instruction: that is, about 12 or 13 studies on average in each category. Certainly these numbers are sufficient for drawing some reasonable conclusions. But they are far from the much-heralded "100,000 studies" and, most importantly, not sufficient numbers for establishing restrictive national policy. There were members of Bush's education advisory committee who were familiar with the NRP report and knew the 100,000 figure was a misrepresentation. But given their interest in foisting their brand of teaching on the nation, it is not surprising that no one told the president that the figure would mislead the public and Congress.

Appraising the Research

The primary method of evaluating the research was a meta-analysis, a statistical method that pools a group of studies and estimates the average effect something has on something else, in this case, the effect of aspects of instruction on achievement. A meta-analysis can provide useful information, but it also can have substantial deficiencies, such as not uncovering the quality of, and reasoning in, the studies pooled. Although the panel's conclusions were derived from its meta-analysis, its appraisal of the quality of the research and its reasoning on behalf of its a priori decisions about instruction can be gleaned from the report's detailed descriptions and interpretations of a number of studies. Because of space limitations, I can only discuss two that appear at the beginning of the report's first section. I believe they are representative of the panel's entire appraisal of its studies.

Correlation Versus Cause

The panel concluded that "results of the experimental studies allow the Panel to infer that [phonological awareness] training was the cause of improvement in students'" reading. (Phonological awareness refers to the ability to separate and manipulate speech sounds mentally and orally, as when blending or separating phonemes in order to identify words.) The report states, for example, that one study[1] showed that phonological awareness was the top predictor along with letter knowledge (knowing the names of letters) of later reading achievement. The panel's description suggests that these two predictors are "causes."

However, the accuracy of this conclusion becomes questionable when one includes the third strongest predictor of reading achievement. The panel did not mention this predictor, possibly because it has no apparent relationship to written language. That predictor is the degree of success on a "finger localization" test, in which a child whose vision is blocked identifies which of her or his fingers an adult has touched. Despite its predictive correlation with future reading achievement, finger localization skill in itself could not be considered "causal" to learning to read, and no educator would suggest finger location training as a beginning reading method.

Zip codes are also good "predictors" of academic achievement. A student's zip code (an indication of family income and education, quality of schools in the area, a child's access to educational experiences, etc.) is strongly correlated with future school success. However, this correlation does not make zip codes a cause of academic achievement. Unfortunately, given the failure of some reading researchers to understand the difference between correlation and causation, it is possible that one of them might concoct an experiment to see if the reading achievement of children in a poor, urban area with terrible schools improves if they are given the zip code of children in an affluent, suburban area with excellent schools.

The NRP report also fails to mention that the researchers who did the study offered an explicit caveat about confusing correlation with causation. Yes, they did find that letter knowledge was a strong predictor of future reading, but they emphasized its predictive strength did not mean that beginning readers needed to know letter names in order to get off to a fast, secure start in reading.

Although "knowledge of letter names has been traditionally considered the single best predictor of reading achievement, there appears to be no evidence that letter-name knowledge facilitates reading acquisition," the researchers said in their report.

Letter-name knowledge is likely to be part of and represent experience with early written language that contributes to literacy attainment. That knowledge — like the knowledge of various skills, such as phonological awareness — can be considered to be a "marker" of these experiences and accomplishments.

None of this complexity and these distinctions are captured in the report's simplistic summary that the study "showed that phonological awareness was the top predictor along with letter knowledge."

No Need for Skills Training

A striking example of congruence between the panel's interpretation of the research and its a priori conclusions about the best reading instruction is its description of a study supposedly showing that a phonological awareness "treatment group" was "compared to one no-treatment group" and the "effect size was impressive."[2] This provides evidence, wrote the panel, that the training program being studied could be "used effectively in American classrooms."

This group comparison was correct as far as it went, but the report did not tell readers that there were two control groups, not one. Besides the one control the panel described, another control group learned phonological awareness in an informal, "as needed" way similar to the way skills are taught in a whole language approach. In other words, we have in this study an opportunity to compare children learning these phonological awareness skills either through an explicit skills training program or an implicit, as-needed, approach. Although this comparison would have allowed the panel to delve into the question of how these skills should be taught and learned, it did not do so.

Therefore, we will. At the end of the school year, the skills training group did significantly better on phonological tests, but the researchers found there were "no significant differences between the [skills training and implicit teaching] groups on the tests of word reading and spelling." (Interestingly, the NRP report neglected to mention this finding.) The researchers who did the study observed, moreover, that "the significantly superior scores achieved by the training group in this study on tasks of phonemic awareness suggest that this group should also achieve higher scores on the reading tasks, but this was not in fact the case." Again, the conclusions were not quoted in the NRP report.

The researchers went on to propose that the "writing experiences" of the informal learning group might have accounted for their reading success. On average, they "wrote longer stories than either" the training group or the "normal" kindergarten group. These conclusions too were omitted from the report.

In other words, the study showed that children can learn rhyme, syllable synthesis, word reading, and spelling without needing an explicit skills training program. Furthermore, extensive writing activities are likely to be effective for attaining the literacy knowledge for which the researchers tested. This study also lends some support to a holistic written language approach, insofar as it indicates that phonological skills can be readily learned within a rich array of reading and writing activities. And it further demonstrates that there not only is no need for a step-wise approach to literacy learning, but that such an approach can reduce time spent on essential and productive literacy activities, such as "writing experiences."

The 'Scientific Method'

Despite the lack of scientific evidence for a heavy emphasis on direct instruction of skills in beginning reading instruction, the term "scientifically based" appears 31 times in the House version of President Bush's reading bill and almost as many in the Senate version. To be sure that no one reading the bills is confused about the meaning of "reading," its "components" are enumerated in a list that starts with phonemic awareness and is followed by phonics, vocabulary, reading fluency, and, at the end of the list, reading comprehension.

For skills-first proponents, "comprehension" is always part of their definition of learning to read, but like this definition, the "components" are always designed to be learned in a sequential, stepwise, systematic, scripted, managerial instructional program. The list never runs in the opposite direction, and the components never are described as interactive from the start of learning to read.

The judicial coup d'état that brought us the second Bush Administration has many permutations, one of which is seizing the power to design and enforce the standards of literacy education, and thus to coerce schools into using "scientifically based" reading programs — especially if they hope to receive federal money. In pursuing and exercising this power, talk about "scientifically based" instruction has been no more than a string of infomercials justifying the legitimacy of that power. In legislative hearings, critical voices are locked out.

---

[1] Share, David, et al. "Sources of individual differences in reading acquisition." *Journal of Educational Psychology,* (76)6 1984, pp. 1309-1324.

[2] Brennan, F. and Ireson, J. "Training phonological awareness: A study to evaluate the effects of a program of metalinguistic games in kindergarten." *Reading and Writing,* (9), 1997, pp. 241-263.

Bush's Bad Idea for Bilingual Education

Stephen Krashen

The most significant feature of President Bush's plan for bilingual education is the requirement that there be a three-year limit on bilingual education. As outlined in Bush's education blueprint "No Child Left Behind," after three years students must attain "English fluency" and schools "will be required to teach children in English after three consecutive years of being in school."

Why would anybody think this is a good idea?

One obvious reason is the feeling of some people that children stay in bilingual classes too long. The media have certainly given the public this impression. During a broadcast in 2000 of National Public Radio's "All Things Considered" program, reporter Claudio Sánchez said: "Too many [English learners], some say half, languish in bilingual programs for six years or more and never learn how to read or write in English." This was followed within a few days by two articles in *The New York Times*. Reporter Lynette Holloway wrote that in New York, "many students remain in bilingual education programs nine years or more," and Jacques Steinberg reported that "many students [take] six years or more to exit bilingual programs." *The Times* also claimed that in New York City, "just 45% of the students who entered the bilingual programs in middle school and 15% of those who entered in high school achieved sufficient English proficiency to leave those classes during their school career." This accusation was repeated in *Newsweek* a few months later.

No Evidence of 'Languishing'

These accusations are not true. There is no evidence that significant numbers of children are "languishing" in bilingual programs.

In 2001 the New York City Board of Education issued a report on the progress of English learners in the New York City schools. The report showed that for children entering the New York school system in kindergarten and first grade (86% of the children studied in the report), only 14% were still in bilingual education after six years and only 10% remained in bilingual education after nine years. As for children who spoke Korean, Chinese, and Russian, all were exited from bilingual education within five years. In Texas, according to my estimates (Krashen, 2001), only about 7% of students who started early are still in bilingual education after fifth grade, and after eighth grade practically no early starters are in bilingual programs.

Acquiring enough English to do grade-level classwork in a monolingual classroom is quite an accomplishment. It means knowing enough English to understand story problems, read textbooks, and write compositions and reports. This kind of knowledge of language is called "academic language," and takes considerably longer to acquire than "conversational" language (Cummins, 1981).

But, one might ask, what about non-English speaking students who enter in high school?

The New York Times and *Newsweek* accusation — that only 15% of those who entered bilingual education in high school achieved English proficiency — is wrong. The New York Board of Education did indeed report that after four years of high school, only 15% of those entering at ninth grade had acquired enough English to do classwork in the mainstream. But this figure included those in all-English programs as well as those in bilingual education. There is no evidence in the board report that bilingual education is less successful than all-English education in dealing with late-arriving students.

Latecomers face a daunting task. Many come with inadequate preparation in their country of origin and need to acquire English as well as assimilate years of subject matter knowledge. Many studies, including the New York Board of Education report, have confirmed that those who come with better preparation in their first language do much better in acquiring academic English (see Krashen, 1999).

Other (Bogus) Reasons

Even if policymakers and the media were aware that "languishing" is not a problem, there still might be support for a time limit on bilingual education. There are several possible reasons for this and all, except one, are invalid. The one valid reason has a solution.

First, policymakers may feel that bilingual programs are effective, but that after three years children have already acquired enough English to do well in the mainstream. In other words, the children are being unnecessarily held back. One view is that they are held back by teachers and administrators who regard bilingual education as a "cash cow" and want more students in order to maintain their programs and their power. There is absolutely no evidence supporting this outrageous claim, which amounts to an insulting accusation of unprofessionalism. Moreover, bilingual educators have no need to increase the number of students in their programs: The number of new students arriving in U.S. schools with limited English proficiency is enormous and constantly increasing. If anything, bilingual educators are suffering from having far too many students to deal with.

It could also be maintained that the students themselves are holding back. Here again there are several possibilities. One is that they have acquired a considerable amount of English but don't want to leave the comfort of the bilingual education program, where things are easy (or more accurately, where instruction is comprehensible). Another is that they simply don't want to acquire English and are resisting it. The first possibility is plausible; the jump from bilingual education into the mainstream can be difficult. The solution to this problem is not an arbitrary time limit, but programs that make the transition more comfortable and comprehensible. (For an example see the description of a gradual-exit program in Krashen, 1996.) The second possibility, that children are resisting English, is simply false. The drive to acquire English is very strong and often results in a preference for English over a student's heritage language (Tse, 1998).

Politicians also might feel that bilingual programs are simply not effective and that children, especially after the first three years, are much better off in all-English mainstream classes. This is not true. Nearly every published review of the effectiveness of bilingual education has concluded that bilingual education is at least as effective for the development of academic English as English-only alternatives, and is usually more effective (see especially Willig, 1985 and Greene, 1999).

Nor is there any evidence that less bilingual education is more effective than more bilingual education.* One study reported that students in a "late-exit" program, which continued substantial instruction in the first language until sixth grade, continued to show clear gains in English language development well after grade three. It concluded that "providing LEP [limited-English-proficient] students with substantial amounts of instruction in their primary language does not impede their acquisition of English language skills, but that it is as effective as being provided with large amounts of English" (Ramirez, 1992).

Thus there is no evidence that children are "languishing" for excessive periods of time in bilingual education, no evidence that teachers and administrators are holding them back, no evidence that English immersion is faster, and no evidence that continued instruction in the primary language hurts English language development.

One must conclude that there is no evidence supporting the three-year limit on bilingual education. In fact, there is plenty of reason to drop all time limits. Instruction in the first language, at worst, causes no harm, and there is evidence that it accelerates English language development. Moreover, continued development of the first language has clear advantages. Numerous studies show that those who develop both languages to a high degree have cognitive advantages. Also, it is in the national interest to encourage bilingualism; we need, after all, interpreters, sales personnel, and diplomats (Krashen, 1998).

How to Speed Things Up

Bilingual education has done well, but it can do better. If the Bush administration is serious about improving English language development,

---

*One study found that three years of bilingual education was more effective than two years (Saldate, Mishra, and Medina, 1985), while other studies have found that five years was just as effective as four years (Bacon, Kidd, and Seaberg, 1982) and three years was just as effective as two years (de la Garza and Medina, 1985).

here are some suggestions.

Perhaps the biggest problem is the absence of books, in both the first and second language, in the lives of students in these programs. Many LEP children have little access to books in any language.

The average Hispanic family with LEP children has about 26 books in their home (Ramirez, Yuen, Ramey, and Pasta, 1991).* This refers to the total number of books in the home, including the Bible, cookbooks, and dictionaries, and is about one-sixth the U.S. average (Purves and Elley, 1992). School is not helping. An investigation of school libraries in schools with strong bilingual programs in Southern California, for example, found that books in Spanish were very scarce (Pucci, 1994). Those that were available, while often of high quality, were usually short and for younger children.

The access problem is also present with respect to books in English. Children from low-income families have little access to books in school libraries, public libraries, or their communities (Neuman and Celano, 2001).

Simply providing access to books does not guarantee reading, but there is no question that those with more access to books read more. And those who read more also read better, write better, spell better, and have larger vocabularies. In fact, it is now firmly established that reading for meaning, especially free voluntary reading, is the major source of our literacy competence (Krashen, 1993). Reading is also an important source of knowledge: Those who read more usually know more.

When children read a lot in their first language, they build first language literacy quickly. It is much easier to learn to read in a language you understand, and once you can read, this ability transfers rapidly to other languages. Thus, developing reading ability in the first language is a shortcut to English literacy (Krashen, 1996). Once children can understand texts in English, free-reading in English is a powerful tool for accelerating progress. Also, continuing to read in the primary language helps provide the advantages of bilingualism, mentioned earlier. In addition, more reading

---

* These are data on Spanish-speaking children.

means more knowledge of the world and subject matter knowledge; more knowledge means better comprehension of English and faster acquisition of English.

My suggestion is a massive book flood in the child's home language as well as in English, a suggestion that is relatively inexpensive to implement. Enriching the print environment is not the only recommendation one can make in discussing improvement of bilingual education, but it is a great place to begin.

References

Bacon, H., Kidd, G., and Seaborg, J. "The effectiveness of bilingual instruction with Cherokee Indian students." *Journal of American Indian Education*, 1982. 21(2): 34-43.

Cummins, J. "The role of primary language development in promoting educational success for language minority students." In C. F. Leyba (Ed.), *Schooling and Language of Minority Students: A Theoretical Framework*. Los Angeles, CA: Evaluation, Dissemination and Assessment Center, California State University Los Angeles, 1981. pp. 3-49.

de la Garza, J. and Medina, M. "Academic achievement as influenced by bilingual instruction for Spanish-dominant Mexican-American children." *Hispanic Journal of Behavioral Sciences*, 1985. 7(3): pp. 247-259.

Greene, J. "A Meta-Analysis of the Russell and Baker review of bilingual education research." *Bilingual Research Journal*, 1997. 21(2,3): pp. 103-122.

Krashen, S. *The Power of Reading*. Englewood, CA: Libraries Unlimited, 1993.

Krashen, S. "Heritage language development: Some practical arguments." In S. Krashen, S. 1999. *Condemned without a Trial: Bogus Arguments Against Bilingual Education*. Portsmouth, NH: Heinemann Publishing Company.

Krashen, S. "How many children remain in bilingual education 'too long?' Some recent data." *NABE News*, 24(5), May/June 2001, pp. 15-17.

Krashen, S., Tse, L., and McQuillan, J. (Eds.), *Heritage Language Development*. Culver City, CA: Language Education Associates, 1998.

Neuman, S. and Celano, D. "Access to print in low-income and middle-income communities." *Reading Research Quarterly*, 2001. 36(1): pp. 8-26.

New York City Board of Education. *Chancellor's ELL Education Report*. Division of Assessment and Accountability, 2000.

Pucci, S. "Supporting Spanish language literacy: Latino children and free reading resources in the schools." *Bilingual Research Journal*, 1994. 18: pp. 67-82.

Purves, A. and Elley, W. "The role of the home and student differences in reading performance." In W. Elley (Ed.), *The IEA Study of Reading Achievement and Instruction in Thirty-Two School Systems*. Oxford: Pergamon, 1994. pp. 89-121.

Ramirez, D. "Executive summary (Longitudinal study of structured English immersion strategy, early-exit and late-exit transitional bilingual education programs for language-minority children) " *Bilingual Research Journal*, 1992. 16 (1-2). pp. 1-62.

Ramirez, D., Yuen, S., Ramey, D. and Pasta, D. *Final Report: Longitudinal Study of Structured English Immersion Strategy, Early-Exit and Late-Exit Bilingual Education Programs for Language Minority Students, Vol. I.* San Mateo, CA: Aguirre International, 1991.

Saldate, M., Mishra, S., and Medina, M. "Bilingual instruction and academic achievement: A longitudinal study." *Journal of Instructional Psychology*, 1985. 12(1): pp. 24-30.

United States Government, 2001. *Transforming the Federal Role in Education So That No Child Is Left Behind.* (A link to the full text of this report is available online at www.rethinkingschools.org/rsr.)

Tse, L. "Ethnic identity formation and its implications for heritage language development." In S. Krashen, L. Tse, and J. McQuillan (Eds.), *Heritage Language Development.* Culver City, CA: Language Education Associates, 1998.

Willig, A. "A meta-analysis of selected studies on the effectiveness of bilingual education." *Review of Educational Research*, 1985. 55: pp. 269-316.

Let Them Eat Tests: NCLB and Federal Education Policy

Stan Karp

" **S** tock up on number 2 pencils."

That may be the only reliable advice for public schools to follow in the wake of the No Child Left Behind Act (NCLB). More standardized tests are on the way, and they carry "high stakes" — and high hurdles — with them.

Just four years after Republican presidential candidate Bob Dole campaigned on a platform of abolishing the Department of Education, the new Bush administration made a massive expansion of the federal role in education its number one domestic priority.[1] It also began an effort to replace the federal government's historic role as a promoter of access and equity in public education with a conservative agenda that comes wrapped in rhetoric about "leaving no child behind," but which may ultimately hurt poor schools most.

The euphemistically named Bush education bill was passed in December 2001 with overwhelming Republican and Democratic support, 381-41 in the House, 87-10 in the Senate. Two senators, Ted Kennedy (D-Massachusetts) and Judd Gregg (R-New Hampshire) and two House representatives, John Boehner (R-Ohio) and George Miller (D-California) were largely responsible for guiding the legislation through Congress in a process that bypassed some of the usual advocacy input and compromise that normally raise alarms about dramatic shifts in federal policy. The bill's far-reaching implications came into public focus only gradually, as its provisions were turned into specific federal regulations and as schools and districts read the fine print with growing alarm.[2]

Mandated Testing

Federally mandated annual testing is the cornerstone of the legislation, which reauthorized the Elementary and Secondary Education Act (ESEA), a consolidation of the major K-12 federal education programs including the Title I program that reaches 47,000 high-poverty schools.[3] The tests are central to a greatly expanded and revised role for the federal government in local schools and districts. Among the law's major features:

* Mandated annual tests in reading and math from grades 3-8 and at least once in grades 10-12.

* Additional tests in science beginning in 2007, given once between grades 3-5, 6-9 and 10-12.

* Use of these tests to determine whether schools are making "adequate yearly progress" (AYP) towards the goal of 100% proficiency for all students, including special education students and English language learners, within 12 years (2013-2014).[4]

* Sanctions for schools that don't reach their AYP goals, which will be increasingly impossible to meet (see below). The sanctions include now-familiar "corrective measures" like outside intervention by consultants, replacement of staff, or state takeover. Other sanctions reflect the administration's privatization agenda, which lurks just below the surface of the legislation. These include use of federal funds to provide "supplemental services" to students from outside agencies, imposing school transfer or choice plans, or turning management of schools over to private contractors.

The law does target more federal money to the poorest schools, and mandates changes in testing and reporting requirements that will focus attention on the racial dimensions of the achievement gap, the academic performance of English language learners and special education students, and the widespread use of underqualified and uncertified teachers.

But while the legislation turns up the spotlight, and the heat, on low-performing schools, the extra dollars the Bush administration promised have been undercut by its "war budget" and tax cuts. A $1.4 billion increase in Title I funding in the first year of NCLB was followed by administration proposals to eliminate 45 federal education programs and more than $1.5 billion in other education spending in the 2004 budget (including money for small schools, comprehensive school reform efforts, and K-12 math and science education). The president's 2004 budget fell $6 billion short of the totals authorized in the original NCLB Act. Even with targeted increases, the legislation still doesn't provide full funding for Title I, which currently reaches less than half of all eligible low-income students. And despite the new testing and performance requirements that NCLB puts on special education students, the federal budget doesn't come close to providing the 40% of special education funding called for in the federal Individuals with Disabilities Education Act. In fact the gap between NCLB's lofty goals and its low-rent resources suggests its proper title would have been "The Unfunded Federal Mandates Bill."[5]

Simple-Minded Approaches

Equally alarming, the remedies NCLB offers to struggling schools and districts, particularly an obsessive over-reliance on standards and tests in the name of "accountability," have proven ineffective, even harmful. The law's fundamental premises about how to promote school improvement are both simple and simple-minded.

Thanks to two decades of governors' education summits and the persistent urging of the Clinton administration throughout the 1990s, virtually all states have adopted new curriculum standards. These standards are of widely varying educational quality and relevance to what takes place in real schools. But states, districts, and schools are now under federal mandate to enforce the standards above all other considerations, through annual tests, or face losing federal funds.

All schools are required to plot a path from current levels of achievement to 100% proficiency within 12 years — theoretically, in steady, equal steps forward. "Adequate yearly progress" goals will be set for districts, schools, and individual subgroups. Public reporting of scores is designed to identify schools and students that are not "proficient," while highlighting gaps between genders, races, and other sub-categories (special education, new language learners, low income students, etc.).

Any school or district that doesn't meet all its goals in all its subgroups for two consecutive years will be put in the "needs improvement" category, and if it is receiving Title I money, will face an escalating scale of "corrective action." (The "corrective" steps are mandated only for high-poverty schools receiving federal Title I funds, though states are directed to develop their own sanctions for other schools).

The "adequate yearly progress" formulas are so convoluted and unrealistic they seem designed to create chaos and new categories of failure. An early survey in *Education Week* suggested that as many as 75% of all schools — not just Title I schools — could be placed in the "needs improvement" category.[6]

"It's going to really be a nightmare for states," Cecil J. Picard, the superintendent of education in Louisiana, told *Education Week*. He estimated that as many as 80% of Louisiana schools would fail to meet the targets. Wyoming officials predicted more than half would fail. In North Carolina, a state that is frequently cited as an example of the progress that standards and testing can bring, one researcher calculated that only about 25% of all elementary schools would have met the new standard if it had been in place during the past three years. The Rhode Island Department of Education concluded that there was "virtually no school in the state over the past four years that would actually meet that kind of criteria." Had these standards been in effect while then-Governor Bush was running for president as an education leader, his home state of Texas would have been high on the list of failing states.

Even schools that score well initially will find it easy to slide into the "needs improvement" category, as the performance targets rise each year and significant numbers of students continue to struggle. An Hispanic special education student who is also living in a low-income home, for example, could be counted four times in a school's AYP calculations. If even one group is not meeting the AYP target, the whole school fails. These formulas invite failure by reducing the measure of school success to a single test score and using achievement gaps to label schools as "failures" without providing the resources or support needed to eliminate them.

"The bottom line," says Scott Marion, the director of assessment and accountability for the Wyoming education department, "is that we're going to end up identifying, by any stretch of the imagination, incredibly more schools than we believe the resources are there to serve."[7] The longer the list of "failing schools," the more diluted the limited resources that NCLB provides for school improvement efforts will be. As Paul Houston, executive director of the American Association of School Administrators, said: "What happens is you create a situation where there are so many schools failing that there is no support for them."[8]

Predictable Effects

It's fairly safe to predict the effects of this scheme, as it mirrors the standardized testing plague that swept states in the 1980s and 1990s. Test preparation will dominate classrooms, especially in struggling schools, and curriculum focus will narrow. Already some states are de-emphasizing social studies because history is not one of the federally mandated measures. Statistical "accountability" to bureaucratic monitors from above will take precedence over real accountability to students and their communities, and the huge resources poured into testing programs will do nothing to increase the capacity of schools or districts to improve their educational services. Attention and resources will be diverted from more promising school improvement strategies like smaller class size, creative curriculum reform, and collaborative professional development.

The culture of testing in schools will be strengthened in many ways. The legislation requires that 95% of all students participate in the mandated assessments. While this will challenge the common practice of boosting scores by excluding large numbers of students from the testing pool, it will also increase the pressure that has led to cheating scandals and to grade retention policies that push students out of school.

Monty Neill, executive director of the advocacy group FairTest, called the Bush plan "a major threat to assessment reform efforts that will particularly harm poor children....This unnecessary and unhelpful federal intrusion into the process of school reform will force more states to direct resources toward turning schools into test-prep programs. Yet research has demonstrated that the states which administer the most tests and attach the highest consequences to them tend to have the weakest education programs."[9]

Educators and researchers know that test scores alone provide a very incomplete picture of educational success or failure. Researchers at Arizona

State University who completed the largest study to date on the issue concluded that "rigorous testing that decides whether students graduate, teachers win bonuses and schools are shuttered, an approach already in place in more than half the nation, does little to improve achievement and may actually worsen academic performance and dropout rates."[10]

If the goal is educational accountability, standardized tests are of limited value. To assess the effectiveness of a particular school or education program requires multiple measures of academic performance, classroom observations, project- and portfolio-based assessments, a range of indicators from attendance and drop-out rates to graduation rates and post-graduation success, measures of teacher preparation and quality, and surveys of parent participation and satisfaction. In addition, legitimate assessment strategies would measure "opportunity to learn" inputs and equity of resources so that the victims of educational failure would not be the only ones to face "high stakes" consequences.

However, if the goal is a political one — to posture about "getting tough"; to drive multicultural curriculum reforms, equity concerns, and more pluralistic, bottom-up approaches to school reform out of the system; or to create a widespread general perception of school failure that can be used to justify "breaking up the public school monopoly"— then over-reliance on standardized testing may be just the thing.

The new law appropriates about $400 million each year for six years to develop new tests. Yet according to estimates reported in *Time* magazine: "Full implementation of the Bush plan, with high-quality tests in all 50 states, could cost up to $7 billion."[11] No wonder an executive at one of the major testing firms responded to Bush's proposals by declaring: "This almost reads like our business plan."[12]

The law explicitly mandates tests that attempt to measure progress in meeting state curriculum standards, as opposed to more commonly used general knowledge exams. At the time NCLB was passed, only nine states gave annual tests tied to their standards. One testing expert, Matthew Gandal, writing in a discussion paper for the conservative Thomas B. Fordham Foundation, estimated that the new law would require the creation of "well over 200 new state level tests" and force most states "to more than double the number of tests they are now giving."[13]

Such an explosion of testing will severely tax the capacity of the $700-million-a-year testing industry, currently dominated by four major firms — including McGraw-Hill, which has close Bush family ties.[14] As Gandal noted: "The normal cycle for creating a new assessment in just one state is 2-3 years. This now needs to happen in two subject areas in at least 34 states." Inevitably this will lead to poor quality tests, even by the industry's dubious "scientific" standards. Some states are already seeking to add a few "standards-based" questions to the off-the-shelf products they now use as a relatively cheap and easy, if unreliable, way to meet the new mandate.

While FairTest has pointed out that the language of the law does allow room for better, classroom-based assessments, the Department of Education's implementation regulations specifically emphasize standards-based testing. FairTest concludes: "States which seek to use high-quality, largely local assessments, particularly if they will use classroom-based assessments and portfolios, will have to struggle to use these assessments."

NCLB's testing mandates are exposing some of the contradictions inherent in the movement for educational standards. In the face of strong resistance to the imposition of a single national curriculum, the Bush plan calls for each state to define its own curriculum standards and proficiency levels. But NCLB's insistence on using these different standards to compare and label schools is already having bizarre effects. In the first year of the plan's operation, more than 8,600 schools nationwide were identified as "failing schools" (including 19 of the Department of Education's elite "blue-ribbon schools"). Michigan led the nation with more than 1,500 schools "needing improvement," partly because it has relatively difficult standards that include writing and science scores, instead of just the federally required reading and math, and because it set relatively higher state benchmarks. On the other hand, Arkansas and Wyoming, with comparatively lower standards, reported no failing schools.[15]

Accordingly, some states may be motivated by NCLB to dilute their standards or give "dumbed-down" tests to avoid penalties. Other states, like Vermont, Minnesota, and Iowa, have considered the drastic step of refusing federal education aid completely to avoid having to comply with NCLB. In

March 2003, *New York Times* education columnist Michael Winerip wrote: "As I travel the country, I find nearly universal contempt for this noble-sounding law signed last year by President Bush. Tom Horne, the Republican state education commissioner of Arizona, and Tom Watkins, the Democratic commissioner of Michigan, sound virtually alike in their criticisms."[16]

New Categories of Failure

One obvious question is: Why would the federal government adopt narrowly prescriptive strategies that will label huge numbers of schools as failures on the basis of test scores? This is a far cry from the historic tradition of federal intervention on behalf of racial equity, inclusion for students with disabilities, or equitable distribution of resources. It is also a major reversal of traditional Republican rhetoric about "local control" of schools, and reflects the larger political agendas at work.

Conservatives are not blind to the likelihood that this test-and-label strategy will lead to a large number of Fs on the new school report cards. For example, conservative critic Abigail Thernstrom, who sits on the Massachusetts State Board of Education, declared: "Getting all of our students to anything close to [proficient] is just not possible. It's not possible in Massachusetts or in any other state....Neither the state nor the districts really know how to turn schools — no less whole districts — around....I don't know how we're going to have effective intervention within the public school system as it's currently structured."[17]

"As it's currently structured" may be the key phrase. The new federal law was a compromise between right-wing and centrist political forces in Washington that linked an increase in federal funding for low-income schools to a narrow vision of school improvement based almost exclusively on state standards and tests. The funding increases are not enough to make dramatic improvements in conditions of teaching and learning, especially with economic recession feeding a new round of state and local cutbacks, and federal dollars still providing only about 7% of all school spending.

When this new federal testing scheme begins to document, as it inevitably will, an inability to reach its unrealistic and underfunded goals, it will provide new ammunition for a push to fundamentally "overhaul" and reshape public schooling. Conservatives will press their critique of public education as a "failed monopoly" that must be "reformed" through market measures and steps towards privatization. The U.S. Supreme Court's June 2002 voucher decision, which endorsed the transfer of state and federal dollars to private and religious schools, will accelerate this trend and give greater momentum to the rightward turn in federal education policy.

What's significant about the policies enshrined in NCLB is not their content — they are neither new nor promising as school improvement strategies — but their federal endorsement and political packaging. Essentially, NCLB codifies at the national level policies that have already wreaked havoc at the state level: punitive high stakes testing, the use of bureaucratic monitoring as the engine of school reform, and "accountability" schemes that set up schools to fail and then use that failure to justify disinvestment and privatization. It's George W. Bush's dubious "Texas miracle" gone national. (For a detailed discussion of Bush's Texas education record, see "The Educational Costs of Standardization" by Linda McNeil, p. 215.)

For Bush, this rightward turn in federal education policy has several sources. As a dubiously elected president who came into office with historically low levels of support among African Americans and a well-deserved anti-poor, pro-business image, education is an "outreach" issue. It's one of the few areas that allows a Republican president to posture, however disingenuously, as an ally of poor communities of color, particularly those that have been badly served by public education.

During his presidential campaign, Bush railed against the "soft bigotry of low expectations" to promote a school reform strategy based on punitive high-stakes testing. By focusing on the lowest performing schools and the racial dimensions of the achievement gap, he gave his education rhetoric an edge and an urgency it would have otherwise lacked. However, Bush has used this rhetoric to frame policy proposals that actually reinforce the "hard bigotry" of institutional racism in education, for example by promoting higher dropout rates and failing to redress persistent funding inequities. In fact, combining rhetorical concern for the victims of inequality with policies that perpetuate it may be an operative definition of Bush's "compassionate conservatism."

While inequality in test scores is one indicator of school performance, test scores also reflect other inequalities in resources and opportunities that persist in the larger society and in schools themselves. About 12% of white children live in poverty, while more than 30% of black and Latino children live in poverty. The richest 1% of all households have more wealth than the bottom 95%. Students in low-income schools, on average, have thousands of dollars less per year spent on their education than those in wealthier schools. About 14% of whites don't have health insurance, but more than 20% of blacks and 30% of Latinos have no health insurance. Unemployment rates for blacks and Latinos are nearly double what they are for whites.[18]

Yet we do not hear the Bush administration demanding an end to this kind of equality or proposing that other institutions which serve poor communities should be dismantled or replaced. Can you imagine the federal government saying all crime must be eliminated in 12 years or we'll privatize the police? All citizens must be healthy in 12 years or we will shut down the health-care system?

Ideological Aims

Instead of an appropriate educational strategy, the Bush administration's approach is part of a calculated political campaign to leave schools and children behind as the federal government retreats from the commitment to improving universal public schooling for all kids. For years a number of Bush's advisors have proposed just such uses of education standards and testing in the service of larger, ideologically driven policy objectives.

Nina Shokraii Rees, a former Heritage Foundation researcher and later an advisor to Vice President Dick Cheney, saw an opening to remake federal policy on a broad scale. "Standards, choice, and fiscal and legal autonomy in exchange for boosting student test scores increasingly are the watchwords of education reform in America," Rees has written. "The principle can be used in programs that apply to whole districts as well as entire states. Importantly, it lays the groundwork for a massive overhaul of education at the federal level in much the same way that welfare reform began."[19] Echoes of this strategy have been evident in the legislative debates over the Individuals with Disabilities Education Act, the National Assessment of Educational Progress, and Head Start as each came up for renewal.

Part of the effort to promote these goals involves a special appeal to parents, particularly in poor communities. In their voucher campaigns, conservatives learned how to repackage market "reforms" that privatize public services as a form of "parental choice." Similarly they are promoting NCLB as a "new federal law that gives parents in failing schools more choices," especially with regard to the school transfer and supplemental tutorial services provisions. Department of Education regulations issued in fall of 2002 require that students be given the right to transfer out of "failing" schools even where no other seats in the district exist. It declared that "local school officials may not use lack of space as a reason to deny students the option to transfer…so districts must either add capacity or provide other choices."[20]

This is a key political pressure point. The new law gives parents the right to take students and money out of struggling schools and to leave those schools behind. But it does not guarantee them any new places to go. In districts where some schools are labeled "failing" and some are not, the new law may actually force increased class sizes by transferring students without creating new capacity. NCLB does not invest in building new schools in failing districts. It does not make rich districts open their doors to students from poor districts. And it doesn't give poor parents any more control over school bureaucracies than food stamps give them over the supermarkets. The transfer regulations are a "supply-side" formula designed to manufacture a demand for alternative school placements, and ultimately to transfer funds and students to profit-making private school corporations through vouchers. Jeanne Allen, president of the conservative Center for Education Reform, predicted that the regulations would produce "constructive chaos….You've got awareness of options, frustration that there aren't enough options, and more awareness of failing schools," she said. "That combined with the fact that in some states we have completely new legislatures that are more reform-minded may spark them to look into capacity as an issue, and creating more supply."[21] While Bush's 2004 budget proposals signficantly underfunded key provisions of NCLB, he did propose $75 million for a new voucher plan and a $226 million program of tax credits to encourage students to leave "failing" public schools behind.[21]

The ideological bent of the new law is evident even in its relatively benign programs, like those promoting teacher quality and increased reading instruction. While attention to these two areas has generally drawn broad support, the specific provisions of the legislation echo problems in other areas.

The new law mandates that all teachers be fully certified and licensed in their teaching areas by June 2006. It also requires all paraprofessionals to have at least two years of college beyond high school or pass a "rigorous" local/state exam. New hires must meet these provisions immediately, while existing staff have several years to comply. As with the "adequate yearly progress" goals, however, there is near universal acknowledgement that these goals cannot be met, particularly given current levels of underfunding.

Most states already have similar teacher licensing requirements on the books, but can't find enough qualified candidates due to low pay scales, rising enrollments, and other aspects of the well-documented teacher shortage. Finding fully qualified teachers is especially difficult in rural and poor areas, and in some subjects, like math and science.

Even reading instruction is ideologically framed in NCLB. The new law puts more than $1 billion into expanded reading, literacy, and library programs designed to help every student read proficiently by third grade. These programs will support needed professional development for teachers and provide materials to promote essential literacy skills. But the effort is linked to dubious language restricting funding to "scientifically based reading programs," which may be narrowly interpreted to endorse only certain phonics-based approaches or commercial reading packages. (See "Learning to Read "Scientifically"" by Gerald Coles, p. 184.)

Also damaging is the legislation's wholesale attack on federal bilingual education programs, which the new law recasts in the spirit, if not the name, of "English only" intolerance. (See "Bush's Bad Idea for Bilingual Education" by Stephen Krashen, p. 192.) The new bill transforms the Bilingual Education Act into the "English Language Acquisition Act." It will assess schools on the basis of the number of students reclassified as fluent in English each year, and severely discourages native-language instruction. It also promotes a number of inappropriate educational practices for English language learners, including forcing them to take content area exams in languages they do not yet understand.

The Act is littered with assorted right-wing nuggets, including a provision preventing districts from banning the Boy Scouts from using school facilities because of their anti-gay policies, a requirement that districts accepting federal dollars open their doors to military recruiters, and the promotion of "constitutionally protected" school prayer.

NCLB is the culmination of a very active conservative mobilization around schools over the past several decades. It is also part of a larger political agenda that seeks to erode and privatize the public sector. The federal government provides only 7% of school funding, but today the Bush administration is using federal regulation to drive school policy in conservative directions at the state, district, and school levels.

What's changed is not the federal commitment to "leave no child behind," but the ideological commitment of some politicians to reform public education out of existence through a strategy of "test and burn." As researcher Gerald Bracey has put it, NCLB "is a weapon of mass destruction, and its target is the public schools."

---

[1] See 1996 and 2000 National Platforms of the Republican Party.

[2] "Senate Approves a Bill to Expand the Federal Role in Public Education," Diana Jean Schemo, *New York Times*, Dec. 19, 2001.

[3] American Federation of Teachers briefing papers on 2001 renewal of the Elementary and Secondary Education Act.

[4] See provisions of NCLB legislation, available from U.S. Department of Education at www.ed.gov/offices/OESE/asst.html.

[5] "Critics Say Money for Schools Falls Short of Promises," Diana Jean Schemo, *New York Times*, February 5, 2003; and "On the Block," *Education Week*, March 5, 2003. Also Bob Chase, NEA President, Congressional testimony before House Committee on Education and the Workforce, June 10, 1999.

[6] "Inadequate Yearly Gains Are Predicted," Lynn Olsen, *Education Week*, April 3, 2002.

[7] See Olsen, *Education Week*, April 3, 2002, for individual state projections.

[8] "States Worry New Law Sets Schools Up to Fail," Michael A. Fletcher, *Washington Post*, January 2, 2003.

[9] *FairTest Examiner*, Winter 2000-2001.

[10] "More Schools Rely on Tests, But Study Raises Doubts," Greg Winter, *New York Times*, December 28, 2002.

[11] "Bush Education Bill One Step Closer to Law," Andrew Goldstein, *Time* magazine, Dec. 14, 2001.

[12] "Reading Between the Lines," Stephen Metcalf, *The Nation*, Jan. 28, 2002.

[13] "Multiple Choices: How Will States Fill in the Blanks in Their Testing Systems?" Matthew Gandal, Thomas B. Fordham Foundation, February 2002.

[14] See "Reading Between the Lines," Stephen Metcalf, *The Nation*, Jan. 28 2002.

[15] See "Schools May Lower Standards to Stay Off Federal Watch List," Adam Emerson, *Lansing State Journal*, Oct. 24, 2002; Schemo, *New York Times*, Nov. 27, 2002; and "School 'Excellence' Thrown a Grading Curve," Karen Thomas and Anthony DeBarros, *USA Today*, Aug. 5, 2002.

[16] "A Pervasive Dismay on a Bush School Law," Michael Winerip, *New York Times*, March 19, 2003.

[17] Abigail Thernstrom, Comments, in "No Child Left Behind: What Will It Take," Thomas B. Fordham Foundation, Feb. 2002.

[18] See Current Population Survey of the Bureau of Labor Statistics and Bureau of Census (http://ferret.bls.census.gov/macro/032002/pov/new01_003.htm); Edward N. Wolff, "Recent Trends in Wealth Ownership," New York University, December 1998; U.S. Census Bureau, Health Insurance Coverage 2001; Bureau of Labor Statistics, Employment Situation Summary, April 2003.

[19] Nina Shokraii Rees, "Improving Education for Every American Child," The Heritage Foundation, Feb. 5, 2001.

[20] "Escape Hatch for Poor Students Is Identified," Associated Press, Washington, DC, Dec. 9, 2002.

[21] "New Federal Rule Tightens Demands on Failing Schools," Diana Jean Schemo, *New York Times*, Nov. 27, 2002.

[22] "Itemizing the Budget," Erik W. Robelen, *Education Week*, March 5, 2003.

PART 4

Standards and Testing

The Educational Costs of Standardization

Linda McNeil

The following examines how high-stakes testing has affected teaching and learning in Houston, the fifth-largest public school system in the United States.

Texas is the second largest state, and its educational policies help set the national agenda. Furthermore Texas has often been cited, particularly by backers of President George W. Bush, as a positive example of how high-stakes testing can act as a catalyst of education reform. Under the Texas Assessment of Academic Skills (TAAS) program, students cannot graduate if they fail the TAAS exams. Further, a principal's pay is tied to the school's performance on TAAS.

This article provides an overview of how an emphasis on high-stakes testing affects teaching and learning in the classroom — particularly in schools with large percentages of African-American and Latino students, who have traditionally scored lower on standardized tests than white students in more affluent areas.

The article is condensed from the final chapter of Linda McNeil's book Contradictions of School Reform: The Educational Costs of Standardized Testing *(Routledge, 2000). The book is based McNeil's research at a set of magnet schools. She visited the schools prior to the implementation of centralized accountability measures and then again after the reforms were imposed, documenting the effects on classroom practice.*

> The town's head librarian loved to encourage the children of his small, isolated farming community to read. He frequently went to the local school to read to the children. Most recently, he had been reading to a class of "at-risk" eighth-graders — students who had been held back two or more years in school. They loved his reading and his choices of books. He reports feeling very frustrated: The department chair has told him not to come any more to read to the students — they are too busy preparing for their TAAS test.
>
> — *unsolicited correspondence*

Three in a row? No, No, No!
[Three answers "b" in a row? No, No, No!]
— *one of several cheers taught to students at their daily*
pep rallies on test-taking strategies for the TAAS test.

In many urban schools, particularly those whose students are predominantly poor and minority, the TAAS system of testing reduces both the quality of what is taught and the quantity of what is taught. Because the principal's pay (and job contract) and the school's reputation depend on the school's TAAS scores, in those schools where students have traditionally not tested well on standardized tests the regular curriculum in these subjects is frequently set aside, so that students can prepare for the test.

The TAAS tests include reading skills, writing, and math. Common sense would suggest that if a teacher followed a traditional curriculum, even using the state's textbook, the teaching of regular lessons would be preparation for success on the test. If students were able to do math problems, explain math concepts, and apply math skills in the regular sequence of lessons, then it should follow that they would do well on the test.

The tests, however, are not necessarily consistent with traditional teaching and learning. First, they are multiple-choice: They call for selecting among given answers. Second, they call for accurately darkening a circle beside the selected answer, without making stray marks on the paper.

In minority schools, in the urban school district where the magnet schools are located, and in many schools across the state, substantial class time is spent practicing bubbling in answers and learning to recognize "distractor" (obviously incorrect) answers. Students are drilled on such strategies as the one in the pep rally cheer quoted above: If you see you have answered "b" three times in a row, you know ("no, no, no") that at least one of those answers is likely to be wrong, because the maker of a test would not be likely to construct three questions in a row with the same answer-indicator. (The basis for such advice comes from the publishers of test-prep materials, many of whom send consultants into schools — for a substantial price — to help plan pep rallies, to "train" teachers to use the TAAS-prep kits, and to ease the substitution of their TAAS-prep materials for the curriculum in classrooms where teachers stubbornly resist.)

Teachers, even those who know their subjects and their students well, have much less latitude when their principals purchase test-prep materials to be used in lieu of the regular curriculum.

One teacher, a graduate of an Ivy League college with a master's degree from another select school, had spent considerable time and money assembling a rich collection of historical and literary works of importance in Latino culture. She had sought titles especially related to the American Southwest for her classes at a Latino high school. Her building of a classroom resource collection was extremely important, given the school's lack of a library and its lean instructional budget. Her students responded to her initiative with a real enthusiasm to study and learn.

She was dismayed to see, upon returning one day from lunch, that the books for her week's lessons had been set aside. In the center of her desk was a stack of test-prep booklets with a teacher's guide and a note saying "use these instead of your regular curriculum until after the TAAS." The TAAS test date was three months away.

(The prep materials bore the logo "Guerrilla TAAS," as in making war on the TAAS test; the booklet covers were military-camouflage colors; the Guerrilla TAAS consultants came to the school in camouflage gear to do a TAAS pep rally for the students and faculty.)

This teacher reported that her principal, a person dedicated to these students and to helping them pass the TAAS in order to graduate, had spent almost $20,000, virtually the entire instructional budget for the year, on these materials. The cost was merely one problem. Inside the booklets for "reading" were single-page activities, with brief reading selections followed by TAAS-type answer choices. These students, who had been analyzing the poetry of Gary Soto and exploring the generational themes in Rudolfo Anaya's novel *Bless Me Última,* had to set aside this intellectual work to spend more than half of every class period working through the "Guerrilla TAAS" booklet.

Teachers in urban schools say that to raise questions about the TAAS and about artificial test prep is characterized as being against minority students' chances to get high test scores. Or it is portrayed as "not being a team player." The test scores generated by centralized, standardized tests like the

TAAS, and by the test-prep materials which prepare students for those tests, are not reliable indicators of learning. It is here where the effects on low-performing students, particularly minority students, begin to skew the possibilities for their access to a richer education.

At this school and other minority high schools where TAAS prep replaced the curriculum, teachers reported that even though many more students were passing TAAS "reading," few of their students were actually readers. Few of them could use reading for assignments in literature, science, or history classes; few of them chose to read; few of them could make meaning of literature or connect writing and discussing to reading. In schools where TAAS reading scores were going up, there was little or no will to address this gap. In fact, the rise in scores was used to justify even more TAAS prep, even more pep rallies, even more substituting of test-based programs for the regular curriculum.

TAAS and Reading

Advocates of TAAS might argue that passing the reading skills section of TAAS is better than not being able to read at all. However, there is first of all no evidence that these students cannot "read at all." Second, teachers are reporting that the kind of test prep frequently done to raise test scores may actually hamper students' ability to learn to read for meaning outside the test setting. In fact, students report that in the drills on the TAAS reading section, they frequently mark answers without reading the sample of text. They merely match key words in an answer choice with key words in the text. The definition of "reading" as captured on the test ignores a broad and sophisticated research base on the teaching of reading and on children's development as language learners. When teachers are able to draw on this professional knowledge base, it does not lead them to testing formats like TAAS for help with their children's reading.

Elementary teachers have expressed the concern that extensive prep for the reading section of TAAS actually undermines children's ability to read sustained passages. The prep materials in reading, again purchased by principals eager to protect their performance contract or perhaps to help children pass the test, feature brief passages. After reading a passage, students are to answer practice questions ("Which of the following is the main idea?" "Which of the following would not make a good title for this paragraph?" "Which of the following was described as '...'?"). The selected passage is not something they will see again; it is not even linked to the subsequent practice passage.

Students who practice these reading exercises day after day for months (many principals have had teachers begin TAAS prep in September and have not let them revert to the "regular" curriculum until after the TAAS test in March) show a decreased ability to read longer works. A sixth-grade teacher who had selected a fourth-grade Newbery Award book for her class, thinking all the students could read and understand it, found that after reading for a few minutes the students stopped. They were accustomed to reading very brief, disjointed passages; they had difficulty carrying over information from the first chapter to a later one. Discussions with other upper-elementary and middle-school teachers confirmed that students accustomed to TAAS prep, rather than literature, may be internalizing the format of reading skills tests, but not the habits needed to read for meaning.

TAAS and Writing

The teaching of "writing," also a subject tested by TAAS, has been reduced in many schools to daily practice of the essay form being tested that year. A teacher who is African-American and always alert to good educational opportunities for her sons was very pleased that her second son would be able to have the same excellent fourth-grade teacher under whom her oldest son had thrived. She was not prepared for the TAAS-based transformation of the fourth grade in the intervening years. She said that although the principal and teacher remained the same, the entire fourth-grade curriculum had been replaced by TAAS prep. Writing had become daily practice in "the persuasive essay," consisting of five five-sentence paragraphs, a form which clearly qualifies as "school knowledge" in the most limited sense. What students had to say in these essays was of virtually no importance; conforming to the form was the requirement, and the students practiced every day. This mother knew that in Anglo schools, while there was some abuse of teaching through TAAS prep, most of the children were nevertheless learning to tailor their writing to their subjects, to write in different voices and formats for different audiences, and to write in order to stretch their vocabularies.

A principal of a middle- to upper-middle-class elementary school explained to an audience at a school reform conference that her teachers had heard that teachers at other schools were having their students practice the five-paragraph essay every day. They were concerned to hear that it had become the only form of writing done that year in their school. This principal, under much less pressure to contrive passing rates for her students on the TAAS, worked with her teachers to include the TAAS as one of many "audiences" when they teach students to develop voice and a sense of audience in their writing.

Similarly, several high school teachers told of discussions they'd had with their students about the TAAS writing exam. After learning more about TAAS, the students had decided to think of the audience for their TAAS writing test as "bureaucrats sitting in little offices, waiting to count sentences and paragraphs." These teachers, usually in high-performing schools and therefore not required to do TAAS prep, are in a similar way trying to make the test the subject of critical inquiry. This is not typical in low-performing schools where teachers and principals are using pep rallies and incentive prizes to get students to "buy in" to these forms of evaluation.

The younger children growing up with TAAS prep may not always know (unless they compare with friends in private schools or have an older sibling whose learning was more substantive) how TAAS-prep reading and writing differ from good instruction. Older children, however, are not without skepticism that this system of testing is altering what they and their teachers jointly regard as important learning. Elaine, an eighth grader, knows firsthand the artificiality of "TAAS writing." In a previous grade, she won the citywide short-story writing award conferred by the local chapter of the National Council of Teachers of English. The next spring she received notice that she failed to pass the eighth-grade writing section of the TAAS because she "failed to provide sufficient supporting detail." Elaine and her teacher both know that she is known in her school as a writer. What distinguishes her writing is its rich detail. They could speculate that perhaps the scanning of her TAAS writing missed, by its haste or its rigid format, the elaborative and "supporting" detail that characterizes her writing. The TAAS, and not the quality of her writing nor her English teachers' judgment, lost credibility for her and for her parents as an indicator of her writing skills.

An eighth-grade class in a predominantly poor, Latino middle school demonstrated pointedly the intellectual subtraction resulting from the TAAS system of testing when the emphasis is on raising minority scores. In mid-September, a group of community visitors stepped into Mr. Sanchez's class just as he was covering the blackboard with rules for semicolon usage. Using semicolons in writing seemed a useful and worthy lesson for eighth graders working on their writing, so at first the visitors watched without comment. While the students were copying the semicolon rules, the teacher explained: "We are having to do grammar until after the TAAS. I'm so excited — this year we have a whole nine weeks after the TAAS to do eighth-grade English. I always do Shakespeare with my students. And I have many stories that they love to read. Last year we didn't have much time, but this year I will have a whole nine weeks." The visitors were just then realizing the import of his words: He was to do TAAS prep from September until March, and then "teach eighth-grade English" only in the remaining nine weeks. And the teacher was made to feel grateful for all nine of those weeks. He explained that it was the will of the principal that they get the scores up and that everyone in the school was feeling the pressure. He knew that by focusing on TAAS alone, his students would be getting far less than the eighth-grade curriculum studied by students in schools where the student demographics (middle class, predominantly white) would carry the scores, and they would be learning even less than his own students in the years before TAAS.

TAAS and Math

Under the TAAS-prep system, the teaching of mathematics is also highly truncated. TAAS tests math by having students choose among four or five possible answers. They are not asked to explain their answers, so if students have alternative ways of working a problem, their reasoning is not made visible on the test. Nor are their reasons for selecting "correct" answers. Being able to conceptualize in mathematics, being able to envision a solution and select among possible approaches, being able to articulate the reasoning behind the answer — none of these is tested by TAAS. Instead TAAS tests computational accuracy and familiarity with basic operations.

The reductive mathematics on the test is not adequate preparation for courses in more advanced mathematics. The TAAS-prep booklets, which emphasize test-taking strategies over mathematical reasoning, again create a gap between the content learned by poor and minority students in schools investing in TAAS-prep kits and the students in well-provisioned schools. In these latter schools, principals assume students will pass because of their family background and their having attended "good" schools in lower grades. They therefore support the teaching of the regular academic curriculum without substantial risk that to do so might lower the TAAS scores.

Trying to Circumvent TAAS

If a teacher wanted to avoid TAAS prep and focus on the students and the curriculum, then it would seem that the answer would be to teach a subject not yet tested by TAAS. At the Pathfinder school, Ms. Bartlett had claimed a space for teaching complex biology topics by shifting some of her teaching out from under the controls of the proficiency system (the predecessor of TAAS). She created elective courses and independent study seminars around such units of study as ecology and habitats (enabling her to integrate concepts and topics that were fragmented and sequenced separately under the proficiencies). She taught a biochemistry elective (using knowledge she gained though a mentorship program with a medical school and crossing traditional subject boundaries) and, in some semesters, marine biology.

Under the TAAS system of testing, teachers reported that there were fewer and fewer venues in which they could do authentic teaching, even when officially only three subjects — math, reading, and writing — were tested. In poor and minority schools, especially, teaching untested subjects such as art, science, or social studies was not exempt from the pressures of TAAS prep. An art teacher with a reputation for engaging her Latino students in serious studio work, and for getting students excited about being in school, was required to suspend the teaching of art in order to drill her students daily in TAAS grammar. By the time the grammar drills were completed, there was no time to set up for art projects.

Her students were doubly losing: Their treatment of grammar was artificial, aimed at correctness within the multiple-choice format of the test, rather than at fluency in their own writing; and they were denied an opportunity to develop their sense of color and design in art.

A history teacher in an under-resourced Latino high school worked with his colleagues to create a history curriculum that would maintain authentic content and yet incorporate some of the skills their students would need to do well on the TAAS. They included the writing of essays on historical topics and gave attention to reading skills. They had at first been given permission to create this curriculum on their own but later were told that they needed to set aside the teaching of history entirely in order to "cooperate with the rest of the faculty" in getting students to pass the TAAS. This history teacher's assignment was to drill his students every day on math, a subject outside his field of expertise.

Science teachers who spent a year in the Rice University Center for Education Model Science Lab (located in an urban middle school) — updating their science knowledge and upgrading their capacity for laboratory-based teaching — entered the program with the consent of their principals to implement what they had learned when they returned to their schools. Many of these teachers discovered, on returning to their home schools, that they were required, for as much as two to four months of the school year, to suspend the teaching of science in order to drill students on TAAS math. Again, the students in these urban schools were doubly penalized, first for losing out on the science that their peers in suburban schools were learning, second by having to spend extra periods on low-level, disjointed math drills — math divorced from both the applications and conceptual understandings they will need if they are to hold their own later in upper-level math classes with middle-class students. It is unlikely that the middle-class students were doing "math" from commercial test-prep booklets, rather than from math books, manipulatives, calculators, computers, and peer study groups. The TAAS, then, lowered the quality and quantity of even subjects not being tested in those schools where students had traditionally not tested well, the students who are poor and the minority.

Race, Testing, and the Miner's Canary

Lani Guinier

The following is condensed from a speech at the annual convention of the Wisconsin Education Association Council in 2001.

I want to talk this morning about the subject of a book I have co-authored called *Who's Qualified?* What does it mean to be qualified? And within that, how do we measure success in our democracy?

Surveys have reported that 75% of college students say that one of the major things they hoped to get out of college was the opportunity to make money. To be completely truthful, 60% say they want to make money and 15% say they want to make a hell of a lot of money. So we find that winning and losing is depending on how much money people make — and that becomes the value of success. We don't really talk about other values that measure the worth of a democratic society.

I'd like to focus on these other values, and do so by looking at the so-called losers of society — because it is the losers who have the most to tell us about what is happening in the larger society. And the metaphor that I use for this paradigm shift is the miner's canary.

The miners used to take the canary into the mines to alert them when the atmosphere was too toxic for the miners. And the play that I am making is that the experience of those who have been left out — people of color, women, poor people, the disabled, gays and lesbians — is the experience of the canary. If we trap their experience, we can discover something about the atmosphere in the mine.

Unfortunately, our society takes the view that we don't need to worry about the losers; we just feel sorry for them. We pathologize the canary, as if the canary's distress is caused by the canary. And then the solution is to fix the canary — to outfit the canary with a little pint-size gas mask so it can endure the toxic atmosphere.

But we need to heed the signal of the canary and fix the atmosphere in the mines. Taking from the margins, we need to rethink the whole.

Rethinking One's Teaching

Let me give you a relatively easy example. Uri Treisman taught calculus at the University of California-Berkeley and he noticed that his African-American calculus students were not doing as well as his Chinese-American calculus students, and he wanted to know why. He went to his colleagues and asked if they noticed anything similar and they said they [the African-American students] were not prepared, they came from single-parent families, and they were not studying. He decided not to accept the stereotypes of his colleagues without at least testing them and so he hired some researchers to follow around the African-American and Chinese-American students. It turned out that his colleagues were wrong — the African-American students were actually studying harder than the Chinese-American students, if you count the time sitting in your dorm room with a calculus book open in front of you as studying. But the way the Chinese-American students were studying was to talk about calculus with one another, in their rooms, over lunch, on their way to the study hall, in and out of the library.

It turned out that the practice of engaging one's peers as a way of learning a conceptually difficult task was crucial to the mastery of calculus. It was the process of learning to ask questions when you don't know the answer. The Chinese-American students were developing that skill and the African-American students were not.

So Uri Treisman decided he was going to fix the canary. He took from what he'd observed the Chinese-American students doing and he set up a peer workshop where he gave the black students problems to solve, arranged the students around the table, served food — because the researchers had seen the Chinese-American students studying problems over lunch, which seemed to create an informal atmosphere — and he brought recent past learners, people who had taken calculus and done well, to the workshops so that they would be available to answer questions. And he encouraged students to work through the problems collaboratively and to ask questions.

Within the first semester of the peer workshop, the African-American students' low scores in calculus went up, and by the second semester they were among the highest scoring calculus students in the class.

You might say he fixed the canary — except that at that moment, he had an epiphany. He realized the problem is not in the African-American calculus students, the problem was in the way he, Uri Treisman, the sage on the stage, was teaching calculus to all of his students. He was using the "chalk and talk" method, and his students were sitting there half-asleep, listening. He was not incorporating the insight of the Chinese-American students in his classroom: that the best way to master concepts is through a process in which students have to learn to ask questions when they do not know the answers and to be intellectually engaged with their peers. And he introduced those concepts into his class.

Treisman took from the margins to rethink the whole, which suggests that we can learn if we study the experiences of those we dismiss as the losers. Because they have insight into ways in which we are conducting ourselves that affect everyone but visibly converge first around those who are the canaries.

Admissions Requirements

What if we were to rethink our assumptions in the context of standardized tests and admissions requirements? What would we find?

I have studied the LSAT quite extensively, and have also looked at the SAT. How well you do on the SAT is seen as a measure of qualifications, a measure of success, a measure of merit. What does that say about the assumptions that we hold in terms of what an educated person is supposed to be able to do?

Let's look at the findings of a study at the University of Michigan Law School, where they tried to see if there was a relationship between the incoming credentials of the law students and what the students actually did as lawyers once they had graduated. They studied all the classes of University of Michigan since 1970 and looked at three measures of success: financial satisfaction, career satisfaction, and leadership in the community. (They picked those three measures because that's part of the law school's mission statement.) They found there was no relationship between entry-level credentials and income as an attorney. Basically everyone who went to University of Michigan Law School made a decent living.

They also found that those with higher entry-level credentials and the highest LSATs were the least likely to enjoy their career or employment. The theory is that the test-taking, and the socializing effect of doing well on tests, creates people who think there's only one right answer, that the objective is to find the right answer, that the right answer is in the mind of the test drafter. But this process undermines creativity and it undermines problem-solving ability, because the only problem you were trying to solve is how the mind works of the person writing the question, rather than looking at the various ways of solving the problem presented.

The most interesting finding is the relationship between high incoming credentials and leadership: Those with the highest LSAT and entry-level credentials were the least likely to become leaders in their community. The students most likely to become leaders in their community, other than those who had been out of school the longest, were the black and Latino students who had been admitted under affirmative action, in part because those students who had been admitted under affirmative action were admitted based on their leadership skills and their leadership commitment. So part of what this study shows is that when you admit for a particular quality, you may find people who demonstrate that quality over time.

When you admit for the quality of doing well on tests, that quality doesn't have a particularly useful relationship to the real world. What the tests actually test is quick, strategic guesses with less than perfect information. That can be a useful power. When you don't have good information and you have to make an executive decision quickly, you often have to guess.

However, as a teacher myself, I am much more concerned with training people how to solve problems when time is not of the essence, how to create a situation in which they can get more time to get more information, because the more information you have, the better problem-solver you will be. So, do research.

Many of my colleagues have great faith in the LSAT, number one because they did very well on it, and number two because we have almost a religious attitude toward testing. It's what I call the testocracy.

It turns out that many students of color do not do as well on the SAT or the LSAT. Same thing with women, although the variation is not as strong. But it is also true in terms of class. Within each race and ethnic group, as your parental income goes up, so do your SAT scores. In fact, the SAT correlates more strongly with your parent's socioeconomic status than with your first year college grades. Indeed, it correlates strongly with your grandparents' socioeconomic status. It becomes a test of how much money your family has, how many resources your family has to prepare you to take this test.

What has happened is that the testocracy has been manipulated to reproduce and credentialize the social hierarchy. We haven't really interrogated why we value test smarts when they don't actually predict workplace smarts, or, what is most important to me, leadership smarts. Who is going to play a contributing role in a multiracial democracy to help all of our society solve complex problems?

Ten Percent Plan

A group of black and Latino professors, activists, and legislators were concerned that if there were no affirmative action at the University of Texas — which had been sued in the 1950s because it deliberately excluded blacks and Mexicans —the school would be resegregated. They started looking at the evidence that the LSAT actually does not correlate with first-year law school grades, and that the SAT is not a strong predictor of first-year college grades. There is a relationship but it is a modest relationship.

They looked at what does predict first-year grades, and it turns out that those who do well in school in one domain do well in another; so the best predictor of success, at least better than the standardized aptitude tests, is grades. They then introduced the idea of the ten percent plan, which means that anyone in the top 10% of their graduating high school class, anywhere in Texas, would be automatically eligible to attend the University of Texas-Austin or Texas A&M University. They put this bill before the legislature and it passed by one vote.

That one vote came from a white Republican legislator who represented a West Texas constituency. None of his constituents had been going on to Texas A&M or the University of Texas-Austin, because he represented a poor and working-class white constituency and they had not been doing well on the SAT either. Of the 1,500 high schools in Texas, 150 schools — primarily suburban public schools and independent schools around Dallas, Austin, and Houston — were providing 75% of the first-year freshman placement at the University of Texas-Austin. Once that information became obvious to this legislator, he supported the bill.

Texas now admits its class using many different vehicles, but particularly the ten percent plan. The freshman class at the University of Texas has been able to retain the same number of black students as when they were using affirmative action, and has a higher number of Latino students and white working-class students. By the way, the GPA of the freshmen who were admitted under the ten percent plan is higher across racial groups than the GPA of the freshmen who were admitted using the SAT.

I am not here pushing for the ten percent plan. That may work in Texas because of its demographics. But I am suggesting that it is very important that we begin a much larger conversation about what it means to be qualified, and that we don't rely on a test or any of the uniform and single devices to determine who is qualified to do complex tasks in a multiracial democracy.

This is a challenge about problem-solving. This is a challenge about linking the values and function of education to the values and function of democracy. If we don't have an educated citizenry, we don't have a democracy. If we don't have people who have learned how to think critically, to ask questions when they don't know the answer, we don't have a functioning democracy. If we don't have people who are committed to becoming leaders in their community, we don't have a functioning democracy.

To me, the issue of qualification and the issue of the miner's canary is really an issue of how we are going to not only survive, but also thrive, in a multiracial democracy.

Standards and Multiculturalism

Bill Bigelow

Proponents of "higher standards" and more testing promise raised expectations for all students and increased "accountability." In practice, their reforms are hostile to good teaching and pose a special threat to multiculturalism.

Oregon, where I teach, has joined the national testing craze. Recently the Oregon Department of Education field tested its first-ever statewide social studies assessments. Many teachers were dismayed to discover that the tests were a multiple-choice maze that lurched about helter-skelter, seeking answers on World War I, constitutional amendments, global climate, rivers in India, hypothetical population projections, Supreme Court decisions, and economic terminology. Evidently, for many standards-makers in Oregon and elsewhere, social studies knowledge is little more than acquiring piles of disconnected facts about the world.

If it prevails, this brand of standardization will undermine hard-fought efforts to move toward a multicultural curriculum — one that describes and attempts to explain the world as it really exists; that speaks to the diversity of our society and our students; and aims not only to teach important facts, but to develop citizens who can make the world safer and more just.

In a sense, the entire effort to create fixed standards violates the very essence of multiculturalism. Multiculturalism is, in the words of Harvard professor Henry Louis Gates Jr., a "conversation among different voices," to discover perspectives that have been silenced in traditional scholastic narratives. Multiculturalism attempts to uncover "the histories and experiences of people who have been left out of the curriculum," as anti-racist educator Enid Lee emphasizes. Because multiculturalism is an undertaking that requires new scholarship and constant discussion, it necessarily is ongoing. Yet as researcher Harold Berlak has written, "standardization and centralization of curriculum testing is an effort to put an end to a cacophony of voices on what constitutes truth, knowledge, and learning and what the young should be taught. It insists upon one set of answers." Curriculum standardization is, as Berlak indicates, a way to silence dissident voices, "a way to manufacture consent and cohesion."

Creating official, government-approved social studies standards is bound to be controversial, whether at the national or state level. Thus, according to the *Portland Oregonian*, state education officials "tried to stake a neutral ground," in order to win approval for their version of social reality. "We have tried so hard to go right down the middle between what teachers want, what parents want, and what the [Republican-dominated] Legislature wants," according to Dawn Billings, a Department of Education curriculum coordinator. Not surprisingly, this attempt to be "neutral" and inoffensive means that the standards lack a critical sensibility — or an emphasis on conflict and diversity of interpretation — and instead tend towards a conservative, "Father Knows Best" portrait of history and society. For example, one typical tenth-grade benchmark calls for students to "understand how the Constitution can be a vehicle for change and for resolving issues as well as a device for preserving values and principles of society."

Is this the only way students should understand the Constitution? Is this how, say, Frederick Douglass or the Seminole leader Osceola would have seen it? Shouldn't students also understand how the Constitution can be (and has been) a vehicle for preserving class and race stratification and for maintaining the privileges of dominant social groups? For example, in the 1857 *Dred Scott* case, the Supreme Court held that a slave could not sue for his freedom because he was property, not a human being. Chief Justice Roger Taney declared that no black person in the United States had "any rights which the white man is bound to respect." The Abolitionist William Lloyd Garrison called the Constitution an "agreement with Hell" for its support of slavery. And in 1896 the Supreme Court ruled in *Plessy v. Ferguson* that segregation — "separate but equal" — did not violate the Fourteenth Amendment.

Constitutional Realities

Almost 40% of the men who wrote the Constitution owned slaves, including George Washington and James Madison. In my U.S. history classes we look at the adoption of the Constitution from the standpoint of poor white farmers, enslaved African Americans, unemployed workers in urban areas, and other groups. Students create their own Constitution in a mock assembly, and then compare their document to the actual Constitution. They discover, for example, that the Constitution does not include the word "slave," but instead refers euphemistically to enslaved African Americans, as in Article 4, Section 2: "No person held to service or labor in one state, under the laws thereof, escaping into another, shall in consequence of any law or regulation therein, be discharged from such service or labor, but shall be delivered up on claim of the party to whom such service or labor may be due." It's a vicious clause, that sits uncomfortably alongside the "preserving values and principles" rhetoric of Oregon's standards.

It is probably inevitable that school curricula will reflect the contradictions between a society's myths and realities. But while a critical multicultural approach attempts to examine these contradictions, standardization tends to paper them over. For example, another benchmark — "Explain how laws are developed and applied to provide order, set limits, protect basic rights, and promote the common good" — similarly fails the multicultural test. Whose order, whose basic rights, are protected by laws? Are all social groups included equally in the term "common good"? Between 1862 and 1890, laws in the United States gave 180 million acres (an area the size of Texas and Oklahoma) to privately owned railroad companies, but gave virtually no land to African Americans freed from slavery in the South. Viewing the Constitution and other U.S. laws through a multicultural lens would add texture and depth to the facile one-sidedness of Oregon's "neutral" standards.

Indeed the "R" word — racism — is not mentioned once in any of the seven 11th-grade field tests used in 1998 nor in the social studies standards adopted that year by the state board of education. Even if the only yardstick were strict historical accuracy this would be a bizarre omission: The state of Oregon was launched as a whites-only territory by the Oregon Donation Act and in racist wars of dispossession waged against indigenous peoples; the first constitution outlawed slavery but also forbade blacks from living in the state, a prohibition that remained on the books until 1926. Perhaps state education officials are concerned that introducing the concept of racism to students could call into question the essentially harmonious world of "change, and continuity over time" that underpins the standards project. Whatever the reason, there is no way that students can make sense of the world today without the idea of racism in their conceptual knapsack. If a key goal of multiculturalism is to account for how the past helped shape the present, and an important part of the present is social inequality, then Oregon's standards and tests earn a failing grade.

Despite the publication of state social studies standards and benchmarks, teachers and parents don't really know what students are expected to learn until they see the tests, which were developed by an out-of-state assessment corporation, MetriTech. As Prof. Wade W. Nelson pointed out in a delightfully frank 1998 article in *Phi Delta Kappan*, "The Naked Truth about School Reform in Minnesota" (that might as well have been written about Oregon):

> The content of the standards is found only in the tests used to assess them. Access to the tests themselves is carefully controlled, making it difficult to get a handle on what these standards are. It seems ironic to me that basic standards — that which every student is expected to know or be able to do — are revealed only in tests accessible only to test-makers and administrators. This design avoids much of the debate about what these standards ought to be....

— a debate which is essential to the ongoing struggle for a multicultural curriculum.

Discrete Facts

It's when you look directly at the tests that their limitations and negative implications for multiculturalism become most clear. Test questions inevitably focus on discrete facts, but cannot address the deeper, multifaceted meaning of facts. For example, in the field tests Oregon piloted, one question asked which constitutional amendment gave women the right to vote. Students could know virtually nothing about the long struggle for women's rights and get this question right. On the other hand, they could know lots about the feminist movement and not recall that it was the

Nineteenth and not the Sixteenth, Seventeenth, or Eighteenth Amendment (the other test choices) that gave women the right to vote.

Because there is no way to predict precisely which facts will be sought on the state tests, teachers will feel pressured to turn courses into a "memory Olympics"; teachers simply cannot afford to spend time probing beneath the headlines of history. One year my students at Franklin High School in Portland performed a role play on the 1848 Seneca Falls, New York women's rights conference, the first formal U.S. gathering to demand greater equality for women. The original assembly was composed largely of middle- to upper-class white women. I wanted my students to appreciate the issues that these women addressed and their courage, but also to consider the limitations imposed by their race, class, and ethnicity. Thus in our simulated 1848 gathering, my students portrayed women who were not at the original conference — enslaved African Americans, Cherokee women who had been forcibly moved to Oklahoma on the Trail of Tears, Mexican women in the recently conquered territory of New Mexico, poor white New England mill workers — as well as the white middle- and upper-class reformers like Elizabeth Cady Stanton and Lucretia Mott who were in attendance.

In this more socially representative fictional assembly, students learned about the resolutions adopted at the original gathering and the conditions that motivated those, but they also saw firsthand how more privileged white women ignored other important issues — such as treaty rights of Mexican women, sexual abuse of enslaved African Americans, and the workplace exploitation of poor white women — that a more diverse convention might have addressed.

The knowledge that my students acquired from this role play consisted not only of "facts" — although they learned plenty of these. They also exercised their multicultural social imaginations — listening for the voices that are often silenced in the traditional U.S. history narrative, becoming more alert to the importance of issues of race and class. However, this kind of teaching and learning takes time — time that will be lost to the fact-packing pedagogy required by multiple-choice tests. And after all their study, would my students have recalled whether it was the Sixteenth, Seventeenth, Eighteenth, or Nineteenth Amendment that gave women the right to vote? If not, they would have appeared ignorant about the struggle for women's rights.

Likewise, my Global Studies students spend the better part of a quarter reading, discussing, role-playing, and writing about the manifold consequences of European colonialism. They read excerpts from Okot p'Bitek's poignant book-length poem *Song of Lawino*, about the lingering psychological effects of colonialism in Uganda; role play a trial on the colonial roots of the potato famine in Ireland; and examine how Asian economies were distorted to serve the needs of European ruling classes. But when confronted with Oregon's multiple-choice question that asks which continent was most thoroughly colonized in 1914, would my students answer correctly?

As these examples illustrate, in a multicultural curriculum it's not so much facts as it is perspective that is important in nurturing a fuller understanding of society. And sometimes considering new perspectives requires imagination as much as or more than memory of specific facts. For example, my history students read about the people Columbus encountered in 1492, the Taínos — who themselves left no written records — in excerpts from Columbus's journal and articles like Jose Barriero's "Taínos: Men of the Good." I ask students to write a story or diary entry from the point of view of a Taíno during the first few days or weeks of their encounter with Spaniards that draws on information in the readings, but goes further. It's necessarily a speculative undertaking, but it invites students to turn the "Columbus discovers America" story on its head, encourages them to appreciate the humanity in the people usually marginalized in tales of "exploration." In response, students have written pieces of startling insight. Sure, a multiple choice test can assess whether students know that Columbus first sailed in 1492, where he landed, or the name of the people he encountered. But it is ill-equipped to assess what students truly *understand* about this encounter.

Not surprisingly, Oregon's "one best answer" approach vastly oversimplifies and misrepresents complex social processes — and entirely erases ethnicity and race as categories of analysis. One question on a recent test reads: "In 1919, over 4.1 million Americans belonged to labor unions. By 1928, that number had dropped to 3.4 million. Which of the following best accounts for that drop?" It seems that the correct answer must be A: "Wages increased dramatically, so workers didn't need unions." All the other answers are clearly wrong, but is this answer "correct"? Since when do workers leave unions when they win higher wages? Weren't mechanization and scientific management factors in undermining traditional craft unions? Did the post-World War I Red Scare, with systematic attacks on radical unions like the Industrial Workers of the World and deportations of foreign-born labor organizers, affect union membership?

And how about the Oregon test's reductive category of "worker"? Shouldn't students be alert to how race, ethnicity, and gender were — and are — important factors in determining one's workplace experience, including union membership? For example, in 1919 professional strikebreakers, hired by steel corporations, were told to "stir up as much bad feeling as you possibly can between the Serbians and the Italians." And more than 30,000 black workers, excluded from American Federation of Labor unions, were brought in as strikebreakers. A multicultural awareness is vital if we're to arrive at a satisfactory answer to the above Oregon field-test question. But the state would reward students for choosing an historical soundbite that is as shallow as it is wrong.

This leads me to an aspect of these tests that is especially offensive to teachers: They don't merely assess, they also instruct. The tests represent the authority of the state, implicitly telling students, "Just memorize the facts, kids. That's what social studies is all about — and if teachers do any more than that, they're wasting your time." Multiple-choice tests undermine teachers' efforts to construct a rigorous multicultural curriculum because they delegitimize that curriculum in students' eyes: If it were important, it would be on the test.

Core of Multiculturalism

At its core, multicultural teaching is an ethical, even political, enterprise. Its aim is not just to impart lots of interesting facts, to equip students to be proficient Trivial Pursuit players, but to help make the world a better place. It highlights injustice of all kinds — racial, gender, class, linguistic, ethnic, national, environmental — in order to make explanations and propose solutions. It recognizes our responsibility to fellow human beings and to the earth. It has heart and soul.

Compare that with the sterile, fact-collecting orientation of Oregon's standards and assessments. For example, a typical 49-question high-school field test piloted in 1998 included seven questions on global climate, two on the location of rivers in India and Africa, and one on hypothetical world population projections in the year 2050. But not a single question in the test concerned the lives of people around the world, or environmental conditions — nothing about increasing poverty, the global AIDS epidemic, disappearance of the rain forests, rates of unemployment, global warming, etc., or efforts to address these crises. The test bounded aimlessly from one disjointed fact to another. In the most profound sense it was pointless.

Indeed the test's random amorality may reveal another of its cultural biases. Oregon's standards and assessments make no distinction between knowledge and information. The state's version of social education would appear to have no raison d'être beyond the acquisition of large quantities of data. But for many cultures the aim of knowledge is not bulk, but wisdom — insight into meaningful aspects about the nature of life. Writing in the Winter 1998/99 issue of *Rethinking Schools*, Peter Kiang makes a similar point about the Massachusetts teacher test that calls into question the validity of enterprises such as these. He writes that "by constructing a test based on a sequence of isolated, decontextualized questions that have no relationship to each other, the underlying epistemology embedded in the test design has a Western-cultural bias, even if individual questions include or represent 'multicultural' content. Articulating and assessing a knowledge base requires examining not only what one knows, but also how one knows."

Students "know" in different ways, and these differences are often cultural. Oregon nonetheless subjects all students to an abstract, data-heavy assessment device that does not gauge what or how they have learned. As Kiang points out, test-makers address multicultural criticism by including individual questions about multicultural content — for example, by highlighting snippets of information about famous people of color like Dr.

Martin Luther King, Jr., César Chávez, and Harriet Tubman. But these "heroes and holidays" additions cannot mask the fundamental hostility to multicultural education shown by standards and assessments like those initiated by Oregon.

Standardization efforts like these are attempts to turn teachers into deliverers of approved social information. Instead, teachers should be getting support to collaborate on curriculum that deals forthrightly with social problems, that fights racism and social injustice. We should help teachers construct rigorous performance standards for students that promote deep thinking about the nature of our society. These efforts should acknowledge the legitimacy of a multicultural curriculum of critical questions, complexity, multiple perspectives, and social imagination. They should recognize that wisdom is more than information — that the world can't be chopped up into multiple-choice questions, and that you can't bubble in the truth with a number-two pencil.

Testing Slights Multiculturalism

Makani Themba-Nixon

As a parent active on a local school council, I watched with apprehension as Virginia's high-stakes testing program unfolded. But it was not until the day my third-grade son came home sad and dejected that I realized my worst fears about the tests were true.

My son's class was studying explorers — his favorite subject — and he wanted to write a report on Matthew Henson, his favorite explorer. Henson, an African American, was the first man to set foot on the North Pole. He was a self-taught sailor and astronomer who rose above the racism and prejudice of his day to become one of the most important explorers of the 20th century.

Imagine my thrill as my son, without any urging on my part, went to the computer to do research on Henson. I was particularly pleased because after a tough first grade and difficulty reading in second grade, in third grade my son was at last learning that school could be fun.

While researching on the computer, my son took great delight in finding obscure facts about Henson. He fantasized out loud about how impressed his teachers and classmates would be once they saw his great report.

I had never seen him so excited about school work. He really identified with Henson, not only because he and Henson are both African Americans, which was clearly important to him, but also because he was excited about the opportunity to be an explorer himself. What excited him most was the novelty of the information and the fact that Henson wasn't one of the explorers the class as a whole was studying. As he said to me, "Mom, I'm being an explorer in social studies!"

When he turned in his report, he got a much different reaction than he expected. His teacher patiently explained that although his hard work was obvious and it was a great report, he would have to do another report on Christopher Columbus instead.

It turned out that Matthew Henson wasn't on Virginia's high-stakes test, known as the Standards of Learning (SOL).

Like any mother, I called the teacher. I tried hard to be understanding. She said she felt bad about her decision and admitted that she knew what it meant to my son to be so excited about school. But, she rationalized, it wasn't her fault. She was trying to make sure he passed the Virginia test. After all, so much was on the line.

In that regard, she is right. The SOLs are high-stakes tests, with winners and many more losers.

The tests, and the curriculum acrobatics schools undertake to adapt to them, literally determine what's important to know and what's not. Books, methods, and coursework that don't support test standards are thrown by the wayside. For example, students at my children's elementary school who do not meet SOLs in math must forego art classes for extra tutoring. And, of course, any historical figures that don't fit within the mostly white framework of the state standards are lost as well.

I worry about my children in this new world of high-stakes testing. How will they remain creative or sustain an interest in lifelong learning? Further, if the tests are to ensure that our students are better prepared, it's completely confounding that multicultural education is ignored in the development of learning standards.

Teaching in Dangerous Times

Gloria Ladson-Billings

In the popular book *Dangerous Minds*, the former-Marine-turned-teacher LouAnne Johnson is credited with turning around the "class from hell" — a group of urban African-American and Latino students on the road to failure in school and life. This book and the subsequent motion picture were more of the "teacher-as-savior" genre that constructs an image of teachers, particularly white teachers, as "rescuing" urban students of color from themselves, their families, and their communities.

Unfortunately, most of the teachers in this genre pay little or no attention to the academic achievement of their students. Thus, while many audiences applaud the Hollywood teacher-images' amazing social work, interpersonal, and cross-cultural communications skills, few real-life educators would point to any of these histrionic teachers as exemplary classroom instructors.

Given the changing demographics of the student body in the United States and the bifurcation of public school student populations into groups of haves and have-nots, it is important to understand that, rather than confront dangerous minds, teachers of urban students of color are teaching in dangerous times.

One of the most urgent issues facing this perilous era, and the cadre of teachers who serve in it, is that of being able to more accurately measure what students know and are able to do. Communities of color, which historically have raised questions about the potential biases built into traditional test measures, have challenged the purpose and design of many of the assessments. This scrutiny has been accompanied by a focus in the educational community at large on teacher assessment. Rather than rely on the old "input" model, in which teacher-worthiness is judged by the kinds of courses teachers have completed, there have been increasing calls for more authentic forms of assessment for teachers. These new assessments target "outputs" — what teachers know and are able to do.

Educational researchers and scholars of color have long suspected that traditional teaching assessment techniques systematically screen out teachers of color from the teaching field. For example, in 1997 I was personally told that during a recent round of testing for the National Board for Professional Teaching Standards, no candidates of color passed the Early Adolescence/English Language Arts Assessment.

Do proposed new, "authentic" teacher-assessment techniques continue in this vein? And, if so, do alternative assessments need to be formulated, and what proficiency or skill areas must these assessments address?

In this article, I would like to look briefly at problems in some of the most popular teacher assessment techniques and then propose other possible measures that can be used to assess teachers.

Testing Teachers

Since the mid-1980s, the nation has seemed fixated on testing its teachers. Predictably, these testing measures have had an adverse impact on the already shrinking pool of African-American teachers. Though none would argue that school districts certify incompetent teachers, those states calling for teachers to be tested typically fail to engage in a process that holds schools and colleges of teacher education responsible for ensuring that their graduates meet minimum standards.

The problem of teachers not passing competency tests seems inconsequential when compared to the larger issue of what these tests reveal about teachers' ability to teach. For example, all California teachers who have received regular teaching certificates within the past 10 years have passed that state's teacher competency test. Yet would one argue that all of California's teachers are good teachers? Creating tests as screens or barriers to admission seems to appease the public outcry for higher standards, even when those standards have no relationship to performance.

The more relevant question might be: How equitable and reliable are teacher assessment measures for ensuring that teachers will be effective in classrooms of urban children of color?

Many new teacher assessments fail to consider the very different contexts in which teachers find themselves. More pointedly, teachers of color are more likely to find themselves in poor, urban school communities than are white teachers.

The example of one assessment activity that I personally critiqued describes a case in point.

In this instance, the videotape prepared and presented to the assessors by an African-American teacher — who taught in an overcrowded, under-funded urban public school — yielded assessor discussion only about how stark and bare her classroom seemed compared to those of other exami-nees. This teacher did not have an intricate, handmade "spider's web" draped across her classroom as a visible reminder of a reading unit's insect theme, as did the suburban teacher who submitted a video. Nor did the African-American teacher have a big comfortable sofa, beanbag chairs, pillows, and a carpeted floor, as did the teacher from a school in a college-town district.

In my later conversation with the African-American teacher, I learned that because of overcrowding she did not have a real room for her classes and instead taught out of a makeshift closet. Additionally, the school was on a year-round schedule. This meant that every nine weeks she was re-quired to take down everything in her "room" and reassemble it after the break. Nothing in the teacher assessment process was designed to take into consideration teaching under these circumstances. Further, if new assess-ments continue to discount the inequities already built into schools by virtue of unequal funding and other material resources, they will continue to discount the creative ways some teachers deal with scarcity and push students to higher intellectual heights.

Videotapes and Portfolios

I'd like to briefly touch on two popular innovations in teacher assess-ment: videotapes and portfolios.

Because videotaping gives us the luxury of "seeing" teaching, it has gained increased credibility. However, videotaping a classroom also reveals how cameras do, indeed, lie.

At best, a video is an artificial representation of teaching. Even un-edited, a video reveals but a partial view of the classroom setting and what transpires there. It can capture only selected slices of classroom life.

Teachers cannot yell "cut" and re-teach a "scene" each time a student is confused or behaving inappropriately. Teaching is more episodic, random, and unpredictable than movies. The dynamic of the classroom creates ups and downs, zigs and zags, that may come across as confused and unfocused through the flat, unforgiving lens of a video camera.

Further, when a videotape is used for assessment and evaluation, teachers, as vested participants, often choose to "create" a tape that features the best of their teaching. Schools and districts with resources and personnel equipped to produce high-quality videotapes can make mediocre teaching appear much better than it really is. Conversely, excellent teachers with limited access to good equipment and videographic skills may be left with poor-quality tapes that fail to illuminate any of the magic that transpires in the classroom.

Similar problems can emerge with portfolio assessment.

On the surface, this seems a fair and equitable way to assess teaching: Allow teachers to show what they believe is their best work, and/or the products of that work, and judge it. However, this also has its equity pitfalls.

Imagine, for example, a teacher who was prepared at one of the nation's Research I institutions. She probably heard about teaching portfolios; perhaps she was both taught and required to construct a portfolio during her student teacher semester. By contrast, her colleague who was prepared at a small, historically black college did not have the same access to portfolio preparation training. Both are good teachers, but one is more capable of using a portfolio to document her abilities and skills.

A Culturally Relevant Approach

If the most common teacher assessment techniques fall short, especially for students and teachers in urban areas, what proficiency or skills areas must the assessments address?

My previous work with teachers who are successful with African-American students suggests that some ways to rethink teacher performance include looking at teachers' abilities to engender success among their students in three key areas: academic achievement, cultural competence, and sociopolitical consciousness.

Additionally, assessments that consider aspects of teachers' culture might prove more equitable for teachers of color.

Student Achievement

Regardless of the elegance of one's teaching performances, the bottom line is always how much learning takes place. Do students demonstrate competence in academic areas? Are they able to formulate questions, propose solutions, apply knowledge to new and different situations?

Most portfolio assessments require teachers to supply examples of individual students' work. Rarely do they set performance criteria for a teacher's entire class. However, a central focus on helping as many children as possible achieve academically is one of the hallmarks of culturally relevant teaching. Consequently, assessment of culturally relevant teaching practice would require teachers to show evidence of academic achievement for all their students, or to provide educationally defensible explanations of why any students do not meet this criteria (e.g., consistently poor attendance, identified special needs, and so forth).

One way to determine teachers' ability to enhance students' academic achievement is to collect baseline data at the beginning of the school year and compare those findings to end-of-year data. Often, students from upper-income, dominant-culture communities come into a classroom knowing much of what their teachers purport to teach them. Thus, their typically superior performance on standardized measures is actually an indication of what they already know.

Unless a teacher's students are demonstrating academic progress, one cannot contend, with good conscience, that the teacher is exemplary. Indeed, it is not the teacher method or strategy that should be the criteria for good teaching, but rather the academic accomplishments of students. Do students who were previously unable to read demonstrate an ability to read after spending a year in a teacher's classroom? Can students who were not able to compute and solve problems at the beginning of the school term provide evidence that they can do so by the end? These students' performances should be the benchmarks upon which we put our confidence in teacher effectiveness. They do not have to be demonstrated solely on standardized tests, but effective teachers must be prepared to provide powerful examples of what their students know and can do.

Cultural Competence

Cultural competence does not lend itself to conventional forms of measurement. Its goal is to ensure that teachers support the home and community cultures of students, while helping students become proficient in the cultures of schooling and education.

What makes this difficult is the finding that far too many teachers in U.S. schools possess only a surface understanding of culture — their own or anyone else's. As noted in one of my earlier studies, many middle-class white American teachers fail to associate the notion of culture with themselves. Instead, they believe that they are "just regular Americans," while people of color are the ones "with culture." This notion of regularity serves a normalizing function that positions those who are "not regular" as "others." Not recognizing that they, too, are cultural beings prevents these teachers from ever questioning taken-for-granted assumptions about the nature of human thought, activity, and existence.

Culturally relevant teachers know when to introduce relevant examples from their students' backgrounds and experiences to make learning more meaningful. For example, when the African-American students of a teacher I will call Ms. Deberaux indicated that the only females who could be princesses were white, blond-haired, and blue-eyed, she quickly brought out a copy of John Steptoe's *Mufaro's Beautiful Daughters* for them to read. This lavishly illustrated children's book, with its richly detailed story of African royalty and traditions, provided her students with the necessary counter-knowledge to challenge their misguided notions about nobility and people of African descent.

The goal of fostering cultural competence requires teachers to help raise students' awareness of prejudice and discrimination, as well as their ability to react to and constructively cope with these negative social realities. For example, before a teacher I will identify as Ms. Lewis took her inner-city African-American students on a camping trip, she talked candidly with them about the fact that they would be coming in contact with white students and counselors. She encouraged them to think proactively about what they might do if any white person exhibited insensitive or racist attitudes toward them.

Fostering cultural competence also requires teachers to support students' home language/dialect while simultaneously teaching them Standard English. That is, rather than chastise students for using the language/dialect they use when speaking with family and friends and in their communities, effective teachers help students understand when and where code-switching, or the alternate use of Standard English and home language/dialect in formal and informal settings, is preferable or necessary.

Unfortunately, nothing in the current teacher assessment battery addresses how well teachers foster cultural competence within their students. Perhaps this is because few test constructors have ever considered the importance of cultural competence for students, nor would they even recognize it when it is being demonstrated by teachers.

One example that came to my attention involved an art teacher in a predominantly African-American high school. The classroom video submitted by this teacher depicted a demonstration lecture by a cosmetologist whom the teacher had invited to her class to discuss the intricate hair braiding done by black African women as an art form. The assessors rated this teacher's submission poorly, claiming that cosmetology belongs in vocational education, not art. Their lack of understanding of the relationship between hair and art in African societies kept them from accepting a broader notion of the relevance of this demonstration.

Sociopolitical Consciousness

In addition to ensuring that students achieve academically and are culturally competent, culturally relevant teachers develop a sociopolitical consciousness in their students. The use of the term "sociopolitical consciousness" is important, lest readers equate it with the more simplistic, almost vacuous term "critical thinking."

Whereas there certainly is nothing wrong with critical thinking per se, what often masquerades as critical thinking in most classrooms is a set of prescriptive steps and practices that may reflect important processes but that are attached to relatively inane content. For instance, students might be asked to imagine that they are legislators who must decide whether or not to provide aid to a country that is deforesting its rain forest. Although this is a serious ecological issue, how can students come to think critically about it given only vicarious knowledge?

A different kind of critical thinking — what I term sociopolitical consciousness or an activist civic and social awareness — is demonstrated by William Tate in his focus on a teacher he calls Sandra Mason. According to Tate, Ms. Mason's middle school mathematics students came to class upset each morning because their route to school was impeded by indigent panhandlers who aggressively approached them for money to purchase cheap liquor from one of the many liquor stores near the school. Instead of ignoring the students' concerns, Ms. Mason decided to incorporate the problem of negotiating around these alcohol-dependent throngs into a classroom lesson.

Her students examined city zoning ordinances and learned that their city was divided into "wet" and "dry" zones that determined where alcoholic beverages could be sold. The schools that served poor communities of color were located in wet zones. The students calculated the amount of money that was being generated by the liquor stores in the school neighborhood (and lost to the community since most of the store owners lived elsewhere), and they developed an action plan for rethinking zoning in the city.

This involvement with real problems raised the students' sociopolitical consciousness and made mathematics a more meaningful activity for the students. It also made teaching more challenging for Ms. Mason, but it enabled her to help her students understand that what happened in school had relevance for their everyday lives.

How should teachers' abilities to develop students' sociopolitical consciousness be assessed? Certainly, this is a more complex skill than can be exhibited on a pencil-and-paper test. Yet if we say that students must exhibit this trait, then teachers have to demonstrate their ability to teach in ways that support that kind of learning.

Concluding Thoughts

In the longer essay upon which this article is based, I outline some possible ways in which one might promote assessments for teachers that value and reward culturally relevant teaching. Here, I want to underscore a question that looms over any assessment practice: Who gets to handle whose business?

If assessment practices both powerful and subtle enough to evaluate academic achievement, cultural competence, and sociopolitical consciousness could somehow be devised, who would carry them out? The complexities of the new types of assessments required will demand assessors who are capable of cultural translations of pedagogical expertise. These assessors would have to be able to answer several questions, such as the following:

- When is direct instruction the right methodology to use?
- How does one determine the difference between a teacher who is unduly harsh or one who is warmly demanding?
- What difference does it make if teachers slip in and out of a students' home language to make a point to their students?
- Can all assessors determine the pedagogical significance of teachers' culturally specific behaviors?
- How is it that African-American teachers so regularly and predictably fail current assessments, yet the presence of white teachers is no assurance that African-American or other students of color will achieve?
- What is the nature of the technical problems related to designing culturally relevant teacher assessments? Can teacher assessments be considered without a concomitant look at student assessment? In other words, can failing students have successful teachers?

These questions are important because more states and local districts continue to look at new ways to assess both preservice and inservice teachers. What these assessments will look like, what opportunities teachers will have for demonstrating teaching competence, and how these assessments will include or exclude potential teacher candidates need careful and critical examination.

The work of teaching is both complicated and complex. How we educators come to understand it has implications for how we assess it. If we construct teaching as a set of technical tasks, then we will devise assessments designed to score these tasks. However, if we understand teaching as a highly complex endeavor undertaken by professionals, then we are compelled to develop assessments that are highly sophisticated and nuanced. Regardless of how we construct teaching as a profession, the challenge of ensuring high-quality performance from teachers and students remains. Without improvement in both, we will continue to live in dangerous times.

This article is condensed from a longer piece in The Journal of Negro Education, *67(3), pp. 255-267.*

Their Report Card — and Ours

Portland Area Rethinking Schools

Several years ago, Oregon, like many states, began issuing school "report cards" which judge a school almost exclusively on the basis of standardized tests. In response, members of the group Portland Area Rethinking Schools (PARS) drafted an alternative "report card" as an example of how concerned educators and community members can work together to set up and implement a meaningful system of accountability. The questions this "report card" raises are not designed to produce a label or a numerical rating, but to promote a thoughtful collective dialogue about a school and its programs. A complete copy of the PARS Report Card, which elaborates on each item, is available at www.rethinkingschools.org/rsr.

How do we know if schools are doing a good job? And how can we make them better?

According to Oregon's Department of Education, state-mandated standardization of curriculum and increased testing will inspire — or frighten — educators and students into performing at higher levels. This strategy emphasizes measurable objectives and scores that can be compared from student to student, school to school, community to community. It emphasizes the necessity of holding all students to "high standards."

In practice, this strategy increasingly turns schools into test-prep academies. Test-led reform sucks the joy out of learning and discourages both teacher and student creativity. What is not measured on the tests — for example, critical thinking, discussion skills, the arts — is more and more neglected.

Of course, equating student achievement with higher test scores may, in fact, raise test scores. But it will not help nurture more knowledgeable, motivated, or caring students.

The Oregon Department of Education's school "report cards" exemplify the hollowness of this reform strategy. The state judges "student performance" strictly in terms of standardized test results; "school characteristics" are assessed based on one criterion: the percentage of a school's students taking state tests. We're reminded of the saying, "Not everything that matters can be measured, and not everything that can be measured matters." If one aim of school reform is to make schools more "accountable," then surely we need to capture a fuller portrait of school life.

Portland Area Rethinking Schools developed an alternative school reform strategy. Unlike state testing, which is premised on a belief that all learning can and should be quantified and assessment results used to compare, reward, and punish, we believe that assessments should be collaborative endeavors, grounded in school communities. We believe that school life and student achievement can only be assessed — and improved — with participatory inquiries that offer rich descriptions of a school's educational practice.

Below is a draft of our alternative "report card." In important respects, the process of collecting data for the report card is itself an essential part of the product. Real school reform must be democratic, drawing on the collective efforts of teachers, students, administrators, parents and the broader community. We encourage school communities to use the questions below as the basis of discussions to assess and improve school life.

Curriculum

- How is the content of the curriculum meaningful, interdisciplinary, multicultural, and academically rigorous for all students?
- How are high academic expectations communicated to and maintained for all students?
- How are historic, artistic, and scientific contributions of diverse cultures, families, social classes, and genders represented in each content area?
- How does the curriculum encourage all students to see themselves as social and environmental problem-solvers capable of making the world a better place? Does the curriculum have real-life links?
- Are there sufficient resources available to meet the curricular mission of the school? For example:
1. What is the range of actual class sizes?

2. Do students have access to mentors and tutors?

3. Are specialists in reading, writing, math, and/or other areas available for students and staff?

4. What school time is scheduled for teachers to plan, develop, and discuss curriculum?

Student Assessment

- How is it ensured that assessment allows students multiple ways to demonstrate their learning?

- How is it ensured that the frequent use of feedback from assessments offers students the opportunity to grow?

- How do assessment results influence subsequent instruction in the classroom and program modification in the school?

- What actions are taken to avoid misapplication of assessment results through tracking or stigmatization?

Equity for All Students

- Historically, so-called ability grouping has discriminated against poor and working-class students and students of color by offering educational programs of unequal quality to different students. How does the school group its students (e.g., honors, advanced, remedial, scholars, International Baccalaureate)? How does the school know that these grouping practices do not result in unequal educational experiences?

- What accommodations are made for the needs of students with attendance and tardiness problems: students who work to support their families, travel to home countries, take care of younger or older family members?

- Is there evidence of historical, literary, artistic, and scientific contributions of diverse cultures represented in each content area? In teachers' lesson plans? In the book room? On bulletin boards? During assemblies?

- Who is represented and honored in the school? Consider the hallways, library, and overall school environment. Does the racial, ethnic, linguistic, and class composition of extra-curricular leadership and special academic programs reflect the student body? How are low-income, minority, or second language students encouraged to participate?

Health and Safety

- ◆ Describe your discipline policies and programs that promote respect and conflict intervention and resolution. Specifically, how are students involved in these programs?
- ◆ How does the school promote the physical safety and the emotional well-being of students? Are programs built into the curriculum addressing such needs as the prevention of violence and sexual harassment, suicide intervention, sex education, and prevention of drug and alcohol abuse?
- ◆ How are marginalized students identified and protected at your school? What policies and strategies are used to counter racist, sexist, or homophobic language and put-downs? How is respect taught in the school curriculum?
- ◆ How accessible are mental health and crisis services at the school? Is nursing staff provided? Describe safe places students can go during personal distress. Describe any formal or informal mental health services available to students.
- ◆ What is the selection and quality of cafeteria food?
- ◆ How often and under what criteria is the water tested in the school?
- ◆ How is the student environment protected from other chemical ingredients of unknown or potentially harmful effects — e.g., in cleaning solutions, herbicides, pesticides, or airborne contaminants?

Parents and Community in the Life of the School

- ◆ How does the school include parents, students, and community in decision-making?
- ◆ What adaptation and/or encouragement is made for working, non-English speaking, marginalized parents and/or parents of color?
- ◆ What power does the community have in decision-making?
- ◆ When and how are parents informed and included regarding student progress (e.g., academic assessments, absences, tardiness, and misconduct)?

- How does the school ensure parents understand their student's progress?
- Is there broad representation of community organizations in the life of the school: unions, women's organizations, religious institutions, senior centers, environmental and social justice organizations, businesses, etc.?
- How is school networked to other community services? How does the school facilitate connecting students and families to community and governmental resources?
- How does the school reach out to the community during transition points — i.e., from preschool into kindergarten or first grade? From elementary to middle school? From middle school to high school? From high school to college?
- In the school, how are parents and/or community members invited to give feedback on student work or portfolios? Are there student author presentations, science fairs, gallery displays, etc.?
- What informational events does the school hold?

District and State Support

- In what ways do the school district and state support the school community in achieving the above aims?
- In what ways do the school district and state hinder the school community in achieving the above aims?
- What strategies are being pursued by the school community to challenge any policies or practices that hinder efforts to provide all students with quality education?

PART 5

Roads to Reform

Drive-By School Reform

Stan Karp

In 1991, my school district was taken over by the state. It was the second large urban system seized by the New Jersey Department of Education under the state's "radical" initiative for addressing "educational bankruptcy" in long-failing districts. Low test scores and fiscal mismanagement led to the replacement of the superintendent, central office administrators, and the local school board by a new state-appointed superintendent with broad powers to implement reforms. Today, New Jersey's three largest school systems, Paterson — where I've been a high school teacher for more than two decades — Jersey City, and Newark, remain under state control.

Since the takeover began, I've participated in site-based management reforms, school-based restructuring projects and endless meetings about school reform. For three years I chaired the district's site-based management (SBM) committee, which attempted to define what SBM would mean in Paterson. I served two terms on the local union executive board, an outgrowth of my work on the SBM project. After the SBM project stalled, I began to lead a team charged with expanding my journalism elective courses into a theme-based, communications "school-within-a-school." The project was part of a plan designed to restructure my comprehensive high school of about 2,500 students into smaller units led by interdisciplinary teams of teachers. This effort, in turn, was later folded into a larger, districtwide effort to create a system of small, theme-based "career academies" at the high school level.

As I write, I still hope that our Academy project will succeed and, over time, provide a more collaborative and productive educational environment for the several hundred students and the dozen or so teachers involved. But these hopes have been tempered by frustrating experience with a reform process that often seems to push schools two steps back for each one forward. It's a phenomenon I've come to call "drive-by school reform."

Why Drive-By Reforms Fail

The telltale signs of this hit-and-run approach to educational change are painfully familiar in urban public schools. Drive-by reform is invariably generated by something outside the school: a new state law, a directive from the Department of Education, the agenda of a new governor or a recently hired central office administrator. The school community becomes the wary target of intervention, rather than the initiator of change or an active partner in it. External agendas are often imposed without developing any shared assessment of a school's problems or the common priorities needed to make reform credible.

Since all sponsors of reform want to claim the "investment of the stakeholders," there is often considerable lip service paid to "parent/community involvement" and "teacher input." But in practice, the experience and concerns of teachers, parents, and even school-based administrators can be marginalized in many ways. Too often they seem to count only insofar as they serve the agenda imposed from the outside.

One way this is done is by introducing reform with little context or connection to a school's recent history. In New Jersey, reform trends wash over urban districts like waves on the Jersey shore, frequently erasing all traces of past efforts to make room for a few more short-lived footprints (or worse, depositing new forms of debris or toxic waste). Abrupt changes in direction are announced with little attempt to sum up the lessons, pro or con, of recent experience. This failure to speak directly to the real experience and frustrations schools have had with previous reform projects feeds cynicism and reduces the credibility and prospects for success of new programs.

Similarly, schools can be set up to fail by the imposition of absurd time lines. Drive-by reform asks school staff to form site councils in a matter of days, asks parents and teachers with little experience to develop school budgets in a few weeks, and asks schools to choose from a grab bag of reform models after a cursory survey and one or two site visits by a small delegation. Such time frames suggest that the "democratic processes" that accompany many reform efforts are designed primarily to create the appearance of legitimacy rather than the common ground and broad coalitions that reform needs to succeed over the long haul.

Another sure sign of drive-by reform is when a district allows educational consultants or outside "experts" to define reform agendas rather than play a supporting role. In my district, the first state takeover administration began by sending in teams of external monitors to evaluate schools using criteria that the schools and teachers had no role in formulating or even reviewing. Teachers read the results in the local papers, where they were labeled as "failing," "adequate," or "successful" without any chance to respond or question the findings. Such alienating, bureaucratic practices squander valuable energy and good will that might otherwise be constructively mobilized for change.

To be sure, consultants, coaches, and "comprehensive school reform models" may have valuable expertise and resources to draw on. But in order for reform to take root, it's necessary to create a level of school-based leadership and commitment that in many schools and districts does not readily exist. Building this capacity for leadership, facilitation, team-building, planning, community outreach, trouble-shooting — in a word, school-based organizing — is one of the often unacknowledged missing links in the process of reform. Too often, the time-consuming leadership tasks of new reforms are added to the duties of reluctant building administrators, where they may compete or even conflict with existing priorities and past practice. Alternately, reform may rely on an unsustainable level of (often unpaid) voluntarism on the part of individual teachers, or be contracted out to consultants. None of these approaches is adequate.

Moreover, in some districts this raises issues about the need to rethink the roles of central office administrators, supervisors, principals, vice principals, department chairs, deans, and other non-teaching personnel that are often unexamined. A top-heavy administrative apparatus can reflect bureaucratic patterns of organization that have developed over many years and may be unsupportive of, even incompatible with, school-based initiative. In such systems, administrative leadership often lacks the vision and "classroom credibility" needed to mobilize teachers and other key constituencies behind authentic reform.

Successful reform often requires rethinking job descriptions, with classroom teachers taking on leadership roles and administrators giving higher priority and more time to classroom and curriculum concerns. Over the long term, the rigid division between teaching and non-teaching responsibilities inside school systems needs to be re-examined and hierarchical patterns of management need to be reduced. The division of labor between central office, school-based administration, and classroom teachers needs to be renegotiated so that those closest to classroom realities have more influence in setting reform agendas and those responsible for providing teachers with the leadership and support they need are more accountable to students, teachers, and communities. Similarly, bureaucratic, top-down authority needs to be replaced with more collaborative processes that include room for school-based priorities and initiative.

This is not to minimize the importance of districtwide leadership and central office resources in sustaining reform and addressing equity concerns, like fairness in the allocation of resources or affirmative action in staffing, that may get lost at the level of a single school or project. Effective reform also requires imposing coherence on the sprawling bureaucratic turf that defines urban public school systems, and harmonizing confused, often competing agendas. Aligning district and school-based priorities so that reform efforts reinforce rather than undermine each other is crucial.

It is not unusual for urban schools to be told to simultaneously implement mutually incompatible initiatives. The restructuring project in my high school, for example, is still wrestling with the contradictions of creating interdisciplinary Academy teams of teachers without overhauling the school's organization by academic departments, or of encouraging teachers to develop new "student-centered, theme-based curriculum" while huge chunks of instructional time, curriculum planning, and professional development remain narrowly driven by the state's standardized tests. Some years it hasn't even been possible to place Academy students in common homerooms or core classes because grouping policies issued by central office mandated their placement on the basis of test scores.

Such confused agendas can cripple reform initiatives in areas like curriculum planning, staff development, school-based budgeting and technology. Drive-by reforms typically paper over these problems with little more than shared rhetoric or top-down directives, which is one reason they fail.

More fundamentally, however, the failings of drive-by reform cannot be blamed simply on the misuse of consultants or central office bureaucracy. Instead they reflect deeper contradictions at the core of many school reform efforts and, indeed, at the core of public schooling itself. The bureaucratic process, the inconsistent support from the top, the token community and staff participation, the confused and competing agendas, the avoidance of hard issues, and the absence of staying power are the expressions of a contradictory reform impulse that lacks the vision and commitment needed to seriously tackle the deeply political questions of democracy and power that lie at the heart of school reform.

The Dual Character of School Reform

If truth be told, there is much about the apparent consensus on the need to reform and improve our urban public schools that is, ultimately, illusory. School reform in urban districts often invokes a common rhetoric: "high standards for all," "all children can learn," "no child should be left behind." These high-minded sentiments resonate with all who care about schools and children.

But like support for motherhood and apple pie, rhetoric about school reform can hide the historic reality that schools have always had a dual character. On the one hand, public schools remain perhaps society's most important democratic institution. They are the product of decades of effort to give substance to the nation's promises of equal opportunity, self-improvement, and success through hard work and achievement. Schools play a key role in American dreams of class mobility and generational progress, and their success or failure has a daily impact on the lives and prospects of millions of children and families.

On the other hand, schools historically have been instruments for reproducing class and race privilege as it exists in the larger society. The low academic performance of schools in poor areas, the inadequate facilities, the toleration of failure, and the disrespect for communities of color reflect real relations of inequality and injustice that permeate our society. Through ideology, gate-keeping, various forms of stratification, and bureaucratic — often authoritarian — administration, schools function as a large sifting and labeling operation that re-creates and justifies existing distributions of wealth and power. In many ways, schools reproduce the very inequality that American mythology professes they are designed to overcome.

This dual character of schooling — its democratic promise and its institutional service to a society based on class, race, and gender privilege — invariably generates contradictory impulses when it comes to reform. At every turn, the gap between the promise and practice of schooling creates a tension: Should curriculum reflect mainstream consensus or a multicultural pluralism? Should schools endorse traditional values or promote independent, critical thought? Are standards being raised to bar the door to some or assure better outcomes for all? Should parents and classroom teachers have as much to say about reform agendas as governors and corporate executives? Should schools be as concerned with promoting anti-racist attitudes as marketable skills? Will new forms of assessment provide better ways to report and improve student performance or more effective ways to sort and label kids for predetermined slots in society?

To be sure, answers to complicated questions of educational policy cannot be reduced to either/or propositions. But the debate over policy options inevitably takes place within this context of the dual nature of schooling. The choices made invariably push schools in one direction or the other, along a continuum from promoting social justice to reinforcing the status quo. Whether any particular reform initiative moves things forward, backward, or into a dead end often depends on how it fits into this larger context.

Take, for example, the current enthusiasm in reform circles for small school experiments. Small schools show promise in large part because they attempt to change the social relations of schooling; that is, they create a more human scale and more supportive environment for collaborative, personalized interaction among students, teachers, and communities. They can nourish creativity and mutual accountability in powerful ways that large, traditional schools cannot. Small schools can also introduce elements of choice, pluralism, and innovation into historically bureaucratized and stagnant systems.

But like most reforms, small schools can also be developed in problematic ways. They can become specialized magnets that "cream" the best students and most committed parents. They can claim a disproportionate share of resources for a relatively small slice of the student population. Instead of providing models that promote systemwide reform, they can be insulated pockets of privilege, resegregation, and tracking. It all depends on which of the system's dual tendencies prevails. This is one reason for keeping a sharp eye on the big picture and asking "who benefits and who does not?" whenever a reform proposal is put on the table.

Finally, this dual character of schooling suggests that reforms should ultimately be judged not by their self-proclaimed goals, rhetorical promises, or short-term effect on test scores, but by their ability to deliver more democratic classroom experiences, and more equitable results and outcomes across the system. In an era of politically motivated "quick fixes" and narrow test-driven reform, changes in school form and structure, however necessary, must also be measured by the extent of their impact on the texture and substance of classroom life throughout the system.

Drive-by approaches to reform will never take schools where they need to go. Until we find the political will and vision to put social justice at the heart of the debate about public education, school reform will continue to be an exasperating tug of war with limited impact on the status quo.

Unfortunate as it may be, schools have never been just about educating children. They are also about constructing social and political power. Real school reform must be about challenging it.

Reconstituting Jefferson: Lessons on School Reform

Linda Christensen

On May 21, 1998, Jefferson High School teachers, cafeteria workers, custodians, secretaries, and administrators lined up to receive our official pink slips, notifying us to vacate our positions. Jefferson was being "reconstituted" because of low test scores and falling enrollment.

Lela Triplett Roberts, the incoming interim principal appointed by the Portland, Oregon school district, told teachers to inventory supplies, books, computers, and pack up our years of teaching materials by June 11 — while we were still teaching. As I took down student pictures, the national awards that *Rites of Passage*, Jefferson's literary magazine, had won, and boxed 22 years of lesson plans for my language arts classes, I felt the twin emotions of anger and sadness about being forced to leave a school I loved.

The decision to leave Jefferson was not an easy one. As part of the reconstitution process, staff could reapply for their positions. In meetings packed with emotion, Jefferson staff members struggled between staying for our students who did nothing to bring this about and leaving because it was an "insult to reapply for a job we did well." I always thought that I would retire from Jefferson. But instead, I packed my boxes because I refused to offer legitimacy to a shallow, mean-spirited educational policy.

The reconstitution of Jefferson was the school district's "get tough" reform strategy for schools that received the lowest numbers on state tests. Reconstitution means replacing the entire staff — administrators, teachers, custodians, secretaries — with a new staff. The logic underpinning this policy is that the problems of the school are caused by the staff's incompetence. Teachers became the scapegoats: Our supposed lack of competence and skill in teaching, as well as our allegedly low expectations for students, were deemed responsible for the low test scores and declining enrollment.

But reconstitution was not the answer to Jefferson's problems. It was a quick-fix solution, the kind now promoted by the No Child Left Behind federal legislation (NCLB), the kind that too many urban school districts use in response to the complex problems in low-performing schools.

Jefferson's history — as a reconstituted school and as a school on the federal "failing schools" list — makes it a perfect place to learn a key lesson about school reform: There are no quick fixes. In order to create a school characterized by vitality, high achievement, and engaged students, teachers need time to struggle collectively to build school structures and curriculum that not only address the academic and social needs of their students, but also lead students to a rigorous examination of a society that allows some students and schools to fail while others prosper.

Scholastic Triage

Located in the heart of Portland's predominantly working-class African-American community, Jefferson is considered the only "black" high school in Oregon. One has to wonder how much this designation contributed to the student flight that has marked the school's enrollment patterns. Jefferson typically loses a significant number of its neighborhood students to schools elsewhere in the city, as a part of a districtwide magnet program initiated in the mid-1970s to desegregate Portland's schools. After the reconstitution, students continued to pour out of the neighborhood and into other schools around the city. In the 2002-2003 school year, 971 "Jeff" students chose *not* to attend the school, leaving only 826 students. The numbers for September 2003 were even lower — only 750 students enrolled. Jefferson rated an "unacceptable" on the state report card and earned a place on the No Child Left Behind hit list. (See "Let Them Eat Tests: NCLB and Federal Education Policy" on p. 199.) Because of this designation, the school is required to send a letter home to parents informing them of Jefferson's failing status and their right to send their children to any other school in the district. As of June 2003, only 116 freshmen students had enrolled for the 2003-2004 school year. Between the district transfer policy and the NCLB legislation, Jefferson is turning into a ghost school.

While external policies encouraged students and families to abandon Jefferson and then dropped the "reconstitution bomb" on the school they'd left behind, other, quite different strategies were available. In a June 1993 *Phi Delta Kappan* article, "Reframing the School Reform Agenda: Developing Capacity for School Transformation," Linda Darling-Hammond recalls an eight-year study conducted by the Progressive Education Association as far back as the 1930s. According to the study, when staff members engage in a collaborative discourse, students and the school benefit. As Darling-Hammond writes:

> Most important, the study found that the most successful schools were characterized not by the particular innovation they had adopted but by their willingness to search and struggle in pursuit of valid objectives, new strategies, and new forms of assessment. It was the *process* of collective struggle that produced the vitality, the shared vision, and the conviction that allowed these schools to redesign education in fundamentally different ways. If the processes and outcomes of education are already defined by those outside of the schools, there is nothing left to talk about. Thus the removal of local responsibility for thinking things through deprives schools and communities of the opportunity to engage in the kind of empowering and enlivening dialogue that motivates change. [Emphasis in original.]

The reconstitution of Jefferson — a top-down reform delivered by the central office — included no such process and yielded disastrous results. The only people engaged in "collective struggle" were the students, teachers, parents, and community members who fought against the forced replacement of the Jefferson staff. Under pressure the school board agreed to meet with the Jefferson community in the school cafeteria prior to the reconstitution, but made it clear that although they came to hear what we had to say, they had already made their decision. After pushing out the old staff and creating a new administration composed of two elementary principals, a high school music teacher with no previous administrative experience, and a first-year vice principal from the previous administration, the folks at central office initially left the school on its own, more or less, to deal with the aftermath.

That, too, has been instructive. In an odd twist of fate, my post-reconstitution job has been working as the district's high school language arts coordinator, so I return to Jefferson regularly to work with new staff members on literacy issues.

Five years later, the stories of chaos — from a "dictionary toss" conducted by students in one first-year teacher's classroom, to a student urinating in a science class because the teacher refused to give him a bathroom pass, to the principal leading students and staff in prayer for a football championship — make for humorous, sometimes painful, dinner-time conversation. "The first year after reconstitution was a nightmare," according to Danica Fierman, who chose to come to Jefferson because as an Americorps volunteer she'd spent time in the community and fell in love with the school. Fierman later became coordinator for the Title III grant for English Language Learners at Jefferson, but she spent her first three years at the school as a language arts teacher. She remembers:

> There was no institutional memory. There were no systems in place for attendance, to check out books, to write referrals on students who misbehaved. Students were scheduled haphazardly into classes. Special Education and ELL students who had previously been in pull-out programs were placed in our classes without notifying us about their conditions or modifications. We didn't know which books to teach at which grade level in language arts. We had no curriculum. And there was no one to ask for help from within the school because there were no veteran teachers on staff in most of the subject areas.
>
> We were all new. We were handed a 50-page school reform document created by the staff members who were forced out of the school, but we had no idea how to implement it. Five years later, I look at the school reform document and I understand it. There was a vision for the creation of collaborative communities where teachers worked together with small groups of students and took full responsibility for their learning, including everything from attendance to teaching them the skills they needed to navigate high school.

As Darling-Hammond reminds us, school reforms must be created by the people who are going to implement them. Fierman recalls further:

> We moved into the structures created by the previous teachers, but we didn't understand how they worked. My time was spent in a ninth-grade academy with a math and science teacher, but as a new language arts teacher, I had no school time to collaborate with other teachers in my discipline. Instead Theresa Quinn, another first-year

language arts teacher, and I spent hours after school and on weekends developing curriculum where there was none. We had to create everything from scratch. The majority of the new staff members were white, recent graduates who had no experience teaching in an African-American school.

A curricular parallel, or second cousin of the reconstitution strategy, also in evidence at Jefferson, was the effort to "teacher-proof" instruction and lesson planning, and package the curriculum in a way that deskills, de-professionalizes, and disrespects classroom teachers. Instead of getting teachers together to model effective teaching strategies, examine student work, or discuss curriculum possibilities, educators in "failing" schools are sometimes not even trusted to create their own lesson plans. Principals, or school district leaders, buy packaged computer programs supposedly designed to teach reading and math instead of building teacher capacity and professional skills.

Since the reconstitution, Jefferson teachers and students have been the recipients of numerous silver bullets aimed at raising their reading and math test scores. For example, the Sylvan Learning Center created a carpeted space on the fourth floor to work with students on the cusp of passing the state test. But in this program of scholastic triage, they didn't want to deal with students with severe reading problems. They promised to raise the test scores for these "nearly meeting" students, so Jefferson could see some quick improvement in reading scores in the post-reconstitution years. The improvement did not materialize, but according to Peter Thacker, Jefferson's instructional specialist, Sylvan Learning Center walked out with $250,000 a year.

In another frenzied effort to raise scores quickly, the school separated out the students with the lowest test scores on their eighth-grade reading tests and gave them a special class to catch them up. Counselors placed these students in a "CIM reading class" which focused on literacy and aimed at improving scores on the Certificate of Initial Mastery (CIM) tests. The majority of these students were boys who fed off each other's negative behaviors. Many of them stopped attending the class by the end of the school year. Fierman recalls the first day of class when the boys walked in and called it the "retarded class." The students in the class had to take a mandatory summer school class to make up for the ninth-grade language arts credit they missed — a year's credit in six weeks. The Plato math lab, a corporate-generated, computer-assisted math program, was also instituted. These heavily tracked approaches mirrored the administrative labeling system that branded Jefferson a failing school in need of reconstitution, and were similarly counterproductive.

Some Positive Steps

After several disastrous post-reconstitution years, Jefferson has started to recover. The leadership of the last two administrations provided space and time for teachers to struggle collectively to create their own solutions to Jefferson's historic problems. And while it is ironic that their solution reflects the academy reorganization that was outlined in the pre-reconstitution school reform documents, it is the teacher talk, the demonstration lessons, the carving out of time — the creation of a *process*— that reflects the collective vitality discussed in the Progressive Education Association's finding from the 1930's.

The school reform document developed by the soon-to-be-reconstituted Jefferson teachers, referred to earlier by Danica Fierman, included a plan for ninth- and tenth-grade academics. The plan demonstrated some success prior to the reconstitution, but the first group of academy students hadn't graduated by the time the school was closed. The current staff resurrected the academies as part of their new school reform efforts.

Jefferson teachers instituted freshmen academies in the fall of 2002 and created sophomore academies in the fall of 2003. These academies consist of an interdisciplinary team of teachers — language arts, social studies, and science — who work with the same group of students, sometimes for one year, sometimes for more than one if the teachers "loop" to the next grade with the students. These teachers share a common planning time to develop curriculum, participate in integrated professional development, and discuss student work, attendance, and behavior. They are also paid to develop relevant curriculum together for two weeks in the summer.

During the 2002-2003 school year, I worked with the ninth-grade academies frequently — at their invitation. Over the course of the year, we examined student writing to find out what students were doing right and what they needed to learn; we shared reading and writing strategies, and brainstormed interdisciplinary curriculum ideas that focused on the Jefferson community. In a recent professional development session, we studied the grammar rules for Ebonics, teachers looked for evidence of it in student writing, and we discussed how to help students code-switch to standard English.

The initial data after the first year of the academies included hopeful signs: More ninth-grade students attended school regularly — an increase from 85% to 95% in the 2002-2003 school year. They also received fewer discipline referrals; they earned higher grades; and fewer ninth graders failed their academic classes. More ninth graders received passing scores on the writing and speaking work samples mandated by the state of Oregon.

While the academies showed promise in both pre- and post-reconstitution Jefferson, I am also wary of cheering too loudly for a structural change that, by itself, doesn't necessarily change the classroom content. Creating support structures for better teaching and learning will not automatically result in improved student learning. Such reforms are necessary, but not sufficient. Unless teachers also rethink and revise the content of the curriculum and use teaching strategies that actively engage students in critical reflections of their lives and society, we will continue to reproduce the same kind of disengaged students we have in traditional high schools.

The majority of failing schools are inhabited by students whose lives are daily impacted by the twin foes of poverty and racism. When teachers construct lessons that tackle these issues, students tend to become more willing learners. If teachers pour the same curriculum and instructional practices into new organizational structures, little will change.

The intense schoolwide conversations that created the academies at Jefferson need to continue. In the first sweep of building ninth-grade academies, the majority of participating teachers *chose* to become involved, to teach in a community. However, not all teachers want to collaborate. What happens when the numbers of enthusiastic teachers dwindle and teachers are assigned to academies? Who chooses the teams? What if a team member doesn't want to participate in daily meetings? Who is responsible for making sure the meetings occur?

Here again, there are no easy answers. To embrace change, teachers need support, time, and resources. They also need models of success, credible reform processes and leadership, and a sense of accountability to a mobilized student and community constituency. Where these elements are lacking, reform may go off track.

For example, in pre-reconstitution Jefferson, administrators tried to replicate the success of the early academies by mandating that teachers participate in these smaller learning communities. One of the communities had to be disbanded because the teachers would not work together. Similarly, in the first year of the post-reconstitution academies, teachers were randomly assigned to "houses." There was no choice, no time for discussion, no time for collaboration, and no curriculum. Those academies were abandoned after the first year. Even potentially good ideas can fail if the leadership and resources needed to make reform work are missing.

School reform doesn't just happen within the school; it happens within the district as well, which is why support from central office is crucial for the long-term success of building initiatives. When district leadership teams are involved in local change, they can highlight exemplary programs across the district, and create opportunities for teachers from different schools to share structures, critical teaching strategies, interdisciplinary teaching units, and common curricular expectations. Central office is also crucial in supporting innovative programs with lower student-teacher ratios, increased meeting times, and more autonomy in hiring practices.

There is no quick fix to the systemic problems that face Jefferson High School. It is a school that has been stigmatized by failure. Because of the district's magnet school policy, now reinforced by NCLB's student transfer schemes, Jefferson's enrollment continues to decline.

The first reconstitution gave the school one year to turn around. NCLB gave the school another year before imposing sanctions. Despite some hopeful signs, the lack of long-term school leadership (there were six principals in the five years following reconstitution), and a rotating crop of new teachers (25 of the 66 new teachers transferred to other schools in 2002), have made Jefferson's progress episodic since the initial reconstitution.

In order for real and lasting change to take place, schools need stability — an intact administration and teaching staff, who are given the time and resources needed to struggle collectively as they work for change. Teachers need space within the school day and during the summer to construct a curriculum that captures the hearts and minds of their students. And they need collective opportunities to analyze their students' essays, lab reports, and research papers to see if their curriculum worked, to fine-tune, revise, or throw out the lessons that failed to produce results. Finally, reform needs patience to work. Perhaps in the next round, Jefferson can hand out pink slips to those who legislate and posture about school change without ever giving the time or the resources needed to make it happen.

Money, Schools, and Justice

Stan Karp

For 30 years, battles over inequities in school funding have been clogging the nation's courts. Ever since the U.S. Supreme Court declared in 1973 in *Rodriguez v. San Antonio* that education was not a fundamental right protected by the U.S. Constitution, equity advocates and public interest lawyers have fought a state-by-state battle against the "savage inequalities" of school finance systems which provide qualitatively different levels of education to students from different class, race, and community backgrounds.

Typically, these inequities have been traced to wide gaps in per-pupil spending among districts, and to finance systems that rely heavily on unequal property tax bases as the source of funds for education. But the inequalities run deeper. They include funding formulas that dispense state aid in ways that perpetuate inequities; state and federal tax policies that disinvest from public services like education while preserving pockets of privilege; a general retreat from civil-rights-era concerns for equity, desegregation, and racial justice; and the growing economic stratification in society at large. In many ways the funding mechanisms that deliver drastically different experiences to kids in different classrooms simply mirror the inequality that exists all around us.

Given its deep roots, it's not surprising that funding inequity has been hard to overcome despite the growing number of high-profile court cases. Since the early 1970s, more than 30 state supreme court decisions have been issued in school finance cases. About half have declared existing funding systems illegal or inadequate and mandated a variety of corrective measures. In the remaining cases, courts have rejected the challenges or refrained from intervening despite acknowledging inequities, contending that the issue is a legislative matter, not a judicial one, or narrowly reading constitutional provisions about the state's obligation to provide education to all.

Even where courts have declared funding systems illegal, however, equitable solutions have been far from certain. As New Jersey's Education Law Center, which has battled the state's funding system for more than two decades, put it: "Law books are filled with wonderful paper victories which have never been implemented." The state Supreme Court has declared New Jersey's finance system legally inadequate in various ways no less than nine times since the early '70s, yet the state is still struggling to devise an equitable funding formula to meet the court mandates. Other states have similar histories of seemingly interminable litigation.

By themselves, court rulings have been insufficient to assure equity for several reasons. While glaring disparities in school funding may persuade judges to order reform, it has been almost impossible to prevent governors and state legislators from evading or limiting the impact of the court orders. Most courts have been reluctant to go too far in specifying remedies. Restrained by separation-of-powers concerns and the prevailing conservative political climate, courts have generally given states wide latitude to proceed with half measures and "good faith" efforts, sometimes promising further review if reforms prove inadequate. At times judges, governors, and legislators have engaged in prolonged, sometimes ludicrous institutional charades about how much inequality is permissible, while generations of school children remain trapped by injustice.

The Impact of Tax 'Reform'

In some states, tentative steps toward equity taken under court pressure have been thwarted by the rising tide of anti-tax populism. California is a prime example. The state's Serrano decision in the early '70s was one of the first requiring a state to correct massive inequities among districts in educational services. Some efforts were made to equalize spending by revising aid formulas and transferring some property tax revenues from wealthier to poorer districts. But these efforts were derailed by Proposition 13, a 1978 ballot initiative that capped property taxes in one of the opening rounds of the "tax revolt" that came to shape local, state, and federal tax policy in the '80s and '90s (and which, despite promises of relief to hard-pressed taxpayers, has succeeded primarily in swelling state and federal deficits, starving public services, and redirecting wealth upward). As a result of Proposition 13, California was forced to assume a greater share of local school spending, which did lead to a degree of greater "equity" among districts. But there was also a dramatic decline in spending on schools relative to other states. In the '60s, California was fifth in per-pupil spending; by the end of the '90s it was 30th, and well below the national average. Class size in California is now among the highest in the nation.[1] Because of Proposition 13 and its offspring, support for California schools has tended toward "equalization" at a level that keeps them in a state of perpetual budgetary crisis and inadequacy. (In addition, a variety of loopholes and privatizing trends, such as the establishment of private educational foundations to subsidize schools in wealthy districts, has meant that pockets of elite spending persist even in the midst of this "leveling effect.")

The balance sheet, then, on 30 years of state litigation for funding equity is, at best, mixed. The legal basis for funding equity is clearly stronger in many places than it was in the past. In states where legal challenges have been successful, some of the grossest inequities in per-pupil district expenditures have been reduced, if not eliminated. School finance reform has become a high-priority issue across the nation, and an unusually broad consensus has been formed around the proposition that a better system of funding schools needs to be created.

At the same time, many of the groups that have come to a consensus on the need for a new system have arrived there with decidedly different agendas. On the one hand are those with essentially a budget-cutting agenda who want to restrain spending on schools, cut property taxes, and eliminate "waste" which, depending on the source, can mean anything from bloated administrative bureaucracy to desperately needed programs, new facilities, and reductions in class size. On the other hand are those with an equity agenda who see school finance reform as an essential ingredient in an effort to reform ineffective school districts while also compensating as much as possible for the devastating effects of poverty, race, and class injustice on the lives of children. These competing perspectives rise to the surface whenever the issue turns to specifics, and suggest that the apparent consensus on the need for fundamental reform of school finance systems may prove illusory.

With courts usually limiting themselves to generalized orders for reform, the focus turns to legislative and public debates about what alternatives exist to funding systems based on property taxes, about how educational equity should be defined, and about what levels and types of spending are appropriate.

The property tax issue is both a root problem and, in some ways, a diversion from the core issue of equity. Local property taxes still supply about 44% of all school funds. State support varies, but on average provides about 49%. The federal government's share of education spending, which peaked at about 9% in the '70s, has dropped to about 7%.[2]

Since the distribution of property in the U.S. has never been more unequal, and since many communities have never been more segregated by race and class, it's inevitable that schools heavily dependent on property taxes will be unequal. In fact, with more than 16,000 separate school districts, the reliance on property taxes functions as a sorting mechanism for class and race privilege, and allows pockets of "elite schooling" to exist within the public system. Any real chance of increasing and redistributing education resources requires fundamentally changing the connection between school spending and local property taxes.

Historically, it's been argued that schools rely on local property taxes because of the strong U.S. tradition of local control of schools. But one issue that has been clarified in the state-by-state litigation over funding inequities is that it is the state, not the local district, that has the legal responsibility to fund the schools. States may allow education funding to be based on local property taxes, but this is not the result of any immutable standing or compelling interest of local districts. Rather it's a product of state decisions about funding policies, and about the taxing power it does or does not make available to local entities like school boards and city councils, and it provides no legal grounds for permitting inequality to exist. Likewise, the state has the power to remake the funding system in any way it sees fit, retaining or modifying district authority in any given area of school policy or oversight. In other words, preserving local control (or even radically extending it, for example, to individual school site councils) does not in any way depend on retaining the link between school funding and local property taxes.

To sever this link, however, will require a political rather than strictly legal strategy that will have to overcome several obstacles. In many respects, the existing system of funding education through local property taxes serves the agenda of the budget-cutters and conservative forces who currently dominate state and local governments. When local communities must assume growing fiscal burdens for schools by more heavily taxing local residential and commercial property, it creates a strong budgetary pressure for austerity. When local school budgets are presented like sacrificial lambs to hard-pressed local taxpayers (who never get to vote on tax abatements for real estate developers or whether the Defense Department should build another aircraft carrier), the budget process for schools becomes driven not by what schools and children need, but by how to keep the tax rate flat. Add to this the fact that only a fraction of the local population generally has children in the schools, and an even smaller fraction (about 15%) usually votes in budget referendums, and you have a system that works well to undercut, not sustain, quality education. Factor in the growing racial divide between those most likely to vote in local elections and the public school population, and you have a system that regularly keeps communities divided. The reliance on property tax funding for schools, then, works at one level to create inequality, and at another as a vise to squeeze local budgets. For these reasons, there are many interests who want to keep it.

Nevertheless, there is still a growing effort to consider alternatives to funding based on local property taxes, fed by court orders, heavy local tax burdens, and the ongoing national debate about education reform. One set of fiscal reforms is geared to "recapturing" or redistributing property tax revenues from richer districts to poorer ones. Another seeks to replace property taxes with other taxes, usually sales taxes, and have the state assume a larger fraction of overall school spending. Still another set of proposals involves redefining state aid formulas so that fewer funds go to districts as "flat grants" regardless of need or local wealth, and more are distributed through "foundation formulas" which guarantee a base level of funding for each student and which are calculated in ways that promote greater equalization.

The problem is that no particular financial mechanism, in itself, guarantees either equity or quality in education. It's true that relying on some taxes, like property and sales taxes, tends to be regressive, while progressive income taxes are fairer ways to raise revenues. But choosing a particular funding mechanism does not assure that adequate funds will be available.

In fact, one danger in the move to reform existing funding systems is that new ones will be adopted which will still deliver inadequate or inequitable levels of education. New formulas promising better, more secure funding have been adopted in a number of states, only to be cut or modified once the higher costs became clear. If the controlling motivation is a desire to cut property taxes or hold down educational spending, rather than promote quality and equity, it may not matter what fiscal mechanism is chosen to do the job.

Another response to court challenges has been to try to define what a "thorough" or "adequate" education means, and then peg funding formulas to the cost of providing those elements. Here again, the budget-cutters often collide with the equity advocates over what level of educational services the state is obligated to provide for all.

Neighboring States, Different Outcomes

This tension is reflected in two key court cases in the neighboring states of New York and New Jersey. These landmark legal battles illustrate why the legal front is but one part of the struggle for equitable school finance.

The *Abbott* decision in New Jersey is arguably the single most progressive school funding ruling in the history of school finance cases. It is the product of more than 20 years of litigation and advocacy by New Jersey's Education Law Center (www.edlawcenter.org), and includes 10 separate state Supreme Court rulings. It also has prompted countless evasive maneuvers by legislators and gubernatorial administrations who have resisted the court's decisions and mandates.

Essentially, the New Jersey court ruled that the state's system of school funding, which relied heavily on unequal property tax bases in more than 600 separate districts, denied children in the state's urban areas equal access to the "thorough and efficient" education guaranteed by the state constitution. The Education Law Center documented gross inequality and pressing need across the state's urban districts, and the court established unequivocally that it was the state's obligation to redress this inequality in its public schools.

Where *Abbott* really blazed new ground was in the standard it set for this equity mandate. Throughout the long years of litigation, the state court had repeatedly pressed the state Department of Education to define and itemize the essential elements of a "thorough and efficient" education. Repeatedly, the Department of Education and successive administrations avoided this request, fearing that a generous definition would obligate them to provide such services to poor districts. At the same time, the Department of Education was wary of defining too low a level of education services for fear that this would open up a Pandora's box in New Jersey's middle-income and wealthy districts, which would then be forced to justify to angry taxpayers expenditures above some state-defined minimum. Moreover, a large gap between a state-defined minimum and the prevailing practice in most New Jersey districts (which collectively averaged among the highest per-pupil spending levels in the nation) would call attention to the very inequality the state court was seeking to address.

Frustrated by the Department of Education's evasions, the state court ultimately took as its standard the level of spending in the state's richest and most successful school districts. Arguing, plausibly, that these districts obviously knew what it took for kids to succeed educationally, the court ordered the state to raise the spending level of the state's poorest districts to the average level of the 100 richest. And, citing deeper social problems and years of deprivation, the court directed the state to compensate by spending money in poor districts above and beyond parity for regular educational programs. *Abbott* remains, as the Education Law Center declared, "the first decision in the 20-year history of school finance reform to establish an equality standard for the allocation of education resources to poor urban children."

By defining equity as equivalency in per-pupil spending with the richest districts, plus additional spending to compensate for greater need, the New Jersey Supreme Court defined equity at the highest levels of spending.

Moreover, the court's decision was phrased in striking language that made clear the implications of the social problems it was addressing: "The fact is that a large part of our society is disintegrating, so large a part that it cannot help but affect the rest. Everyone's future is at stake, and not just the poor's."[3]

This extraordinary decision opened up a new era of reform in New Jersey's urban districts. More than $1 billion was allocated in the five years following the 1998 *Abbott* decision for court-ordered investments in early childhood programs, whole-school reform initiatives, supplemental health and social services, extended day and summer programs, a massive program of school construction, technology upgrades and other improvements.

To be sure, struggles over the implementation and effectiveness of the *Abbott* mandates have continued. Budget pressures pushed the administration of Democratic Governor James McGreevey, which initially came into office in 2001 promising to embrace and improve *Abbott* programs, to return to court seeking to roll back the ruling's mandates and costs. Perhaps more significant in the long run is the fact that while *Abbott* addressed funding equity for poor urban districts, it did not fix the state's overall school finance system. More than 400 so-called "middle districts" remain squeezed by property tax formulas and the state budget crisis. Poor rural districts have had little success gaining access to *Abbott* levels of support. Unless remedies are found for these problems, sustaining *Abbott* formulas may be difficult as urban, suburban, and rural districts are pitted in competition for an inadequate pool of funds. Nevertheless, *Abbott* remains the "gold standard" for school funding equity cases.

But if *Abbott* set an equity standard for the education of poor children in New Jersey, other courts have responded quite differently. Just next door in New York, the Coalition for Fiscal Equity (CFE) mounted a broad campaign of public engagement and advocacy in support of a legal challenge to the state's school funding system. That system delivers more than $1,000 per pupil less to New York City's 1.1 million students, 84% of whom are students of color, than it delivers to other districts in the state. The CFE won a round in January 2001 when a New York judge ruled that the school funding formula was "inequitable and unconstitutional," and failed to meet the state's constitutional guarantee of the right to a "sound basic education."[4]

But in a striking reversal, a state appellate court overturned that finding and held that the state was obligated only to provide "the skills required to enable a person to obtain employment, vote, and serve on a jury" and that these skills are "imparted between grades 8 and 9." In other words, a "minimally adequate" middle school education was sufficient to meet New York legal requirements. "Society needs workers at all levels," the Appeals Court wrote provocatively, "the majority of which may very well be low level." The state and its experts argued that while poverty and related family crises could be reliably identified as the source of unequal educational achievement, New York schools were not obligated to address these needs in their school programs.[5]

In June 2003 the state's highest court of appeals overturned the appellate court's ruling, rejecting the "8th grade" standard and reinstating the lower court's guarantee of a "sound basic education." It found that as a result of New York state's school funding system, "tens of thousands of students are placed in overcrowded classrooms, taught by unqualified teachers and provided with inadequate facilities and equipment....The number of children in these straits is large enough to represent a systemic failure." The court gave the New York state legislature until July 2004 to craft a plan that would provide a "sound basic education" to all students.[6]

This latest New York ruling was a clear victory for equity advocates. But it also left large loopholes for the legislature and the governor (who staunchly opposed the challenge to the state's funding system) to evade its implications. Unlike *Abbott*, the New York decision did not specify the educational programs or spending levels required to deliver the "sound basic education" it said students were entitled to receive, explicitly leaving that determination to the legislative process. The Court also left it unclear whether the decision applies to all New York districts or only New York City schools. This ensures an extended political (and perhaps additional legal) struggle, in the midst of perpetual budget crisis, to turn the court's decision into real educational equity.

With different state courts, at times, giving diametrically opposed answers to the question of what constitutes legal equity in school funding, states have been implementing finance systems that vary widely, from those applying an equity standard to those based on a minimal one. The divergent court decisions reflect some of the underlying limitations of a state-by-state process which, even where it succeeds, usually produces a court ruling that is turned over for implementation to a state legislature dominated by politicians unrepresentative of those on the short end of school spending. While important progress has been made in narrowing some educational inequities and raising key issues, continued and more substantial progress may depend on finding new strategies to promote funding equity.

Seeking New Strategies

Along with legal challenges, aggressive public organizing that mobilizes broad constituencies, clarifies issues, and debates proposed solutions is critical to building the kinds of coalitions and political pressure needed to force action. Even where it suffers setbacks, a strategy of public coalition building is more likely to promote grassroots activism and bring together a progressive constituency for school change on a range of issues including funding.

At the same time, over the long term it will be necessary to open up other fronts in the campaign for funding equity, ones that reach beyond state borders. To really make good on promises of educational equity and excellence will take tens of billions of dollars over many years, the kinds of sums that have been poured into the military for decades. A 1995 federal report documented a need for more than $110 billion in construction and renovation of K-12 facilities alone (and such capital costs, while far greater in poorer areas, are often not even included in the per-pupil expenditures that are generally the focus of equalizing efforts). Only a national effort could generate the necessary funds.[7]

Meanwhile, the United States continues to trail other economically developed societies in educational investment. A 1995 report from the Organization for Economic Cooperation and Development, for example, showed the United States was tied for eighth among highly industrialized nations in the percentage of GNP spent on education.[8] Federal funds for local schools dropped to their lowest post-World War II levels in the '80s, and have risen only slightly since.[9]

Moreover, the willingness of the federal government to support national commitments to equality has been waning since the civil rights era. Increasingly, federal courts have ruled that "separate and unequal" educational programs, in themselves, are not illegal, unless conscious, deliberate "intent to discriminate" can be proved. Combined with persistent inequalities in school finance, this legal doctrine nourishes the existence of a dual school system, in which students of color systematically attend schools with less funding in segregated settings. This has prompted some legal experts to consider a new equity challenge in the federal courts.

"Of all developed countries, only two systematically have spent less money educating poor children than wealthy children," noted Paul Tractenberg, a founder of New Jersey's Education Law Center. "One is South Africa [under apartheid], the other is the United States." Tractenberg argues that taken together, racial segregation coupled with systematic funding inequities amount to a degree of inequality that wouldn't even satisfy the standards of *Plessy v. Ferguson*, the historic 1896 U.S. Supreme Court decision that set a standard of "separate but equal" until the 1954 *Brown* decision mandated school integration. Tractenberg argues:

> In the federal courts, now it's clear that *de facto* segregation alone doesn't violate the federal constitution. And it's clear that unequal funding by itself is not a federal constitutional violation. But if you put the two together, aren't you creating a situation which wouldn't have even satisfied the standards of *Plessy v. Fergusson*? So how could it satisfy a body of contemporary law that is presumably more demanding in these terms than *Plessy* was? The question is whether the federal courts might be made to view this issue differently than they did in the past.[10]

New legal pressure on the courts to make the federal government give tangible substance to promises of equality through greater investment in schools could eventually open up the federal treasury to equity advocates. But like state legal strategies, such success would also likely depend on broader public campaigns to reorder the nation's social priorities. That, after all, is what equity in school funding is ultimately all about.

[1] Ed Fact: California Rankings, Education Data Partnership. http://www.ed_data.k12. ca.us/Articles/calrankings.asp.

[2] Carey, Kevin. "Overview of K-12 Education Finance," Center on Policy and Budget Priorities, November 5, 2002, and Education Commission of the States, "The Changing Role of the Federal Government in Education," http://www.ecs.org/clearinghouse/ 24/19/2419.htm#role.

[3] From *Abbott v. Burke II* decision, quoted by Michael Newman, "Finance System For N.J. Schools Is Struck Down" *Education Week*, June 13, 1990.

[4] "A Landmark School Ruling," *New York Times*, January 11, 2001.

[5] Lovett, Kenneth, Campanile, Carl and Gregorian, Dareh. "9th Grade Good Enough for City Kids, Court Says," *New York Post*, June 27, 2002. Also Schweber, Nate and Barrett, Wayne. "State's Top Expert in Case Has Controversial Racial History," *Village Voice*, August 7-13, 2002.

[6] Associated Press, "New York State Failing City Schools, Court Says," Albany, N.Y., June 26, 2003.

[7] Peterson, Bob. "School Facilities at Crisis Level," *Rethinking Schools*, Spring 1996.

[8] "International Comparisons of Education," *Digest of Education Statistics*, 1999.

[9] Hoffman, Charlene M. "Federal Support for Education: Fiscal Years 1980 to 2002," *Education Statistics Quarterly*, Winter, 2002.

[10] Paul Tractenberg, in an interview by Stan Karp, March 1995.

Teacher Councils: Tools for Change

Bob Peterson

Several years ago African-American educator Asa Hilliard spoke to a gathering of elementary teachers and principals in Milwaukee, stressing the central role of teacher knowledge and attitudes in any reform effort. "Curriculum," he told us, "is what's inside teachers' heads."

The significance of Hilliard's remarks extended beyond the group, which consisted of the entire staffs from seven Milwaukee schools. "That inservice was the start of something big," recollects Steve Baruch, coordinator for the Milwaukee Public Schools (MPS) Leadership Academy and an organizer of the event. "Most people don't know it, but it was from there that many of the teacher councils, particularly the Multicultural Council, got their start."

For most of the 1990s, a network of teacher-led, districtwide councils had a significant impact on reform in MPS. In particular, the councils provided a way for progressive teachers to promote student-centered, anti-racist curricular reform.

The original councils included the Multicultural Curriculum Council, Whole Language Council, Early Childhood Council, Ungraded/Multi-Age Council, and the Humanities Council. Eventually a Bilingual Council, Library Council, Reading Council, and Health Council formed. In 1994, a Council of Councils was organized to coordinate the councils and to improve their ability to learn from one another.

Ultimately the councils fell short of their promise, and the reasons are worth examining. But before they began to fade, the councils did much good work. More importantly, they represented a strategy that contrasts sharply with the top-down approaches that characterize many school reform initiatives. Instead of imposing an external agenda developed far from classroom life, the teacher councils represented an opportunity for teachers to help shape the reform agenda and to bring credibility and leadership to the effort to improve Milwaukee schools.

According to Kathy Swope, former teacher co-chair of the Multicultural Curriculum Committee:

> The councils' strength was that they gave an official forum for classroom teachers to comment on various issues and to influence district policy. The councils viewed teachers as the experts. We had teachers teaching teachers, giving workshops, organizing conferences and inservices, and developing materials. The feedback was almost always that our workshops were more useful than many which were not led by teachers.

The Milwaukee teacher councils were effective because they were integrated into a districtwide curriculum reform effort with explicitly anti-racist goals. This process, discussed below, provided direction and opportunities for the councils to grow. Other strengths of the councils were that they were led by classroom teachers, organized throughout the district and across school lines, and focused on classroom teachers sharing their best practices.

In addition, the councils went beyond one-time inservices, and instead formalized teacher collaboration, mobilization, and training. They also recommended and provided money for classroom resources.

The councils are now largely gone. But the lessons learned from the councils can shape discussion of how to promote grassroots, districtwide reform that focuses on changing classroom practice and promotes a curriculum appropriate for our increasingly diverse and multicultural society.

Districtwide Reform

Each of the councils had separate beginnings but all were tied to teacher-led initiatives and progressive curricular philosophies.

"The Multicultural Curriculum Council grew out of the Asa Hilliard inservice," Baruch recalls. "Representatives from the seven schools got together first as a study group...and then the whole thing blossomed." About a dozen schools that had demonstrated a commitment to multicultural education were invited to send representatives and the Multicultural Council was formed. Eventually the council included members from almost every school in the district.

The Whole Language Council, meanwhile, had its origins in the district's process, in 1987, for adopting an elementary reading textbook. Three members of the textbook committee issued a minority report critical of traditional basal reader teaching methods. That ultimately led to an "opt-out" provision whereby individual schools were permitted to submit a whole language reading instructional plan to replace the traditional basal reader collections of short stories and work sheets. Instead of receiving the new basal readers, the "opt-out" schools received money to buy children's literature, big books, and other materials. Thirteen schools opted for this provision. Teachers from those schools met, held joint inservices, and formed the Whole Language Council in the fall of 1988.

The councils received financial support from the general MPS budget up through 1996, when funding was cut off. They received on average about $25,000 a year, although a few received about $100,000 during their initial years. The larger budgets were either for districtwide inservices, such as those of the Early Childhood Council, or for programs to provide grants to schools. These grants, ranging from $1,000 to $10,000, were used to buy materials, pay for specific staff workshops, or to hire community people for school-based projects.

The councils developed in the context of an even broader curricular reform effort that was sparked by grassroots teacher organizing. In the late 1980s dozens of teachers, many of them affiliated with Rethinking Schools, organized against an "outcomes-based education" reform effort pushed by the MPS superintendent. The teachers argued that imposing hundreds of minute learning objectives for each grade level was going to straitjacket quality teaching and dumb-down the curriculum. The board succumbed to the pressure, rejected the "outcomes-based" education proposal, and hired a new superintendent. The district then embarked on a two-year curricular reform process, which came to be known as the Milwaukee K-12 Reform.

The reform's spirit is best captured in its self-description as "a mobilization to improve teaching and learning in the Milwaukee Public Schools.... It aims to offer all children an equitable, multicultural education, and teach all children to think deeply, critically, and creatively." This reform emerged at a time when the national education climate focused on curriculum inno-vation and embraced our country's multicultural heritage and future. The Milwaukee K-12 Reform involved thousands of teachers and hundreds of parents and community people who worked over many months to develop the initiative's 10 Teaching and Learning Goals. Teachers were involved, energized, and felt "ownership" of the Teaching and Learning Goals. The first goal was particularly groundbreaking for a large district. It stated: "Students will project anti-racist, anti-biased attitudes through their partic-ipation in a multilingual, multi-ethnic, culturally diverse curriculum."

The other goals:

2. Students will participate and gain knowledge in all the arts (visual arts, dance, theater, literature, music), developing personal vehi-cles for self-expression reinforced in an integrated curriculum.
3. Students will demonstrate positive attitudes towards life, living, and learning, through an understanding and respect of self and others.
4. Students will make responsible decisions, solve problems, and think critically.
5. Students will demonstrate responsible citizenship and an under-standing of global interdependence.
6. Students will use technological resources capably, actively, and responsibly.
7. Students will think logically and abstractly, applying mathematical and scientific principles of inquiry to solve problems, create new solutions, and communicate new ideas and relationships to real-world experiences.
8. Students will communicate knowledge, ideas, thoughts, feelings, concepts, opinions, and needs effectively and creatively using var-ied modes of expression.
9. Students will learn strategies to cope with the challenges of daily living and will establish practices which promote health, fitness, and safety.
10. Students will set short and long-term goals, will develop an aware-ness of career opportunities, and will be motivated to actualize their potential.

The K-12 Reform played a significant role in shaping nearly all reform initiatives at the time. It remains official district policy as of 2003.

Four teacher councils — the Multicultural Curriculum, Whole Language, Early Childhood, and Humanities Councils — played especially important roles in the K-12 reform and helped ensure its emphasis on equity and multicultural education.

"The councils are what gave flesh to the [K-12] policy," explained Swope. "In order for policies to actually affect classroom practice, you need teachers to develop strategies, try out resources, collaborate, and share their successes. This was done and led by teachers. That's why the councils were so powerful."

Cynthia Ellwood, the central office administrator who led the K-12 Reform effort, explained: "The councils were about mobilization and identifying people who were particularly competent and insightful teachers. They simultaneously modeled good teaching...and gave very specific teaching ideas, along with the necessary books and materials. In fact, the councils help set the [reform] agenda for the district."

Both the K-12 Reform and the teacher councils were based on the belief that improving classroom practice is the key to districtwide reform. The structures of most schools, however, reinforce teacher isolation. Teachers have little time to collaborate with their colleagues across the hall — to say nothing of getting together with teachers from across the city. Too often, school districts rely on experts who no longer teach in the classroom, or on "teacher-proof" curriculum with predetermined lesson plans that leave little room for addressing the specific needs of one's students. The Milwaukee teacher councils took a different approach. The district viewed teachers as leaders and asked them to chair all the councils. To make this possible, the school district allocated funds for substitutes so classroom teachers could be released during the day to work on council business. The decision to pay for substitutes was key to the councils' success: Without paid substitutes at the elementary level, reading resource teachers and program implementers — who don't have classrooms and thus can leave the building more easily — tended to take the lead on districtwide committees.

Classroom teacher leadership on the councils meant several things. First, the workshops, meetings, and resources that ultimately were developed had a more useful character than those imposed by principals or central-office officials. Second, experienced classroom teachers often were presenters, and even the non-teacher presenters were people committee members knew were of high quality and could connect well with classroom teachers.

Crossing School Lines

The councils promoted ongoing discussion among teachers at different schools. They brought together some of the most committed teachers and gave them time and resources to help educate and mobilize other teachers. Through workshops, conferences, inservice courses, newsletters, and resource vendor fairs, the councils' impact was felt throughout the district. In some schools, teacher council members reported back at staff meetings and helped re-create workshops that they themselves had experienced at council functions. Other members helped shape staff inservices at their school, or helped launch new projects within their schools. For example, in one school teachers who had previously developed a multi-ethnic fair that tended to accentuate stereotypes changed their celebration to focus on commonalities across culture, such as different types of bread and art. In some cases the councils provided a lifeline for teachers who were isolated in schools that had little or no staff collaboration. More than one teacher reported at council meetings that their participation on the council was what kept their faith in quality teaching alive, and in fact kept them teaching.

The most extensive example is the work of the Early Childhood Council, which was founded in 1991. The council coordinated a series of workshops to help teachers improve their teaching and implement the K-12 Reform. In 1992-93, for example, every kindergarten teacher in the MPS district was released for three days to attend workshops led by classroom teachers with outstanding practice. The following year, all first-grade teachers attended similar professional development; a new grade level was inserviced each year for two more years. The workshops addressed a variety of issues, including how to construct curriculum that builds on children's cultural and family backgrounds, how to work successfully with limited-English learners, how to detect stereotypes in children's literature and classroom practices, and how to integrate multicultural children's books into different subject areas.

"The workshops touched every early childhood [K-third grade] teacher," said Mary Randall, a kindergarten teacher who was chair of the Early Childhood Council. "We had teachers — new ones and experienced ones — learning about the very best techniques from people who were excellent classroom teachers."

Rita Tenorio, a veteran bilingual teacher who presented at those workshops, recalled: "The workshop presenters were classroom teachers who shared what worked in multiracial classrooms, but who at the same time challenged the participants. For example, we looked at how thematic approaches need to go beyond bears and dinosaurs to more substantive issues."

Tenorio continued:

> We talked about how teachers need to be aware of multiple perspectives and present them even to the youngest children. We had to share with the teachers themselves how the "official" versions of historical incidents — like Columbus's landfall and the Battle of the Alamo — are too often told only from the perspective of the [eventual] victors. It's not until teachers understood that it was the United States who stole half of Mexico, and not the other way around, that they could start to create classroom situations that helped kids see things from a different perspective.

Sharing Best Practices

The councils didn't rely only on inservices to promote quality teaching. The Whole Language Council provided funding so that entire staffs from participating schools could attend workshops of the National Writing Project. The Multicultural Council held quarterly after-school meetings and an annual weekend conference, which highlighted exemplary teacher practice. Most councils put out newsletters highlighting resources and inservice opportunities sponsored by area colleges or by the councils themselves. For a while the Whole Language Council hosted a radio show about literacy teaching on the district's FM radio station. The Humanities and Multicultural councils both created menus of quality multicultural literature and teaching guides. The councils provided schools with the funds to

buy materials from the menus and then held workshops on how to effectively use the materials in the classroom.

Some of the councils also put out specific teacher guides. The Multicultural Council, for example, published a "Guide for Implementation of
Goal 1 of the MPS K-12 Teaching and Learning Initiative." Despite its lack-
luster title, the guide provided both a theoretical explanation and specific
lesson plans and resources for teachers to deal with the difficult issue of
anti-racist education. One lesson, for example, was on how to teach inter-
mediate students to critique the bias and omissions in children's books
about Christopher Columbus. The Early Childhood Council piloted early
childhood screening methods and prepared a videotape to help teachers. It
also put out a kindergarten guide to hands-on learning and developmen-
tally appropriate instruction. The Reading Council developed districtwide
reading curricula.

While emphasizing lessons from classroom teachers, the councils also
brought to Milwaukee a number of well-respected experts, such as James
Banks, Howard Zinn, Enid Lee, Gloria Ladson-Billings, Bill Bigelow, Asa
Hilliard, Nancy Schniedewind, and Carlos Cortez.

The Demise of the Councils

Most of the councils ceased functioning during the 1996-1997 school
year. A number of factors contributed to their decline, including budget
cuts, the push for radical, school-based decentralization, a shift away from
the K-12 curriculum effort towards a school-to-work focus, a national reform effort driven by standardized test scores, and some weaknesses within
the councils themselves.

State-mandated revenue caps increasingly squeezed the MPS budget
throughout the mid-1990s. In response, the school board slashed programs
such as summer school and staff development. At the same time, under the
leadership of then-Superintendent Howard Fuller, the school board started
to radically decentralize many services. One result was increasing pressure
to cut money in the Curriculum and Instruction division at central office
that had funded the councils. Without money for substitutes and basic
operating expenses, most council activities slowed down. Moreover, with-

out adequate funds for districtwide inservices, some councils increasingly found themselves preaching to the converted. These factors sapped the vitality of several councils and hastened their dissolution.

One lesson from this is painfully clear: Radical decentralization can undermine progressive reforms that are centrally coordinated. With the defunding of the councils and the ending of inservices paid for by central office, a coordinated emphasis on developing and promoting anti-racist curriculum all but evaporated within MPS.

The councils also were affected by the district's emphasis on "school-to-work" reforms during the mid-1990s. While district administrators presented school-to-work as an extension and deepening of the K-12 reform, in practice the initiative refocused many peoples' energies. Some elementary schools, for example, set up banks and stores instead of organizing multicultural activities. All schools had to identify school-to-work coordinators, and inservice funds were concentrated on school-to-work.

The councils also had their shortcomings. They would have been in a much stronger position to prevent their defunding if they had done a few things differently. For instance:

- The councils could have done a better job of reaching out to a wider network of teachers, particularly connecting council representatives to classroom teachers who were not council members. This problem became exacerbated as budgets were cut, and some councils became too ingrown.
- Some councils could have increased their advocacy role. For example, the Multicultural Council "could have taken a stronger stand in favor of the African-American immersion schools," according to Baruch. At the same time, the Early Childhood Council successfully advocated for an expansion of kindergarten for four-year-olds, and for improved assessment tools in a state-funded class size reduction program.
- The councils could have fought harder to institutionalize their status, perhaps through the teacher union contract. One problem was that, until the end, the councils were dependent on the spending whims of the administration and the school board.

Had a visionary superintendent or school board promoted the councils, conditions in the district might be different today. The mobilization of progressive teachers, so necessary for districtwide school reform, might have continued and expanded.

Relative to the overall budget of MPS, the money spent on the teacher councils was minuscule. The results, however, were immense. The councils inspired hundreds, at times thousands, of teachers. As one member of the Early Childhood Council said, the councils were "the only spark in teachers' lives to learn new techniques and reaffirm the positive things they were doing."

While there is no scientific way to measure the councils' effectiveness, one could argue from the vantage point of Asa Hilliard — that the councils had started to change "what's in teachers' heads." It is an unfinished task.

For Further Reading:

Hilliard, Asa. *The Baseline Essays*, Portland, OR: Portland Public Schools. 1986.

Levine, David. "Forging Curriculum Reform Throughout a District," in *Rethinking Schools, Rethinking Our Classrooms, Volume 1: Teaching for Equity and Justice*, Milwaukee, WI: Rethinking Schools Press, 1994. pp. 168-170.

Milwaukee Public Schools. *Teaching and Learning Goals of the Milwaukee Public Schools*, Milwaukee, WI, 1992.

Peterson, Bob. "Mourn — Organize: Teachers Take the Offensive Against Basals." *Theory Into Practice*, 28(4), 1989. pp. 295-299.

Peterson, Bob. "Total Decentralization: Contradictions and Dangers," *Rethinking Schools*, 9(3), 1995 (Spring). pp 17-18.

'Summer Camp' for Teachers: Alternative Staff Development

S. J. Childs

The voices coming from the Madison High School cafeteria in Portland, Oregon are loud and excited. It is the end of June, but these voices aren't students talking about vacation. They belong to 50 high school teachers from Portland Public Schools, who are starting their summer vacation by attending the Summer Literacy Institute, known unofficially as "Summer Camp."

The Institute is one week of intensive collaboration among teachers to develop curriculum units and workshops around multicultural texts. Teachers are treated as professionals instead of volunteers or enthusiastic martyrs: They are paid their hourly rate to collaborate and create. The summer of 2002 was the Institute's fourth year.

The Summer Literacy Institute differs sharply from many staff development models, which take a top-down approach and rely on non-district "experts." Instead, the Institute is led by Portland teachers, with the goal of developing a collaborative, ongoing staff development process that relies on local teacher-experts to lead future workshops and inservices. The majority of Portland Public Schools' 175 high school language arts teachers have now gone through the Summer Literacy Institute or have led workshops during the year.

Too often, teachers are subjected to staff development that involves outside experts lecturing at us from a distance, ignoring our own expertise and professional knowledge. Stuck in rows of chairs, we passively listen while highly paid outsiders impose their "wisdom" and authority. In the Institute, however, classroom teachers are the experts. The Institute promotes collaboration and fosters a sense of community; it is also a model for new-teacher training, pairing new teachers with veterans to help guide them in developing curriculum.

Districtwide Reform

The Institute's ultimate curriculum goal is to expand the language arts "canon" to include more culturally diverse readings that raise social justice issues, and to create curriculum that engages students in linking the literature to their lives and the broader society.

Such a specific reform isn't successful if it is happening in only a few classrooms or in a couple of buildings. While in many areas of education decentralization and site control are positive changes, in the context of curriculum development and teacher education, a central vision and a districtwide reform effort can have several advantages. The collective power of central reform that pushes for change can provide the opening blow for progressive teachers in their home schools.

For example, having a central agenda to untrack ninth-grade English classes means that parents who are school-shopping find similar policies throughout the district and can't pit one school against another. Teachers can also collaborate with teachers throughout the district to find books, poems, essays, and strategies to help construct rigorous units to teach in untracked classrooms. Also, teachers can point to successful practices in neighboring schools — from interdisciplinary ninth-grade academies to ninth-grade support classes. Second, progressive teachers in traditional departments can use the district aims to move their colleagues to incorporate a more diverse reading list, because they can point to the district booklist, and they can borrow the books held in the district's library.

Linda Christensen — Portland Public Schools Language Arts Curriculum Specialist and a *Rethinking Schools* editor — designed the Institute as an alternative model for teacher education. Christensen assembled a team of teacher-advisors (one from every high school) who meet monthly to assist in the development, planning, and revision of the Summer Literacy Institute and the other staff development workshops that take place throughout the year.

During the Institute, teachers engage in three main activities. First, they read research articles on literacy, language, and achievement.

Second, mornings are devoted to teachers sharing lessons — perhaps an improvisation to understand a character's motives and actions, or a

Socratic seminar to crack a difficult passage. In an effort to move toward reflection and critical analysis, we also devote morning time to issues such as creating independent reading opportunities, integrating English language learners into the classroom, and bridging the achievement gap.

Third, in the afternoon teams of teachers meet to develop units filled with literacy lessons and strategies around a book or theme that are available for other teachers to use throughout the year. The lessons and strategies from these units have become the basis for districtwide staff development workshops.

Opening the Canon

In Portland, the goal is to infuse district classrooms with books and lessons that address issues of race, culture, class, and gender. In various forums throughout the school year, Christensen invites teachers to lead workshops on strategies to improve reading and writing, but she makes a special effort to seek out teachers who will offer workshops that raise questions about social justice and which focus on multicultural literature.

Of course, even the best workshops don't necessarily transform classroom practice. Not all teachers are willing to open their locked boxes of canonical curriculum to admit a few titles not on the dead-white-men list. But every year, more of those teachers retire or leave; and every year new teachers enter the district and try to figure out what they are "supposed" to teach. The Summer Literacy Institute provides institutional support and context for these efforts.

The Institute pairs new teachers with master teachers. And the Institute introduces more titles that deal with issues of social justice and that speak more directly to our students' lives. Because of the Institute, diverse titles are being bought and getting used. Just glancing at the list of some of the books recently purchased by the school district as a result of the Summer Literacy Institute shows us something has changed. These books include *Lesson Before Dying*, *Fences*, *Their Eyes Were Watching God*, *Ricochet River*, *Kaffir Boy*, *Smoke Signals*, *Martyr's Crossing*, *In The Time of Butterflies*, *Krik? Krak!*, *The House on Mango Street*, and many more.

During the first year of the Literacy Institute, the teacher-advisors set guidelines for the literature we would write curriculum around. We wanted to introduce literature that puts traditionally marginalized groups at the center. We adapted guidelines from the San Francisco Unified School District and "Teachers' Choice for 1996: A Project of the International Reading Association." We sought to select titles that:

+ Reflect high literary quality.
+ Have cross-cultural themes.
+ Actively challenge stereotypes.
+ Raise issues of class, race, gender, and justice.
+ Move beyond victimization and show resistance and empowerment.
+ Provide historical context and deepen cultural knowledge.
+ Have the potential for use across the curriculum.

Teachers have developed units around works such as *Bless Me, Ultima* by Rudolfo Anaya, *Slam* by Walter Dean Myers, and *Thousand Pieces of Gold* by Ruthanne Lum McCunn. More than 30 curriculum guides were developed during a period of three years.

For *Thousand Pieces of Gold*, social studies and language arts teachers integrated the study of the novel with its historical, political, and social contexts. The curriculum includes a lesson on Confucian philosophy and invites students to look at their own family structures for similarities. Another lesson asks students to examine the social construction of beauty and how it oppresses women. Using the foot-binding in the story as a jumping-off place, students brainstorm ways our society today compels people to alter their bodies to fit in, and then write personal narratives on the subject. Another lesson requires students to read newspaper articles on current immigration situations and draft fictional pieces about the subjects of the articles, allowing them to link immigration issues of the past with those of today.

Some of us created units to reintroduce African-American classics such as *Their Eyes Were Watching God* by Zora Neale Hurston or *The Color Purple* by Alice Walker. Lessons for *Their Eyes Were Watching God* focus on the politics of language; examine the relationship between art and justice; use the lenses of race, class, and gender to analyze scenes from the novel; and help students write their own "love" stories.

Some teachers in the Institute pair the "classics" with modern pieces to open new doors into the issues. For instance, during the 2000 Literacy Project, language arts and social studies teachers used *The Poisonwood Bible* by Barbara Kingsolver with *Heart of Darkness* by Joseph Conrad in a unit on colonialism that includes simulations, role plays, poetry writing, character logs, and more.

Others have chosen new pieces of literature that give voice to those not often featured in the language arts curriculum — for example, prisoners, Native Americans, Latinos, poor people — with books like *The Skin I'm In* by Sharon Flake, *When I Was Puerto Rican* by Esmeralda Santiago, and *Where the Heart Is* by Billie Letts. All three of these units invite students to make connections between their own lives and the main characters.

A few groups organized their units around a theme. For example, Language, Manipulation, and Globalization is a multidisciplinary unit using film, fiction, and nonfiction to analyze the role of the media and consumerism on cultures and the environment. Texts include *Savages* by Joe Kane, *My Year of Meats* by Ruth Ozeki, *Enemy of the People* by Henrik Ibsen, and *The Legacy of Luna* by Julia Butterfly Hill, as well as films like *Killing Us Softly* and *Wag the Dog*.

A team of teachers I worked with created a Women's Literature Unit, subtitled Women and Resistance, focusing on the power and resistance of women in society and not on their victimization. We use early classic authors like Kate Chopin and Charlotte Perkins Gilman, but also explore newer works like Julia Alvarez' *In the Time of the Butterflies* and Margaret Atwood's *The Handmaid's Tale*. In a series of lessons, students examine the use of silence as a tool of oppression and the power of silence as a form of resistance. From this they write their own narratives about times they were silenced or used silence as a source of power.

Christensen, the Institute organizer, secured foundation grants so that the district could purchase class sets of books featured in curriculum units. Many schools matched these purchases by buying additional class sets of curriculum-featured books. We have also developed a "centralized" collection at the district library and have begun a new era of sharing collections among schools.

But putting books into book rooms is not enough. Without the curriculum guides developed by the Institute participants, many of the new titles and a lot of the old ones would be used by only a couple of teachers and would gather dust the rest of the year. When the structure of school life keeps us isolated during most of the year it is difficult to borrow, steal, and share; but these guides encourage that kind of sharing and make it easier for teachers — novice and veteran — to try new things and to move beyond the comfortable.

Uncovering Weaknesses

To be sure, there are still plenty of teachers ignoring these more multi-cultural titles, still giving fact-chasing multiple-choice tests, never offering students a chance to hear and speak in their own voices, nor inviting them to critique the world around them. But more and more they find themselves at the margins.

While promising as an alternative professional development strategy, this teachers-teaching-teachers model of curriculum development faces many challenges, particularly in large districts and schools. For example, new teachers may have great ideas, but they often lack the critical awareness that comes with years of reflective teaching. The curriculum guides make it less scary to try new titles, but many also reflect the short timetable, limited knowledge base, and uneven teaching skills of some participants. Better "quality control" requires more time, space, and resources.

Teachers are exposed to new literature through the curriculum guides; but unfortunately, they are exposed to some poorly designed lessons as well. In the Institute's first two years, we had clear standards for the texts we chose, but neglected to impose standards on the lessons we included. In order not to destroy the spirit of collaboration and good will, many teacher-teams avoided the harder questions about each other's lessons and strategies. Some units became dumping grounds, where any remotely connected lesson was included: not examined, not tried out, not revised. Some lessons were fun and engaging, but didn't delve into the texts' historical or political realities.

Certainly, there is a need to sustain a critical, collective dialogue around curriculum development. One week in the summer is not enough. Follow-up sessions to discuss and revise the curriculum after we've taught it are necessary, but with dwindling budgets not a current reality.

Just as our own teaching evolves with time and critical reflection, so too the Summer Literacy Institute has evolved. Any district hoping to adapt this model must see it as a continual work in progress.

Recognizing these weaknesses, Christensen and her teacher advisors redesigned the Institute to create an atmosphere of critique and revision. Wanting participants to use their time more reflectively, organizers developed a new format, switching from morning show-and-tell workshops to morning discussions. In heterogeneous discussion groups, teachers — from different curriculum teams, from different schools, with different years of experience — confronted a series of vexing issues.

For example, we talked about the question of home language in the classroom: When should teachers demand that students use Standard English and when is home language acceptable, or even encouraged? What are ways to "correct" that respect students' cultures? Alternatively, how do teachers often correct in disrespectful ways? What do we need to know about the relationship between culture and language to answer these questions? Discussions of these and other issues helped push teachers to consider what, for many, were topics they had not thought deeply about. The curriculum guides were likely better because of this effort.

In addition to morning conversations, teams were encouraged to reflect before developing lessons, and to critique after writing lessons. Groups used critical questions, developed previously by participants, to guide the early discussions. They examined whether the lessons addressed the different needs and abilities of the students. They identified how the lessons developed reading, writing, speaking, and critical thinking skills. They asked how the lessons connected the material to the students' lives, how they connected the unit to society, and how they addressed race, gender, and class issues. Repeatedly, Christensen encouraged us to clarify our goals, revisit old lessons, critique each other's work, and eliminate the weak stuff.

Staff Development

One important feature of the Summer Literacy Institute has been the cross-training that develops within and after the summer. Now, during the school district's inservice days, a cadre of teachers from within the district is available to lead workshops. Because classroom teachers lead these workshops, they speak more directly to teachers' needs. Those attending are less resentful, as teachers can be when a non-teaching or university-based "expert" is brought in to tell them how to teach.

While those teaching the workshops get paid their hourly rate, the expense is far less than flying in experts, and the money saved can be used to do more teacher education, buy more books, and create more curriculum. It also gives teachers a chance to peek into each other's classrooms without having to leave their own, and has developed a certain pride throughout the district.

The ethic of collaboration that has emerged from the Institute and the workshops has been remarkable. Indeed, when reading Institute evaluations and talking with participants, it is hard to extract a comment that is not filled with giddy enthusiasm. One teacher noted: "I had the chance to collaborate with a most gifted instructor to develop a unit I can't wait to teach. What the Literacy Institute makes evident is that working teachers, sharing their best practices, provide the best forum for developing new curriculum. After a long hard year, meeting with my fellow language arts instructors from across the district re-energized me."

Personally, after more than 11 years as a Portland teacher, I have noticed that the community of language arts teachers has grown beyond "that nice teacher down the hall who lent me a lesson." It is now a districtwide community.

When I first started teaching, I often felt like I was all on my own. It took long hours into the night for the first few years to gather all my tricks together. Even with significant staff development opportunities on writing under my belt, I needed more to grow. I needed to work with others on a continual basis — to revisit my practice and revise my lessons.

The Summer Literacy Institute and the workshop days throughout the year give me that chance.

Survival and Justice:
Twin Goals for Teacher Unions

Bob Peterson

Never in our history have public schools been under such relentless attack. Never in the history of teacher unionism has there been a greater urgency to rethink strategy.

To meet these challenges, our public schools and our teacher unions must pursue two closely related goals: survival and justice. Put simply, unless both institutions address more forthrightly issues of social justice, neither our system of public education nor our teacher unions may survive.

The precarious position of teacher unions has sparked debates on strategy within both the National Education Association (NEA) and the American Federation of Teachers (AFT). Former NEA President Bob Chase called for a "new unionism." AFT President Sandra Feldman has called on teachers to take more professional responsibility for school success and failure.

Delegates at state and national conventions have hotly debated many pressing questions: How can teacher unions best defend public schools? How can unions ensure that teachers are treated more professionally? How can unions advocate for the needs of all students while defending the interests of teachers?

In looking at these complicated questions, I have found it helpful to look at three different models of teacher unionism: "industrial," "professional," and "social justice." These are somewhat arbitrary distinctions, most useful in helping to frame discussion. In practice, the models often overlap, blending into one another depending on circumstances. But the essential components of each approach can be summarized as follows:

- The industrial unionism model focuses on defending the working conditions and rights of teachers.
- The professional model incorporates, yet moves beyond, the industrial model and suggests that unions also play a leading role in professional

issues, such as teacher accountability and quality of school programs.

◆ The social justice model embraces concepts of industrial and professional unionism, but also is linked to a tradition that views unions as part of a broader movement for social progress. It calls for participatory union membership; education reform focused on serving all children, with special attention to collaboration with parents and community organizations; and a concern for broader issues of equity throughout society.

Industrial Unionism

It would be foolhardy not to recognize the strengths of the industrial union model. Indeed, it is an unfortunate commentary that many current teachers are unaware of the history of teacher unionism and its role in strengthening teacher rights and public education as a whole. Both the AFT and NEA rose to national prominence in the mid-1960s and early 1970s at the time of a more robust labor movement and a strong civil rights movement. In comparison, the current attacks against teacher unions come in the midst of a 30-year decline in the U.S. labor movement and a waning of many social movements, in particular the modern civil rights movement. Overall, union membership fell from about 31% of the labor force in 1970 to just under 14% in 1998, even though levels of public service (and teacher) union membership have risen.

New teachers need to understand that a key strength of teacher unionism has been organizing and winning the right to collectively bargain. Paying teachers respectable wages and benefits and defending their academic and procedural rights has contributed to raising the overall quality of public education. While some teachers, particularly in the NEA, have been reluctant to admit it, this strength depends on teachers having a degree of "trade-union consciousness," recognizing that teachers, like other working people, sell their labor power in order to survive and need protection from management.

Marjorie Murphy, in her book *Blackboard Unions: The AFT and the NEA 1900-1980* (1990), describes numerous cases of arbitrary dismissal of teachers. The reasons ranged from being married (for women), to belonging to integrated organizations (in the South), to being, or accused of being, a communist (particularly in New York). More recent examples include teachers who have been disciplined for their sexual orientation or their political activism. Without unions, teachers could lose basic rights of academic freedom and due process.

Wages, working conditions, and teacher rights were the main focuses of the industrial-style teacher unionism that became dominant in the late 1960s and early 1970s. The AFT initially was more willing to go on strike and was more successful in convincing teachers from large cities to join its union. This pressured the NEA to adopt a more militant industrial-union model. For the NEA this meant a significant change: Until the mid-1960s, its national leadership was dominated by superintendents and administrators who tended not to see teachers as "workers" in the traditional union sense of the word.

By the early 1970s, both the AFT and NEA were conducting strikes to ensure better wages, benefits, and pensions, as well as job protection from dictatorial principals and school boards. This forced most school districts in the country to bargain collectively (with districts in the South being the notable exception). The two unions grew in size and strength; through their collective bargaining agreements, they helped shape a wide range of policies. Relationships with local school authorities tended to be contentious and adversarial, as unions put a priority on protecting the rights of teachers while district administrators focused on protecting their bureaucratic power and procedures. The best interests of children were, too often, secondary.

There are some key shortcomings to the industrial approach. Often it has led teacher unions to negotiate contracts that fail to address broader educational and professional issues. Some teacher unions have been slow to take any responsibility for issues of school reform and quality. To be fair, this is not simply because of narrow attitudes on the part of union leaders, but also because of restrictive state laws and management's desires to dominate school operations. These factors contribute to a "serve the contract" mentality that narrowly focuses on the employment concerns of individual members, rather than on larger professional or social issues. The current pressures on public education, particularly in poor communities of color, make such a position increasingly untenable.

Professional Unionism

Both at the grassroots and national levels, there has been increasing dissatisfaction with the constraints of the industrial union approach. As a result, there have been calls for "professional unionism" — a phrase used extensively by professors Charles Kerchner and Julia Koppich in their book *A Union of Professionals: Labor Relations and Educational Reform* (1993).

The most effective advocates of professional unionism have retained — yet moved beyond — the strengths of the industrial model. In particular, several pioneering locals have maintained a focus on defending teachers' economic and social well-being, while promoting innovative reforms that speak to the interests of students. These innovators include the Rochester Teachers Association led by Adam Urbanski, the Columbus Education Association led by John Grossman, and the Cincinnati Federation of Teachers, originally led by Tom Mooney. (Ironically, although the AFT traditionally has been viewed as the more militant industrial-type union, and the NEA associated with a more "professional" approach, it has been AFT locals that have tended to be pioneers in radical innovations such as peer review and career ladders.)

In addition to innovative local leaders, a variety of national leaders — mostly significantly the NEA's Chase and the AFT's Feldman — have promoted the move toward a professional model of unionism. But it also includes members of the Teacher Union Reform Network (TURN), a grouping of 21 presidents from large AFT and NEA locals who meet regularly to seek "to restructure the nation's teacher unions to promote reforms that will lead to better learning and higher achievement for America's children."

In my mind, the hallmarks of professional unionism are reflected in several ideas:

- Teachers are professionals who uphold high teaching standards.
- Teachers understand the interdependency of teachers with the local school authorities; collaboration, not confrontation, is the preferred approach.
- Teachers, and not just management, are responsible for ensuring that all students are learning and that all teachers are quality teachers. Quality teaching is the main way to ensure equity for all students.

The clearest articulation of professional unionism can be found in a February 1997 speech by the NEA's Chase, shortly after he became president:

> Simply put, in the decade ahead we must revitalize our public schools from within or they will be dismantled from without....The fact is that while NEA does not control curriculum, set funding levels, or hire and fire, we cannot go on denying responsibility for school quality....Our new directions are clear: putting issues of school quality front and center at the bargaining table, collaborating actively with management on an agenda of school reform, involving teachers and other school employees in organizing their schools for excellence.

For the most part this "professional unionism" is a refreshing addition to both the discussion and practice of teacher unions. It does have its weaknesses, however, including a tendency to downplay matters of social justice, particularly regarding class and race. The main academic proponents of this approach (such as Kerchner, Koppich, and Joseph G. Weeres) rarely mention these matters in their main writing and seem fairly infatuated with marketplace reforms for public schools.

Some of the practitioners of "new unionism," such as Chase, have seemed to equate too easily the need to collaborate with locally elected school boards and a need to collaborate strategically with the corporate owners of America. While a strong case can be made that locally elected officials and public service unions should work to forge alliances around a host of issues, the basis for such an alliance with the Fortune 500 is much more problematic. (See Peterson, 1998.)

Social Justice Unionism

Still others have advocated a new vision of unionism that would go beyond professional concerns and ground itself in a commitment to social justice. A clear articulation of this perspective is found in "Social Justice Unionism: A Working Draft," written in the summer of 1994 during a "union institute" sponsored by the National Coalition of Education Activists and attended by activists from the AFT and NEA, including national staff, state and local officers, and rank-and-file members.

The working draft outlined seven "key components of social justice unionism." The first three components give a flavor of the document, arguing that social justice unionism should:

1. Defend the rights of its members while fighting for the rights and needs of the broader community and students.
2. Recognize that the parents and neighbors of our students are key allies, and build strategic alliances with parents, labor unions, and community groups.
3. Fully involve rank-and-file members in running the union and initiate widespread discussion on how education unions should respond to the crises in education and society.

Social justice unionism moves beyond a "trade-union" or "professional" perspective to a "class-conscious" perspective. This class consciousness recognizes that teachers' long-term interests are closer to those of the poor and working people, whose children are in our public schools, than to the corporate leaders and politicians who run our society. It views parents and the community as essential partners in reform, with an emphasis in urban areas on developing ties with communities of color. It is committed to a democratic, bottom-up, grassroots mobilization of teachers, parents, the community, and rank-and-file union members.

Essential to social justice unionism is a recognition that schools have played a contradictory dual role in society. On the one hand, they have reinforced and reproduced the class, racial, and gender divisions of the larger society they serve. On the other hand, they provide opportunities to overcome those divisions and to reduce social inequality. For all their faults, public schools are among the most local, democratically controlled institutions in society. They are a constant battleground of competing visions and priorities.

A social justice perspective struggles against those practices that mirror and replicate society's inequalities — practices such as tracking, narrowly defined curriculum standards, over-reliance on standardized testing, and privatization and voucher schemes that introduce the inequalities of the market economy into public education. Further, a social justice perspective seeks to mobilize teachers and parents to actively overturn such inequitable policies and to implement alternatives.

For example, a social justice unionism approach would caution against simplistic reactions by teachers and schools to complicated matters like student discipline. Instead of backing rhetorical calls for "get-tough policies," a social justice union would call for community and teacher input into the formation of any code of student behavior, and would call for safeguards against racial or class biases. A social justice approach would also challenge long-established practices that condone and perpetuate tracking, and would demand feasible alternatives. It would be wary of some union leaders' tendencies to uncritically endorse corporate or conservative approaches to the imposition of standards and high-stakes testing.

Teacher Accountability

How might the differences in these three approaches to teacher unionism play out on a particular issue? Looking more closely at the issue of teacher accountability provides some clues.

Those urging teacher unions to take a more "professional approach" have focused on teacher accountability as a primary concern. Authors Kerchner and Koppich note that traditionally, teacher unions have tended toward an industrial union model of accountability. This model sees accountability as the responsibility of principals and supervisors, not teachers. (It is sometimes referred to as an "external" accountability system, because it comes from outside of the teaching corps.)

Clearly, unions have a legal and ethical responsibility to protect the due-process rights of all teachers, even incompetent ones. In practice, however, the traditional industrial approach to accountability has meant that at times, some unions have taken a hands-off approach to doing anything at all about ensuring a qualified teaching corps. The industrial union response generally has been, "That's management's problem." This approach evades the hard issues of teacher quality and instead focuses on the technicalities of the dismissal process.

Those advocating professional unionism argue that teacher unions must look beyond the self-interest of individual teachers and consider the broader needs of schools and children. They should respect and honor the rights of due process, but they should also promote "internal" teacher- and union-based controls on quality. Some of the mechanisms they have used include peer mentoring, peer evaluation, and career ladders. One of the clear advantages of peer review is that it moves the dialogue away from procedural technicalities of the dismissal process, and instead focuses on the substance of teaching and how to improve it.

While a professional approach stresses "internal" accountability over the "external" control of a principal, a social justice approach might add additional components. For example, it might suggest that parents and community members should have input into teacher and school evaluation processes.

The Rochester Teachers Association, for instance, negotiated a specific contract provision to encourage parent input in teacher evaluation. The provision involves soliciting parent input in teacher/home communication and homework matters. It is an important step in recognizing that parents should be more than just homework helpers and pizza fundraisers. A related issue involves overall parent participation in schools, in particular setting up school council structures so parent voices are represented and respected. School-based governance structures can play an important part in building dialogue among unions, teachers, parents, and communities around issues of school quality and improvement.

A social justice perspective also proposes that unions should promote accountability and equity on a districtwide level. For example, the Cincinnati Federation of Teachers conducted a survey to determine which high schools were offering calculus and advanced language courses. The survey found that predominantly lower-income neighborhood schools were not offering these classes, while specialty schools and the college-prep high school were. The union's subsequent organizing around the issue caused a major policy shift in the Cincinnati Public Schools, which instituted a special allocation to schools to ensure the availability of advanced classes at all schools.

The Issue of Race

How to deal with racism and race relations is a daunting problem for any institution in this country. It is particularly difficult for schools and teachers.

Teacher-union relations with communities of color have been particularly affected by an approach that prioritizes the interests and rights of teachers above the concerns of students and community.

Professional unionism, as a whole, tends to downplay issues of race. When asked, advocates will often note its importance. But documents, written discussions, and conference topics generally fail to highlight the centrality of racial issues. For example, in Chase's speech announcing the NEA's new unionism, the issue of race was not mentioned even once. Likewise, documents of the Teacher Union Reform Network rarely talk about race directly.

In contrast, a social justice union approach would directly take on issues of race. A key priority of social justice unionism is building coalitions and alliances with parent and community advocacy groups, often across racial and class divides, that speak to both school reform and ensuring equity in society as a whole. There are, unfortunately, not enough examples of such alliances. But some unions have taken noteworthy and positive steps to reach out to their logical allies. The British Columbia Teacher's Federation, for instance, runs an education program which deals with race on personal, political, and pedagogical levels. Through a combination of workshops, training sessions, policy statements, and youth organizing, the provincial union has encouraged teachers to discuss and deal with race issues. (See "Confronting Racism, Promoting Respect" by Tom McKenna, p. 315.) The California Teachers Association and the Washington Education Association have worked against statewide referenda prohibiting affirmative action. On a local level, some union locals have aggressively supported programs to recruit teachers of color, building ties with community groups in the process.

Conclusion

Historically, teacher unions have operated on the premise that their overarching responsibility is to protect their members. In the long run, unions will be able to do so only if they adopt a social justice model.

Unions are under ferocious attack and will not survive unless they are seen as advocates of school reform. Of necessity they must adopt more responsibility for the teaching profession and the academic achievement of students. Only by building alliances with community and parents will unions be able to withstand the conservative onslaught.

But even the best-run school district in the world cannot, over time, compensate for all the inequalities in our society — which is why a commitment to social justice must go beyond education and reach into all aspects of society. If teachers want true equal educational opportunity for their students, they must work for equal opportunity throughout society, not just in education but in health care, employment, and housing.

Social justice unionism also makes sense on a more individual level. Teachers, like all workers, want to go home at night and know they have been successful during the day. When their students live in poverty or without health care, when their students are without hope because they see unemployment everywhere in their community, teachers' jobs are all the more difficult.

In the past, other unions have faced difficult challenges and set ambitious goals. Today, teacher unions face a similar challenge. We must demand and build a democratic teacher union movement that recognizes its interests are bound up with the interests of the children and communities we serve. Only then will we be able to gather sufficient forces to ensure that public education gets the resources that schools deserve and that children need.

For Further Reading

Kerchner, C. and Koppich, Julia. *A Union of Professionals: Labor Relations and Educational Reform.* New York: Teachers College Press, 1993.

Murphy, Marjorie. *Blackboard Unions: The AFT and the NEA 1900-1980.* Ithaca, NY: Cornell University Press, 1990.

Peterson, Bob. "What Will Be The Future of Teacher Unionism? A Review of United Mind Workers: Unions and Teaching in the Knowledge Society." *Rethinking Schools* 12(4), Summer 1998. (A link to this article is available at www.rethinkingschools.org/rsr.)

Confronting Racism, Promoting Respect

Tom McKenna

I'm a racist. My students tell me so. They claim racism doesn't exist in our society anymore. Therefore, anyone who brings up race when analyzing injustice is a racist. According to them, I fit the bill.

I teach high school social studies in Portland, Oregon. Most of my students are white; so am I. Some still use the word "colored" when referring to African Americans. When I correct them, they think I am trying to be "politically correct." They are working-class kids whose experience of the world rarely extends beyond their immediate community. But they have strong opinions about the world.

When issues of race come up, a typical student comment goes like this: "It's an advantage to be colored or black or whatever you want us to call them."

"Tell me about that, how is it an advantage?" I ask. "How do you know that?"

"I mean, just look, they get all the scholarships," they respond. "And they get hired just because they're black, not because they're qualified."

I ask for examples. A student tells me about an uncle who couldn't get a job as a cop because he was white. I suggest that we probe deeper, that maybe we're not seeing the whole picture. "Do you really think it is easier to be a person of color than white in America today?" I question. "Do you really think there is no racism?"

That's when they lower the boom and tell me I'm racist.

After class, I talk with my student intern. We both shake our heads in disbelief and realize how much work we have to do in order to broaden our students' understanding about issues of race.

"Where do you begin with kids like these who are so far out of touch?" my intern asks. "How do you teach them about race and racism?" Her facial expression speaks volumes about the challenge of such an undertaking. We both fall into a momentary silence.

If I were a teacher in the Canadian province of British Columbia, I would at least know where to start.

A Union Dealing with Racism

The British Columbia Teacher's Federation (BCTF) has a Program Against Racism. I've been a teacher for 25 years and a member of three teacher organizations in the United States. None has had anything remotely similar. Yet a Canadian union has had a Program Against Racism for a quarter of a century. How can that be?

I admit that I knew very little about British Columbia before undertaking an investigation of the Program Against Racism (PAR). Though I live only a 75-minute plane ride away, Vancouver has always felt much more distant than that.

Before my visit, I knew some basics. I knew that Vancouver is quite diverse (its English-as-a-second-language population in the public schools hovers around 50%; approximately 25 different languages other than English are spoken at home), and that the city has a lower crime rate than comparable U.S. cities. I had once thought about moving there during the Vietnam War. Overall, I assumed British Columbia was similar to the United States, just a kinder, gentler version.

My first visit to Vancouver shed light on some of the similarities. I found a provincial premier mired in scandal, a large urban school district faced with a funding crisis, a newspaper decrying an influx of immigrants "who aren't appropriate for this country," and an electrical engineer from India who had to drive a cab to make a living.

My initial research about the BCTF's Program Against Racism was via the Internet. I logged onto their web page and found a wealth of information. The federation's "Lesson Aids" catalogue, for instance, features everything from a Human Rights curriculum, to a Status of Women Program, to a videotape featuring noted linguist and radical commentator Noam Chomsky.

I also found the names of contact people within the BCTF. Using e-mail, I sent them endless questions about the Program Against Racism. How did it start? How does it all work? How do you get curriculum into the classroom?

Some of my questions made no sense to my British Columbia counterparts — either via e-mail or in person. When I visited Vancouver, I asked former BCTF president Larry Keuhn: "Why go through the federation to implement curriculum?" He responded with a prolonged "Hmmm," and a puzzled expression, as if to ask back: "How else would one do it?"

Rather quickly it became clear that the BCTF is a key site for teachers to reflect on classroom issues, as well as a vehicle to address larger social ills.

The Program Against Racism isn't just a program. It is a network of committed and culturally diverse educators engaged in a prolonged struggle to fight racism in their schools and their communities. It focuses on changing the attitudes of both teachers and students, and emphasizes not only understanding racism but also taking action against it.

Many of the educators who helped develop PAR have a history of activism. Some found their lives changed by social movements in the United States: the Civil Rights and anti-war movements. They wanted to change what was taught in the schools and how it was taught, while building coalitions with community groups to eliminate racism. As so many PAR associates told me, they were a family. During my days in Vancouver, they let me be a part of that family. And they told me a remarkable story about a unique program.

Presenting Accurate History

In 1975, Lloyd Edwards, a teacher from Surrey, B.C., stood before the Annual General Meeting of the BCTF and offered a motion. He was concerned about issues of racism in schools. Often when he ventured into the halls between classes he saw Indo-Canadians (Canadians from India) being bullied by students of European descent. The bullied students were not finding much success in the classroom, either.

Edwards, a Canadian of African heritage, thought that teachers and, more specifically, their union should do something to address those issues. He had not organized any support for his motion beforehand. His was a solitary voice. Yet, according to many who were in attendance, he spoke with such a passion for justice that his motion was quickly seconded, a vote was taken, and, to many people's surprise, Edwards' motion passed. As a result, the BCTF established a Task Force on Racism to explore the issue more deeply.

"One of the initiatives of the early Task Force on Racism was the production of a slide-tape presentation on the history of racism in British Columbia," Wes Knapp, one of the original BCTF staff members assigned to the project, remembered. The slide-tape presentation was an attempt to come to terms with British Columbia's racist past, which includes internment of Japanese-Canadians during World War II; a provincial legislature that from 1890 to 1924 enacted at least 36 anti-Asian laws in an attempt to create a British Columbia version of apartheid (most were overturned by the federal parliament); a generation of First Nations* children who were separated from their families and culture while kept for up to 10 years in "residential schools" beginning in the 1930s; and a long history of Native peoples' land claims lost to zealous European expansionists.

The slide-tape presentation met with stiff resistance. Two school boards banned it from their districts, arguing that "talking about racism would cause it to exist." Ironically, the controversy raised awareness about the existence of racism and a coexistent problem of denial. It also shed a positive light on the federation's efforts. According to Knapp, the Task Force on Racism's message "got out in ways that would not have normally been available." The BCTF was able to engage everyone from local school officials to community members in discussions about racism and the roles schools might play in its elimination.

"I suppose," Knapp reflected, "more than any other event, the furor around this production fueled the call for a province-wide program to combat racism."

The union was the logical organization to put the call into action. The BCTF has a rich history of social activism. A University of British Columbia student wrote a doctoral thesis about the history of the BCTF's social justice

---

*The term preferred by the indigenous people of Canada.

work; it was 600 pages long and did not get beyond the 1930s. More recently, in 1972 the union established a Status of Women Program to work on issues of gender discrimination. The program enjoyed strong membership and organizational support.

The Task Force called for a Program Against Racism to be established with a full-time coordinator, an oversight Committee Against Racism, an annual budget of $37,000, and a network of activists in every local throughout the province. The Task Force also understood that an activist network limited to just teachers and schools was not enough to adequately deal with the issue of racism. From the beginning, the community was seen as an integral part of the initiative.

The Task Force's recommendation was not without opposition. Some federation members argued that unions exist for the sake of collective bargaining and professional development only. Social justice, they argued, is the duty of others. But there was also considerable support and significant historical precedent for social justice work. The union held fast and, in 1977, the Program Against Racism was established.

The real work was yet to be done. An actual program had to be built. A network of educators organized through the BCTF with community roots had to be developed. But the field work was undertaken with full support of the union. Larry Keuhn was president of the BCTF during PAR's early years and made sure the anti-racism work was not marginalized. He made it a priority to "always keep PAR connected to the rest of the BCTF," he said in an interview. "We needed to make it as central to the BCTF as it was to people's lives."

Eventually, the original PAR budget of $37,000 grew to more than $300,000 a year.

A Grassroots Program

"It was a grassroots program that sprang from all over the province," former PAR coordinator June Williams said as she spoke about PAR's early years. "Teachers who lived with students daily from all segments of society, who really knew the students...took up the fight."

"You start with a small voice and build on it," added another former

PAR coordinator, Sam Fillipoff. "We built a support system and sustained it." A more recent PAR coordinator, Viren Joshi, likened the early years of PAR organizing to Margaret Mead's axiom: "Never doubt that a small group of committed people can change the world."

Staff members went out on the road, visiting local association meetings, university classrooms, and community groups. They devised strategies to forge relationships with ethnic organizations and First Nations people. Innovative curriculum was created and revised. "There was lots of energy around our efforts," Knapp recalled. "It was really quite exhilarating to be a part of these initiatives. They were certainly the most rewarding years of my work at the BCTF."

Former PAR coordinator Williams particularly remembers the political debates with students and discussions about racism. "Students [were] meeting around the province," she said, "feeling they had permission to talk about this thing they were experiencing."

Curriculum development paralleled the organizing campaign. PAR created a follow-up to the Task Force's controversial slide-tape presentation, a video production and accompanying lesson plans entitled "Life Without Fear." (The video is an excellent classroom tool, as well as a valuable historical document. It can be found in the BCTF lesson aids catalogue. For a link, visit their website at www.bctf.bc.ca.)

The video captures examples of conversations about racism around the province. In the conversations, students and teachers reflect upon their experience and address a broad range of related topics, such as denial, stereotypes, xenophobia, institutional racism, and social action. The lesson plans provide frameworks for analyzing the themes developed in the video and strategies for taking action.

One of the video's most refreshing aspects is that it emphasizes going beyond an understanding of racism to trying to change racist behavior. The video challenges students to ask themselves: "What can I do to eliminate racism, in my school, in my community?" Students are encouraged to become aware of cultural differences and the dynamics of racism, to speak out against racist comments and jokes, and to ally with community members and families.

The emphasis on social action in "Life Without Fear" reflects a fundamental PAR principle. PAR outlines four elements of a racist incident: 1) perpetrator, 2) target, 3) bystanders, and 4) interveners. "PAR brought a paradigm shift," explained Fillipoff. "As educators we said: 'The majority of people are bystanders — let's change as many of them as we can into interveners.'"

In order to take the vision of students as informed social activists even further, PAR created Students Taking Action Against Racism (STAAR) camps. Teacher and PAR associate Carl Beach said the camps' influence was based on the fact that "students bonded around their opposition to injustice."

Chiara Anselmo, a teacher and a former student of PAR coordinator Viren Joshi, said that in one year alone her STAAR camp sponsored as many as 300 students from all over her region for a weekend stay. "We offered Holocaust seminars, human rights work, [workshops on] valuing diversity, problem solving, intervention skills," she said. "The BCTF provided the funding." And for the first time that year, she said, her local board provided the transportation. After the camps, students returned to their schools and communities to create their own activist network.

Teacher Workshops

From the outset, the PAR network also provided teacher conferences and workshops. Educators from all over the province were bused to a lake in northern British Columbia for the program's first provincial training conference. "We were all strangers on that bus," said Fillipoff. "By the time we got to the lake, we were a community. It was an 18-hour bus trip....We were together for six days, we got to see each other's warts and dimples, we built a trust which was reflected throughout the PAR network."

PAR facilitates around 100 workshops a year, with all PAR expenses paid by the BCTF. Any teacher from anywhere in the province has the right to ask PAR to come in and help, and simply has to get a commitment that 75% of his/her colleagues will participate. Teacher commitment means teacher buy-in, and provides the basis for ongoing work after the workshop ends.

Through a special fund, PAR also provided money for individual teachers to implement community-based projects. For instance, a number of communities were concerned about the impact of racist practices on the culture of the First Nations. Having been in the public system for only about the last 40 years, First Nations students were struggling in school, succumbing to self-destructive behaviors, living without much hope. PAR grants funded programs across British Columbia that brought First Nations elders into the classroom to educate a younger generation about their lost oral tradition. With the guidance of elders, high school students learned to tell their stories. Students created books and read them to elementary students. Learning took on a new light, because it was no longer solely the enterprise of an institution that had alienated First Nations people.

A Different Direction

At their 1998 annual general meeting, the BCTF membership voted to take the federation's social justice work in a new direction. It was decided that anti-racism work would be part of a larger umbrella covering a First Nations program and initiatives around homophobia, poverty, and the status of women. The new, broader program was dubbed the Social Justice Network.

Some activists worried about the impact of the change. Fillipoff, like many, feared the possible loss of the network that was the heart and soul of PAR. He worried that PAR would "lose the passion and the principal focus," which he considered both satisfying and necessary "when addressing an evil like racism." He also worried that the changes "are going to return the focus [of anti-racist work] to perpetrators and victims." Finally, he was concerned because "power has been re-centered in the Social Justice Committee within the BCTF and taken out of the local networks."

PAR associate Sandy Dore was likewise afraid that under the new social justice umbrella, "all programs will be shortchanged." But Dore added that despite his fears, like most activists he supported the federation and the new direction. "The federation just can't handle a whole bunch of splinter groups," Dore said. "Putting it all under one umbrella makes it practical for the BCTF."

Keuhn, the former BCTF president, also was optimistic. He said he thought the new emphasis would keep the union's social justice emphasis from becoming marginalized because it wouldn't be left up to the activists alone to get the work done. "Now, as the president of a local, you don't have a choice to say, 'I'm just interested in bargaining,'" Keuhn said. "You have to deal with issues of social justice."

In the past, Keuhn argued, when activists made social justice work their passion, it let others off the hook. It was easy for local leadership to say, "We don't have to deal with issues of race or gender — the activists are."

"A more holistic approach is necessary to make fundamental change.... Social justice is about sexism and racism, but also about many other things," Keuhn asserted. "We've not dealt with First Nations issues until now. Homophobia was never on the agenda. We cannot systematically change things by just focusing on one issue."

Five years after the change, the BCTF was still evaluating the impact of its decision to create the broader Social Justice Network. A formal evaluation was due to be completed in September 2003, said Patrick Clarke, director of BCTF's division for professional and social issues. "But whatever the findings are, we aren't going back to discrete programs," Clarke said. Like many teacher unions in North America, he said, BCTF has been forced in recent years to contend with declining membership and funding, "and the staff and resource issues that come with that." Individual programs like PAR were more costly than conducting activities on racism under the broader program of the Social Justice Network, he said. That would be doubly true if discrete programs sought to continue the work done in recent years on new issues, notably poverty and homophobia, which weren't directly addressed by PAR, he said.

Commemorating and Moving On

Hopefully the new program format will keep alive the spirit and ideals that were always at the center of the BCTF's Program Against Racism. Back in 1998, PAR held a commemoration of its years of anti-racist work. The last scheduled event in the two-hour long program consisted of sixth- and seventh-grade students from Vancouver who, as a result of a PAR grant, had studied with a West African drummer. After their introduction, a cautious group of about 30 young people in the first stages of adolescence filed into the front of a large meeting room filled with unfamiliar adults. They carried a variety of drums, some almost as big the people carrying them. Their teacher said that the Yoruban song they were about to play was about respect: "Respecting ourselves, learning to respect others."

A tall Indo-Canadian girl in the back row began with a single, simple beat. Others joined in: two more in the back row, then four in the front. Before long, the room filled with a polyrhythmic symphony. A boy seated in front put down his drum, leapt from his cross-legged position, and danced wildly across the room. Drummers shouted their support. He reclaimed his place and was followed by another dancer and then another. The audience of PAR associates and supporters stood and clapped in unison.

The music ended and the adults called for an encore. Drummers looked to their teacher. He nodded back. "OK, we will play one more song, but you have to dance." With a sweeping hand gesture, he pointed to every adult in attendance.

Again, the drumming started with a single beat. Adults gathered in front as the rhythm built. They joined hands and they danced. Finally, they celebrated what brought them all together. The final act of the Program Against Racism ended as it should: PAR veterans dancing in unison to the sound of student rhythms. Faced with an uncertain future, they moved forward in a collective embrace.

I watched it all unfold from a seat in the back of the room. I couldn't help but wonder what it might be like to be a member of a union that was committed to social justice; what it might feel like to be a part of the collective movement I was witnessing. One thing was quite clear. If I remember correctly, it begins with a single voice.

For more information about the programs described above, contact the British Columbia Teachers' Federation, 100-550 West 6th Avenue, Vancouver, BC V5Z 4P2, Canada; (604) 871-2283, (800) 663-9163; or visit their website: www.bctf.bc.ca.

Editors

Linda Christensen, author of *Reading, Writing, and Rising Up: Teaching About Social Justice and the Power of the Written Word* (Rethinking Schools, 2000), taught Language Arts for more than 20 years at Jefferson High School in Portland, Oregon. She currently works as Language Arts Coordinator and Director of the Portland Writing Project for Portland Public Schools, and is a *Rethinking Schools* editor. She can be reached at lchrist@aol.com.

Stan Karp has taught English and journalism at John F. Kennedy High School in Paterson, New Jersey for more than 25 years, and currently serves as lead teacher of the school's Communications Academy. He is a former co-chair of the National Coalition of Education Activists and an editor of *Rethinking Schools.* He is a co-editor of *Funding for Justice: Money, Equity and the Future of Public Education* (Rethinking Schools, 1997) and both volumes of *Rethinking Our Classrooms: Teaching for Equity and Justice* (Rethinking Schools, 1994 and 2001). He can be reached at stankarp@aol.com.

***

Contributors

Bill Bigelow teaches social studies at Franklin High School in Portland, Oregon, and is an editor of *Rethinking Schools*. With Bob Peterson he edited the Rethinking Schools books *Rethinking Columbus: The Next 500 Years* (1998) and *Rethinking Globalization: Teaching for Justice in an Unjust World* (2002).

S. J. Childs is a teacher, writer, and activist at Franklin High School in Portland, Oregon, where she teaches Global Studies and Women and Social Issues Literature courses, and is involved in the Portland Area Rethinking Schools Globalization Group. She is a founding participant in Curriculum Camp and has helped develop curriculum around such works as *Their Eyes Were Watching God* and *In the Time of the Butterflies*.

Gerald Coles is an educational psychologist who has written extensively on literacy and learning disabilities. Formerly a professor of psychiatry at the Robert Wood Johnson Medical School in New Jersey and the University of Rochester, he now writes full-time and lives in Ithaca, New York. He is the author of *Reading the Naked Truth: Literacy, Legislation, and Lies* (Heinemann, 2003).

Lisa Delpit is Executive Director and Eminent Scholar for the Center for Urban Education and Innovation at Florida International University in Miami. She was selected as the Antioch College Horace Mann Humanity Award recipient for 2003 and was a MacArthur Fellow in 1990.

Lani Guinier is a Professor of Law at Harvard Law School and co-author, with Gerald Torres, of *The Miner's Canary* (Harvard University Press, 2002).

Annie Johnston has taught history at Berkeley High School in Berkeley, California and serves as a schoolwide coordinator for staff development at that school. She also is co-director of the school's Community Partnerships Academy, a small-school program.

Stephen Krashen is Professor Emeritus of Education at the University of Southern California. His books include *Explorations in Language Acquisition and Use: The Taipei Lectures* (Heinemann, 2003).

Gloria Ladson-Billings is a professor in the Department of Curriculum and Instruction at the University of Wisconsin-Madison and was a Senior Fellow in Urban Education at the Annenberg Institute for School Reform at Brown University.

Robert Lowe is a professor of Education and co-chair of the Department of Educational Policy and Leadership Studies at Marquette University in Milwaukee, Wisconsin. He is a founder and former editor of *Rethinking Schools*.

Tom McKenna is an adjunct professor in the Department of Curriculum and Instruction at Portland State University in Oregon. He also is a teacher on special assignment coordinating Social Studies programs for the Portland Public Schools.

Linda McNeil is a professor of education and co-director of the Center for Education at Rice University in Houston, Texas. She is the author of *Contradictions of School Reform: Educational Costs of Standardization* (Routledge, 2000). She studies the economic, political, and social forces behind highly centralized, standardized accountability systems and their impact on children, curriculum and democratic schooling.

Barbara Miner is former Managing Editor of *Rethinking Schools* and has written articles about education policy and vouchers in Milwaukee, Wisconsin for more than 10 years. She writes a regular column in *Rethinking Schools* called "Keeping Public Schools Public."

Sonia Nieto is the author of *What Keeps Teachers Going?* (Teachers College Press, 2003) and a Professor of Language, Literacy, and Culture at the University of Massachusetts School of Education.

Gary Orfield is a Professor of Education and Social Policy and co-director of the Civil Rights Project at Harvard University. His central interest is the impact of policy on equal opportunity for success in U.S society. He has testified as a court-appointed expert in school desegregation cases and for civil rights lawsuits brought by the U.S. Department of Justice. He recently co-edited, with Daniel Losen, *Racial Inequality in Special Education* (Harvard Education Press, 2002).

Bob Peterson teaches fifth grade at La Escuela Fratney, a two-way bilingual school in the Milwaukee Public Schools, and is a founding editor of *Rethinking Schools*. He is a long-time teacher union activist and also edited, with Bill Bigelow, the Rethinking Schools books *Rethinking Columbus: The Next 500 Years* (1998) and *Rethinking Globalization: Teaching for Justice in an Unjust World* (2002).

Alejandro Segura-Mora taught kindergarten in La Puente, California and teaches sixth-eighth grade Language Arts in Azusa, California.

Ruth Shagoury Hubbard teaches language arts and literacy courses at Lewis and Clark College in Portland, Oregon.

Makani Themba-Nixon is the director of The Praxis Project, a nonprofit organization based in Washington D.C. working for health justice

Howard Zinn is a historian, playwright, and activist. He has taught at Spelman College in Atlanta and Boston University, and is the author of *A People's History of the United States* (Perennial, 1995) and *Terrorism and War* (South End Press, 2002).

***

Acknowledgments

We would like to thank the many people who made it possible for two working teachers to produce this volume.

Like all Rethinking Schools publications, this book in many respects is a collective product. Rethinking Schools editorial board members Bill Bigelow, Kelley Dawson, David Levine, Larry Miller, Bob Peterson, Kathy Swope, Rita Tenorio, Stephanie Walters, and Dale Weiss have all been part of the editorial process that developed the pieces collected here. The same holds for managing editor Catherine Capallero and her predecessor, Barbara Miner. Bob Peterson and Bill Bigelow especially gave ongoing support, advice, and encouragement. David Levine helped define the scope and organization of the project in its early stages. Rethinking Schools' director of book development Leon Lynn and editorial assistant Stacie Williams provided indispensable editorial, logistical, and practical support. Mike Trokan and Lizzi Dahlk spearheaded the marketing and distribution efforts needed to help progressive ideas penetrate the world of commercial publishing. Mary Jane Karp gave the book shape and substance and performed many tasks that went beyond her responsibilities for layout, design, and production. Proofreader Joanna Dupuis found and corrected many of our mistakes.

Finally many of our colleagues and students in the Portland, Oregon and Paterson, New Jersey public schools shared their ideas and experiences. We are indebted to all of the above.

Index

Resources from
RETHINKING SCHOOLS

RETHINKING
OUR CLASSROOMS, VOL. 1
Teaching for Equity and Justice

Rethinking Our Classrooms includes creative teaching ideas, compelling narratives, and hands-on examples of ways teachers can promote values of community, justice, and equality — and build academic skills. For teachers K-12.

ISBN 0-942961-18-8 • 216 pp • **$12.95**

RETHINKING
OUR CLASSROOMS, VOL. 2

The new companion volume to the original *Rethinking Our Classrooms* is packed with curriculum ideas, lesson plans, resources, and inspiring articles about teaching. Another invaluable guide to promoting social justice and high-quality student learning.

ISBN 0-942961-27-7 • 240 pp • **$12.95**

RETHINKING GLOBALIZATION
Teaching for Justice
in an Unjust World

A comprehensive collection for teachers and activists including role plays, interviews, poetry, stories, background readings, and hands-on teaching tools. *Rethinking Globalization* is a treasury of information about the threats posed by globalization.

ISBN 0-942961-28-5 • 400 pp • **$18.95**